Contemporary Issues in Heritage and Environmental Interpretation

David Uzzell and
Roy Ballantyne

Contemporary Issues in Heritage and Environmental Interpretation:

Problems and Prospects

EDITED BY **DAVID UZZELL** AND **ROY BALLANTYNE**

LONDON: THE STATIONERY OFFICE

Applications for reproduction should be made in writing to The Stationery Office Limited, St Crispins, Duke Street, Norwich NR3 1PD.

The information contained in this publication is believed to be correct at the time of manufacture. Whilst care has been taken to ensure that the information is accurate, the publisher can accept no responsibility for any errors or omissions or for changes to the details given.

David Uzzell, Roy Ballantyne and the contributors have asserted their moral rights under the Copyright, Designs and Patents Act 1988, to be identified as the authors of this work.

A CIP catalogue record for this book is available from the British Library
A Library of Congress CIP catalogue record has been applied for

First published 1998

ISBN 0 11 290572 2

Published by The Stationery Office and available from:

The Publications Centre
(mail, telephone and fax orders only) PO Box 276. London SW8 5DT
General enquiries 0171 873 0011 Telephone orders 0171 873 9090   Fax orders 0171 873 8200

The Stationery Office Bookshops
123 Kingsway, London WC2B 6PQ   0171 242 6393   Fax 0171 242 6394
68–69 Bull Street, Birmingham B4 6AD   0121 236 9696   Fax 0121 236 9699
33 Wine Street, Bristol BS1 2BQ   0117 9264306   Fax 0117 9294515
9–21 Princess Street, Manchester M60 8AS   0161 834 7201   Fax 0161 833 0634
16 Arthur Street, Belfast BT1 4GD   01232 238451   Fax 01232 235401
The Stationery Office Oriel Bookshop,   The Friary, Cardiff CF1 4AA   01222 395548   Fax 01222 384347
71 Lothian Road, Edinburgh EH3 9A2   0131 228 4181   Fax 0131 622 7017

The Stationery Office's Accredited Agents
(see Yellow Pages)

and through good booksellers

333·7 U 22

Printed in Great Britain by Antony Rowe Ltd
J66243 C15 12/98

Contents

Frontispiece   ii
List of plates   vi
List of figures   viii
List of tables   viii
List of contributors   ix
Acknowledgements   xi

1 Problems and prospects for heritage and environmental interpretation in the new millennium: an introduction   1
Roy Ballantyne

2 Interpreting our heritage: a theoretical interpretation   11
David Uzzell

3 Selfishness in heritage   26
David Lowenthal

4 Gender and heritage interpretation   37
Briaval Holcomb

5 Interpretation as a social experience   56
Lynn D. Dierking

6 Interpreting 'visions': addressing environmental education goals through interpretation   77
Roy Ballantyne

7 Ecotourism and interpretation   98
Kevin Markwell and Betty Weiler

8 Heritage, identity and interpreting a European sense of place   112
Gregory Ashworth

9 Mediating the shock of the new: interpreting the evolving city   133
Brian Goodey

10 Heritage that hurts: interpretation in a postmodern world   152
David Uzzell and Roy Ballantyne

11 Contested heritage in the former Yugoslavia   172
Marija Anteric

12 Strategic considerations and practical approaches to the evaluation of heritage interpretation   185
David Uzzell

13 Evaluating the effectiveness of heritage and environmental interpretation   203
Terence R. Lee

14 Planning for interpretive experiences   232
David Uzzell

Index   253

List of plates

1.1 Interpreting the previous history of a public space, Delft, the Netherlands   1

1.2 Seeing the world through Rob Roy's eyes, David Marshal Lodge Visitor Centre, Scotland   2

2.1 One war, many memories, Australian War Memorial Museum   17

2.2 Is heritage interpretation a force for division or unification? South African Museum, Cape Town, South Africa   20

4.1 General Sherman led by Angel on foot   42

4.2 Robert Burns in Central Park (although he never visited New York)   42

4.3 The Emily Dickinson Reading Garden, Manhattan   43

4.4 Eleanor Roosevelt Statue in Riverside Park. One of only three statues of 'real' (as opposed to apocryphal) women in public spaces in Manhattan and the only one with a strong connection with New York   44

7.1 The pressures of ecotourism: turtle laying eggs on Mon-Repos Beach, Queensland, Australia   101

7.2 The pressures of ecotourism: bus tours around Fraser Island, Queensland, a World Heritage Site   102

7.3 Treetop walk in a Queensland rainforest   104

9.1 Opportunity lost: the Peabody Trust, whose origins are worth remembering, forgets itself when converting a new hostel in central London. Given the size of the hoardings, more could have been said   141

9.2 Every opportunity organised: overloaded Liverpool heritage sign which manages to merge modern functions (e.g. car parks), recent history (The Beatles) and heritage (Maritime Museum) in one sign   145

9.3 Humanising humour: public seating in 'Cow Town', Calgary, against a thoroughly modern backdrop   147

9.4 A success story: Croydon's Lifetimes Exhibition – at last a reason for living in Croydon and being part of something great   149

10.1 Interpretation in the Campo del Ghetto, Venice. In 1938 approximately 200 Jews, one-quarter of Venice's Jewish population, were rounded up and deported to German concentration camps   153

10.2 Entrance to Oradour-Sur-Glane, France   155

10.3 Port Arthur historic site in Tasmania, Australia   160

10.4 District Six, Cape Town, South Africa   166

10.5 District Six Museum, Buitenkant Street, Cape Town, South Africa   167

11.1 Monument to the fallen local Partisans, Trogir, Croatia, vandalised following the break-up of Yugoslavia. The monument was completely removed in 1997 by the municipal authorities   180

11.2 The controversial 1946 plaque to the 1945 liberators of Sarajevo   181

13.1 A demonstration of sheep shearing at a Farm Open in Scotland   216

13.2 A tractor and trailer ride around a farm, East Sussex   217

13.3 Sellafield Visitor Centre   221

13.4 Sellafield Visitor Centre   224

14.1 The 'real thing': French tourists walk across the 50m high Pont du Gard aqueduct in southern France, built by the Romans 2,000 years ago   234

14.2 Can virtual reality ever capture the corporate imagination that built cities like Venice?   234

14.3 'What is a Mossland?' Risley Moss Visitor Centre, Warrington   245

List of figures

6.1 Major and minor variables involved in environmental citizenship behaviour   80

6.2 Conceptions as a constructive integration of knowledge (K), attitudes/values (A) and behavioural orientations (B), relating to a phenomenon   88

13.1 Behaviour mapping of the Queen Elizabeth Country Park Visitor Centre, Hampshire   207

13.2 Differences in comprehension between pre-visit and post-visit respondents   209

13.3 Smallest space analysis (SSA) of farm data for 'before' condition   222

13.4 Smallest space analysis (SSA) of farm data for 'after' condition   223

14.1 The themes–markets–resources model   237

14.2 Interrelationships between themes, markets and resources   238

14.3 The creation of an interpretive experience and consequent benefits   240

List of tables

12.1 Front-end, formative and summative evaluation   190

12.2 Questionnaire inviting yes/no response   193

12.3 Questionnaire inviting comparisons   194

12.4 Questionnaire to obtain scale response   194

13.1 Mean construct scores and statistically significant changes in 'before' and 'after' scores: dairy farming   216

13.2 Mean scores for image of farming statements (all farms)   219

13.3 Attitude change resulting from Sellafield Visitor Centre   227

14.1 Planning for the visitor experience   242

List of contributors

Marija Anterić graduated in geography from King's College London, where she is currently undertaking research into the historical landscapes and heritage of the Eastern Adriatic and the Balkans. She is also a freelance writer and consultant. A native of Dalmatia, Croatia, and has lived in London for many years.

Gregory Ashworth studied economics and geography at Cambridge, Reading and London. He has taught in Cardiff, Portsmouth and, since 1979, in Groningen, the Netherlands. He is currently Professor of Heritage Management in the Department of Planning, Faculty of Spatial Sciences and Director of the International School of Spatial Policy Studies. His teaching and research interests include heritage management, urban tourism and more generally the management of inner cities.

Roy Ballantyne is an Associate Professor in the Education Faculty of Queensland University of Technology, Brisbane, Australia. He has researched and published widely in the areas of geography education, environmental education and interpretation, both in Australia and South Africa. His particular interest is in pursuing the application of interpretive practice to social and environmental issues as a means of challenging community attitudes and bringing about societal change.

Lynn D. Dierking is Associate Director of the Institute for Learning Innovation, Annapolis, Maryland, working in the field of museums, cultural institutions and other informal learning settings (community-based organisations, libraries, scientific societies and humanities councils). She has published extensively in the area of the behaviour and learning of children, families and adults in informal learning settings. She possesses a PhD in Science Education from the University of Florida, Gainesville. Her research priorities include: learning in diverse settings (with particular emphasis on museums), the long-term impact of informal educational experiences on individuals and families and the evaluation of community-based programmes.

Brian Goodey is Professor of Urban Landscape Design and currently Chair of the Joint Centre for Urban Design at Oxford Brookes University, England. Trained as a geographer and latterly as a landscape architect, he teaches urban design, heritage interpretation and the love of the real rather than the virtual. Recent research includes the townscape surrounding London's new Jubilee Line underground stations, Latvian national/cultural parks and historic sites in Brazil.

Briavel Holcomb is Professor in the Department of Urban Studies and Community Health at Rutgers University, USA. Born and raised in the UK, she is a geographer much of whose work focused on urban redevelopment until she discovered tourism while circumnavigating the world in 1990 with the University of Pittsburgh's Semester at Sea programme. She has directed the Women's Studies programme at Rutgers and has a long-standing interest in gender. Her last book chapter was on marketing cities for tourism; her next is on gender and tourism in Latin America.

Terence R. Lee studied psychology at Cambridge, graduating in 1949. His PhD was concerned with the planning concept of 'urban neighbourhood'. An early pioneer of environmental psychology, he has since conducted many studies on the interaction between people and their physical environments. He has served on a wide range of government and other committees concerned with environmental policy. After lectureship posts at St Andrews and Dundee, he was appointed Head of Psychology (and later Pro-Vice-Chancellor) at the University of Surrey in 1971. On retirement, he has returned to the University of St Andrews, where he directs a small research unit.

David Lowenthal is Professor Emeritus of Geography and Honorary Research Fellow, University College, London and Visiting Professor of Heritage Studies, St Mary's University College, Twickenham. He is the author of *The Past is a Foreign Country* and *The Heritage Crusade and the Spoils of History*.

Kevin Markwell is a lecturer in the Department of Leisure and Tourism Studies at the University of Newcastle, NSW, Australia. He has a particular interest in the way nature is constructed, mediated and interpreted by the tourism industry and has just completed a PhD on this topic.

David Uzzell is a social and environmental psychologist at the University of Surrey, having studied at Liverpool, the LSE and Surrey. He has been carrying out research into the planning, design, management and use of museums and interpretive facilities and services at heritage sites and museums for twenty years. Other active research interests include health and safety issues, urban planning and design, environmental attitudes and architectural appraisal. He was editor of *Heritage Interpretation, Volumes I and II*, (Belhaven Press). He was recently elected President of the International Association for People–Environment Studies (IAPS).

Betty Weiler is Associate Professor of Tourism at RMIT University in Melbourne, Australia. She holds a PhD in Geography from the University of Victoria (Canada) and has spent the last ten years lecturing and researching in Australia, mainly in the area of ecotourism. With the help of a series of grants, she has established a major research programme on ecotour guiding, culminating in her current project developing a national certification programme for ecotour guides. She is currently writing a book on ecotour guiding.

Acknowledgements

We owe a great debt of gratitude to friends and colleagues who have contributed to the writing of this book. It would be an unwarranted fancy and arrogance to believe that we alone were responsible for identifying the issues which have been marked as crucial for contemporary interpretation, or the ideas in the chapters for which we are responsible. Such ideas developed over many years of planning and implementing interpretive projects as well as undertaking research and evaluation studies to assess their impact. These projects and studies were invariably done with the most talented and congenial of colleagues who have contributed to our thinking in significant ways. It is always invidious to single out individuals but special mention should be made of Don Aldridge, Brian Goodey, Jill Harris, Richard Harrison, Robert Jones, Terence Lee and Ian Parkin. We would also like to thank Jan Packer who helped in many ways, not least of which by taking on the task of indexing the book.

1 Problems and prospects for heritage and environmental interpretation in the new millennium: an introduction

ROY BALLANTYNE

Reflecting on the past decade, one cannot help but be struck by the momentous social, political and economic changes that have occurred as humanity approaches the new millennium. Many of these changes have had, and will continue to have, a marked impact upon the purpose and practice of heritage interpretation. Social and political changes almost unthinkable ten years ago have occurred in areas such as Eastern Europe, the USSR and Southern Africa. New areas have opened up for the tourist market – the world of the tourist has truly expanded. This is clearly seen if one compares the choice of holiday package destinations in a 1980s newspaper with those of today. Not only have tourist destinations changed, but also people's reasons for travelling. An interest in life-long educational pursuits has become an increasingly powerful motivator for travel (at local, national and international levels) and has fuelled a boom in the provision of eco and cultural tourism experiences. Underpinning these changes is the ever increasing presence and influence of technology which promotes, supports and reinforces the reality of the world as a global village. How will these changes affect the nature, practice and provision of heritage and environmental interpretation in the coming years? What are the new issues which interpreters need to confront in order to address and meet the demands of visitors in the new millennium? What role and responsibilities do heritage and environmental interpreters have in presenting the past and future to local and global visitors (Plate 1.1)?

Plate 1.1
Interpreting the previous history of a public space, Delft, the Netherlands
Source: Brian Goodey

This book attempts to challenge those who work in heritage and environmental research, teaching and practice to consider the major theoretical issues impinging upon the interpretation of heritage and environmental places, events and artefacts in the new millennium. It seeks to raise questions and alert interpreters to important issues requiring consideration if the design and delivery of heritage and environmental interpretation is to play a positive role in the education of, and for, global citizenship. It differs from many other books in the field in that it asks interpreters to consider the 'why' as well as the 'how' of their craft. Interpreters, it is argued, should spend more time considering the decisions they make concerning choice of themes, stories and messages and their likely impact upon visitor knowledge, attitudes and behaviour. Interpreters who consider their role as simply neutral practitioners and presenters of heritage, operating in a value-free zone, will neither meet the demands of new millennium visitors nor rise to the professional challenge of using their craft to address society's needs. What are acceptable purposes for interpretation? Are some purposes 'better' than others? Are there ethical issues which we need to consider? Does interpretation have a role to play in the education and implementation of social and environmental justice? Surely, interpreters have a responsibility to address major social, political and economic issues in such a way as to encourage visitors to think about and consider different futures. We should not see ourselves just as 'hired hands' – people skilled in the techniques of presenting the messages of other people and organisations. It should not be acceptable to rebuff criticism of our work with the Nuremberg defence, 'we were only following orders' (Plate 1.2).

This book has been written for people working in the heritage and environmental fields – planners, architects, archaeologists, museum specialists, conservationists, environmentalists and interpreters, heritage, tourism and

Plate 1.2
Seeing the world through Rob Roy's eyes, David Marshall Lodge Visitor Centre, Scotland
Source: David Uzzell

"Yon hills were once my guarded lands, the mountains my castles... the glens my home... Today you need not fear

leisure managers as well as academic researchers and students – who wish to seriously consider contemporary issues impacting upon the nature of their practice.

It is intended that this book will cross boundaries of job definition as well as normal national preoccupations and approaches. Accordingly, the book reflects the ideas of authors who work in and originate from differing regions in Australia, Europe and North America. Interpretation is an international experience and the standards of interpretive practice should reflect this. The book is designed to alert, challenge and encourage interpreters to wrestle with important contemporary international issues relating to the purpose and practice of interpretation as we approach the new millennium. These issues are interdisciplinary in nature and are of concern to a wide range of academics and practitioners working in the heritage and environmental field.

Theoretical issues in interpretation

In Chapter 2, David Uzzell challenges interpreters to ensure that their practice is informed by theory. Theory exists in interpretation and is implicit in the principles initially suggested by Tilden (1957). However, few have attempted to articulate such theory and little consideration has been given to extending the theoretical base of the field. Uzzell suggests that serious attention needs to be directed to the development of theory that addresses major areas of practice, such as the problem of place, the problem of time, personal memories and collective representations, visits as social experiences and the divisive or unifying role of interpretation. He maintains that interpretation will only become truly effective when it is built upon firm theoretical and research-based foundations.

One of the major issues confronting heritage interpreters in a time of increasing internationalisation is to whom does the heritage belong? In Chapter 3, David Lowenthal challenges us to contemplate the selfishness in heritage – how do we reconcile the fact that heritage belongs to a particular group which exercises stewardship over it? Does it not belong to us all? As he comments, 'generosity and charity may be laudable traits, but in our chosen stewards they spell betrayal if not treason. Stewards must be fierce watchdogs, not tame poodles.' How do we balance the need to appropriate and own what is ours with the need to share it with others? According to Lowenthal, the answer lies in an appreciation of the differences between self-concern and selfishness. Selfishness is unprincipled, self-defeating and runs counter to global heritage goals. Stewards of heritage need to consider how sharing can strengthen the heritage. If selfishness runs free, heritage will be in danger of becoming sterile.

How is heritage understood and explained? Are there gender differences in the way men and women perceive and interpret heritage? Is the presentation of heritage gender-biased? According to Briavel Holcomb, the answer is an emphatic 'yes' on both accounts. In her chapter on gender and interpretation, Holcomb presents evidence to support her thesis that the interpretation of heritage is largely reflective of male rather than female values and perspectives – *his*tory is *his* story. The interpretation of landscape clearly illustrates the polysemic nature of environmental texts and leads to the conclusion that feminist heritage interpretation could provide 'oppositional readings' to contemporary cultural inheritance. The role of women in contemporary heritage is discussed in relation to the inequalities of the past – the need for the feminisation of memorials and statues, heritage sites which commemorate the actions of women, and the representation of women in museums. Although redressing the gender bias of past heritage interpretation has begun, Holcomb cautions that the process is far from simple and unproblematic. Research is needed to uncover women's past and to explore its presentation. Should women be represented as victims or heroes? Do we use 'add-women-and-stir' recipes in our interpretation of heritage or are more fundamental changes needed?

Internationally, museums attract millions of visitors each year – why do they visit, what do they do there, what do they remember and what role does the social nature of the experience play in the meaning-making process? In Chapter 5, Lynn D. Dierking provides answers to these questions as she discusses interpretation as a social experience. Taking a visitor-centred approach to the analysis of interpretive experiences, Dierking contends that a visitor's experience is determined by the interplay of personal, physical and social contexts. She focuses on the social context of the experience: for example, the people with whom visitors attend, the influence of staff and other visitors and cultural factors. Research findings are presented and social science theories discussed to alert interpreters to the powerful influence that social factors have on visitor meaning-making. Dierking is of the opinion that interpreters can greatly improve visitor experiences by designing exhibitions, interpretive materials and programmes which foster social interaction and provide opportunities for visitors to find their own personal meaning.

Environmental issues in interpretation

Do interpreters have a role to play in preparing future citizens to address environmental issues facing the global community? Should they become involved in interpreting a vision of a sustainable environmental future? If so, how can they facilitate a re-evaluation of society's environmental goals and practices and extend and support the aims of environmental education? In Chapter 6, Roy Ballantyne addresses these questions by discussing the role of interpretation and informal learning in environmental education and analysing the differences and similarities in the aims of environmental education and interpretation. He argues that interpreters have an important role to play in helping to develop an environmentally informed citizenry. To actualise this potential, he suggests that a new partnership be forged between environmental educators and interpreters. Practitioners from both sides have much to gain if they perceive and act on their commonalties rather than their differences. He explores and illustrates some of the ways in which interpreters wishing to promote environmental education goals should proceed. In particular he explains the use of a constructivist approach in the design of learning experiences; how to determine target audience prior learning and use this information in developing environmental conceptions; and how to match interpretive experiences with school-based environmental education goals. Ballantyne concludes by appealing to interpreters to join environmental educators in 'coming out' and actively promoting the vision of an environmentally sustainable future.

In Chapter 7, Kevin Markwell and Betty Weiler discuss the rapid rise of ecotourism as an adult learning experience. What is ecotourism? How does it differ from general tourism? Is ecotourism just a clever marketing exercise by tourist operators? What characterises the role of interpretation in ecotourism? Such issues are comprehensively dealt with as Markwell and Weiler discuss areas where ecotourism theory and practice often part company. Ecotourism is charged with, among other things, being an agent for personal and social change. How should this affect the design and nature of interpretive experiences? According to these writers, one of the most important issues which ecotourist interpreters need to address is to ensure that the educational paradigm underpinning practice actively engages the visitor in a learning experience. Designs which promote personal decision-making and problem-solving are key characteristics of such interpretation. If ecotourism is to achieve the high goals it sets itself, stakeholders in the industry need to be encouraged and supported by training, accreditation programmes and ongoing research in the field.

Issues involving interpreting a sense of place

How does the spatial dimension of heritage influence the interpretation of place? How is heritage used to create place-based identity? In Chapter 8, Gregory Ashworth addresses these questions, discusses notions of place, placelessness and displacement and explores how a sense of place can differ according to layering, identity and scale. Focusing on the recent promotion of a European sense of place, he analyses and discusses notions of heritage and continentality, meanings of heritage, the creators and content of heritage, and the idea that heritage is Europe and Europe is heritage. While acknowledging the tension, dissonance and conflict which exist at different scales in relation to heritage and sense of place, he argues that it is none the less possible to create a European dimension. A European heritage and sense of place, according to Ashworth, needs to reflect the physical, political and cultural differences and overlapping layers of identity and empowerment in the region. He concludes that 'the meaning and consequences of Europeanness are a challenge that the New Europe is beginning to face and heritage interpretation will not escape'. Is Ashworth overly optimistic? Is it possible to identify and encapsulate, through interpretation, a sense of European place which most Europeans would recognise and own? How would the content of such a heritage be determined? Why would interpreters want to contribute their skills to such a creation – doesn't Lowenthal alert us to the problems of appropriating heritage as 'ours'? What is the relevance of Ashworth's thesis for other areas of the world such as the Middle East, Ireland and Eastern Europe where both the nature and ownership of heritage are complex, diverse and contested?

Moving from the continental to a local scale, in Chapter 9 Brian Goodey illustrates the past failures of urban interpretation in developing a personal and valued sense of place. This critique is accomplished by metaphorically 'walking' the reader around evocative sites in London and deconstructing the messages they convey. He argues that interpreters of urban sites have generally failed to enhance visitor understanding of the meaning of place. He identifies and discusses five major factors which have contributed to the present state of affairs: charging, promotion, seeing globally–disappointed locally, virtual places and layering. Goodey exhorts us to seize opportunities to use interpretation to add value to urban sites thereby enriching inhabitants' sense of place. He urges interpreters to use their skills to 'add value to the experience of the city and its buildings past, present and future'. In particular, he wishes to see interpretation play a major part in engaging the public in discussion and action regarding the future use and design of urban space and buildings and not only be concerned with the past. Finally, Goodey discusses a number of initiatives, skills, media and linkages which can be used to bring the city alive and help engage the public in dialogue regarding the form and function of urban places – in the creation of 'future' heritage.

Emotive issues and contested heritage in interpretation

Political and social changes of the past decade have opened up and increased opportunities for the interpretation of controversial or 'hot' issues. Engaging with such issues is not generally a comfortable position for interpreters who often feel that they need to be neutral commentators. Yet how can one interpret an apartheid site in South Africa such as Robben Island, Nelson Mandela's island prison, in a 'neutral' way? How should we approach the interpretation of 'hot' issues in respect of the environment, aboriginal peoples, nuclear power, human rights, recent sites of urban and national conflict? How are controversial places and issues to be interpreted without being subject to accusations of bias and indoctrination? Is there not a very real danger that the interpretation of contentious issues could lead to greater polarisation of public opinion and in some cases conflict?

According to David Uzzell and Roy Ballantyne, interpreters have little choice but to engage with these questions. In Chapter 10, they argue that all interpretation is values laden – even a so-called neutral approach to interpretation demonstrates a values decision. Interpreters need to acknowledge this. They suggest that it would be strange if heritage did not have an emotional effect on us. The degree to which interpretation affects us – engages us emotionally – depends on four factors: time, distance, the degree of abstraction and management. The impact of these factors on visitor emotional engagement is discussed and illustrated with reference to numerous historical and recent 'hot' events. Uzzell and Ballantyne also discuss the touristic and community development functions of hot interpretation. Two examples are presented of how hot interpretation can be used to help facilitate community development in South Africa and Australia. In conclusion, they challenge interpreters to play a positive role in leading and shaping public opinion on the important issues of the day. This is not to suggest that interpreters should seek to indoctrinate ideas, reinforce stereotypes or incite and encourage fear – quite the opposite. They should present perspectives on hot issues which engage visitors in questioning their accepted views and understandings on controversial issues. Hot interpretation should promote personal reflection, leading to a deeper appreciation and understanding of differing viewpoints, attitudes and behaviour.

In Chapter 11, Marija Anterić continues the focus on the interpretation of hot issues. There cannot be many more hot areas for cultural interpretation at present than the former Yugoslavia. Could there be a neutral approach to interpretation in the region? Anterić, drawing on particular events this decade, illustrates the difficulties facing interpreters of the heritage in former Yugoslavia where the understanding of historical events is so disputed and polarised. One would expect that interpreters in Ireland, Israel or Egypt would appreciate and concur with many of her comments. Where the meaning of events is so contested – where such events are very recent and have involved conflict – is it possible or wise to attempt to interpret them? Can hot interpretation of such events bring about community development and healing, as suggested by Uzzell and Ballantyne? Anterić confronts interpreters with the fact that 'the past and its remains never speak by themselves'. She shows the power and dark side of interpretation: how it can be used to exploit past events, highlight perceived past grievances, encourage ethnic nationalism, divide a people and support all manner of barbaric behaviour and human rights abuses. Reflection on the role that interpretation has and will play in the events of the former Yugoslavian region is sobering.

Design and evaluation issues in interpretation

The final three chapters of this book address planning and evaluation issues in heritage and environmental interpretation – topics of central concern if the nature and quality of interpretive provision and practice is to improve. As David Uzzell points out in Chapter 12, although interpreters agree that evaluation is important, for a number of reasons such a concern is more honoured in the breach than in the observance. Why is evaluation usually the last thing to be considered in interpretive planning? Surely evaluation should inform and guide interpretive design and planning? Uzzell explores these questions, explains the difference between research and evaluation and argues the case for evaluation within an interpretive design framework. Six issues involved with the design of evaluation instruments are explored: validity, reliability, bias, vagueness, ambiguity and the systematic sampling of visitors. Uzzell discusses the different stages at which evaluation can be undertaken (front-end, formative and summative) before concluding with an explanation and brief critique of the use of common evaluation techniques such as questionnaires, interviews, focus groups, observation studies, experiments and readability tests.

Are we achieving the aims of our interpretive experiences? How successful are we in communicating our stories and messages? In Chapter 13, Terence

Lee argues that in these days of 'quality assurance', interpreters must be able to present evidence regarding performance. It is not acceptable to feel that it is 'obvious' that we are doing a good job or to question the point of evaluation. He presents ways in which evaluation may be undertaken to achieve more reliable and valid data as a spur and guide to improving interpretation quality. He considers and illustrates from experience methods that interpreters can use to evaluate the attraction and holding power of exhibits, visitor enjoyment, knowledge gain, knowledge restructuring and attitude change. Lee concludes with the observation that evaluation should be an essential part of the design and improvement of exhibitions and visitor centres. The research findings presented in this chapter should contribute to improving interpreter skills in evaluation and thus enable and encourage interpreters to become more accountable for the quality of their work.

In Chapter 14, David Uzzell revisits Tilden's (1957) *Interpreting Our Heritage* and draws the reader's attention to the kinds of words used to impart the value and importance of interpretation: – 'beauty', 'wonder', 'inspiration', 'spiritual elevation', 'treasures', 'discovery', 'provocation', 'inspired'. Tilden was concerned that visitors should experience the 'Thing Itself'. With our sophisticated techniques and technology there is a danger, Uzzell argues, that interpretation will become a surrogate experience; it will become the reason for the visit when it should be a means to an end. Uzzell draws a distinction between two types of experience – the heritage experience (which centres on the heritage) and psychological experience (which centres on the individual/group experience in an environmental or heritage setting) – and suggests ways in which such experiences can and should be planned. In the light of this, he proposes a themes–markets–resources model which addresses Tilden's challenge of developing a set of interpretive principles which will lead to a coherent, educationally stimulating and beneficial experience of heritage. The model is illustrated by reference to a UK case study. Having identified the necessary infrastructure for constructing environmental and heritage experiences, the chapter concludes by attempting to synthesise some of the principal findings from research and evaluation studies in order to provide guidelines for creating high quality, psychological, social and contextual experiences for the visitor.

Conclusion

In an era of increasing technological, political and social change interpreters need to question the relevance of their practice and how successful it is in addressing the needs of society and visitors. The purposes of interpretation, as well as interpretive techniques and experiences, can become dated in a very short space of time. To remain 'relevant', to continue to attract visitors and provide a quality experience, interpreters need to engage in a continual 'evaluation' process. They need to explore their conceptions regarding their role as interpreters as well as to establish on an ongoing basis why visitors come to their interpretive sites and experiences. This book seeks to help them with this task by focusing upon a number of contemporary controversial issues and ideas which arise from such an exploration.

The issues highlighted differ from those confronting interpreters a decade ago which were generally more concerned with answering the 'how' questions of interpretive practice. As interpreters have become more confident they have moved away from such an applied focus and now seek to address the deeper 'why' and 'what' questions. Why do we interpret? What is the role of interpretation and interpreters in society and what should we interpret? The chapters in this book attempt to address these fundamental questions in specific contexts. As such, the book presents many challenges for interpreters wishing to extend the impact, relevance and quality of their practice as well as the importance of their professional role in society. It is hoped that this book will reward all those concerned with critically evaluating the purpose and practice of heritage and environmental interpretation – those wishing to be challenged with ideas and glimpses of the important role that they and their profession can play in addressing the needs of society and promoting the life-long education of visitors.

Reference

Tilden, F. (1957) *Interpreting Our Heritage*, Chapel Hill: University of North Carolina Press.

2

Interpreting our heritage:
a theoretical interpretation

DAVID UZZELL

Introduction

As heritage interpretation reaches maturity, it is timely to stand back and reflect upon the four decades since Freeman Tilden wrote *Interpreting Our Heritage* (1957). Interpretation has played a crucial role in regenerating declining urban, industrial and rural areas through tourism and conservation programmes. Equally though, it has been accused of trivialising history and inculcating within the public a reactionary, superficial and romantic view of the past. It is not difficult to have some sympathy with the criticism that the promotion of heritage has more often than not been little more than a cynical attempt to exploit and satisfy the public's appetite for reconstructing and fabricating comforting and nostalgic images and myths about the past. The alliance between conservation, education and tourism has led to what has been termed the 'heritage industry': 'Instead of manufacturing goods, we are manufacturing heritage, a commodity which nobody seems able to define, but which everybody is eager to sell' (Hewison 1987: 9). Can we say with as much confidence that heritage interpretation has played an important role in enhancing people's awareness, understanding and appreciation of time and place?

Some might argue that the initial challenge of interpretation has been reduced to finding ever more tricksy techniques and sophisticated hardware. If only as much attention had been paid to how we can get the visitors to really question their values, attitudes and actions. To what extent are visitors challenged? Considerations of not upsetting or troubling them often seem to take precedence over the contribution of interpretation to educating the public about moral and ethical issues, social justice and a sustainable environmental future.

Interpretation is no more immune from the contradictions inherent in public attitudes and values than any other area of contemporary society. The conflicting attitudes we have held and continue to hold about the country and the city, at least in Europe (Herzlich 1973; Lowenthal and Prince 1965), are equally reflected in the values that underlie the way in which we interpret them. The origin of interpretation lies deep within the conservation movement. Consequently, it is not difficult to understand why the emphasis of so much interpretation has been on stability and maintenance of the status quo. The interpretation of nature and wildlife has typically looked backwards to a time when the natural world was supposedly under less of a threat from the influence of humans. The message here is that each one of us is destroying plant and animal life, reducing species diversity, and unless we adopt more sustainable economies the world will be in peril. But has interpretation really sought to challenge our thinking about ecological responsibility and the economic development of society?

Ironically, however, our industrial past, with its associated deplorable living and working conditions, has typically been the subject of an interpretation which has sought to make us feel good about human progress over the years. But has interpretation really asked us to question whether we now live in a more enlightened age where the democratic workplace is the norm and economic, racial and sexual discrimination and abuses are things of the past?

Interpretation is, I suggest, stuck in a rut where the how has become more important than the why. Interpretation will only have a significant impact on society and contribute to global citizenship when practice is informed by consciously articulated theory (Machlis and Field 1992; Uzzell 1988, 1989; Uzzell and Blud 1993).

Assumptions underlying Tilden's model

Theory, of course, exists in interpretation but it is often only implicitly stated and assumed. One of the principal theories in interpretation is imbedded within Tilden's dictum: 'Through interpretation, understanding; through understanding, appreciation; through appreciation, protection.' This has considerable intuitive appeal because it seems to suggest that interpretation will have the desired effect and will be successful. Similar thinking lies behind other areas of public information and education such as advertising and health campaigns. In essence, the formula prescribes that information will lead to attitude change, which in turn will lead to behaviour change. We know, however, from personal experience as well as empirical research in psychology that such a programmatic sequence is not guaranteed. Some psychologists have argued, for example, that attitudes are a consequence of the self-monitoring of our own behaviour and the situations in which this behaviour occurs (Bem 1972).

Investigating the relationship between knowledge and information and subsequent attitude and behaviour change has preoccupied psychologists since the 1920s. What we do know is that attitude change has to be seen within a larger context, in particular the constellation of beliefs and ideologies held by people about the nature of change in society, its purpose and efficacy, and the role of different groups in bringing about change. Understandings and beliefs about environmental change have to be seen as intermeshing within a wider set of understandings and beliefs, and it is this interrelationship which enables the prediction of attitudes and behaviour.

But this also exposes another shortcoming in the failure to articulate the theoretical assumptions underlying our interpretive programmes. One theory of attitudes is that they comprise cognitive, affective and behavioural elements (McGuire 1985). If we think in theoretical terms, we would appreciate that interpreters typically address the cognitive dimension of interpretation, placing emphasis on enhancing people's knowledge and understanding of issues. The affective and behavioural dimensions, however, have received comparatively little attention in interpretive planning and design. If emotional and behavioural considerations are essential to attitude formation and change, then any interpretation which excludes these dimensions is less likely to be effective.

The absence of an affective component is evident, for example, in our approach to the interpretation of war, as I have argued before in introducing the concept of 'hot' interpretation (Uzzell 1989: Chapter 10). The interpretation of war is often approached in a sterile and emotionally neutral way as if we have a dispassionate interest in what is, after all, a highly emotional subject. Emotion plays an important part in colouring our attitudes and actions and is central to the very human qualities of affection, conscience, humanity and compassion. Why do we suppress them? Affective responses are, of course, no less relevant to the interpretation of our planet's future in respect of both ecological destruction and conservation.

As for the behavioural dimension, so much interpretation assumes a public which is essentially passive. There is little expectation or exhortation for the public to engage in any action as a consequence of their learning experience. Rarely does interpretation suggest choice or options, or propose ways in which they can act to create a better world. This applies both to historic and nature conservation. One consequence of this is that we quickly become passive victims of our past and fatalistically remain victims for the future. This is disempowering and a form of what psychologists call 'learned helplessness' (Abramson *et al.* 1978). We know from research in environmental psychology examining the perception of global environmental problems in both Britain and Australia, by supposedly informed environmental sciences students, that environmental problems are always seen to be elsewhere (Uzzell forthcoming). There is a denial that environmental problems are serious where they live or even in their own country and that these problems increase in severity the farther away they are from them. The consequence of this is that people believe that there is little they can do about them – out of sight, out of mind, beyond action.

The problem of place and time

Places change over time. The meaning of places also changes over time. Lowenthal (1985) argues there are three levels of historical analysis – memories, historical records and artefacts – which in turn correspond to the three academic disciplines of psychology, history and archaeology. For example, when the war generation first visited battlefield sites after World War II, it was to pay homage and to remember. As that generation ceases to be with us, the motivations to visit change. Places become less to do with remembrance and more to do with a day-trip excursion, less of a memorial and more of a tourist attraction. Places move from being a memory to being an historical record and artefact. This may not be the case, of course, for the inhabitants of communities close to those sites for whom the heritage may mean something different altogether.

Our knowledge of and access to places has changed dramatically over the last thirty years. The information to which the public in the West had access with regard to the Communist bloc countries between 1950 and 1990 was controlled and partial. The majority were reliant on the mass media for their understanding of the conditions, attitudes and politics on the other side of the Iron Curtain. Times have changed. The mass media are still an important source of information, but over the last thirty years we have seen a revolution in tourism and personal mobility. People can now go to Eastern Europe and find out for themselves about those countries and ways of life – partly, of course, because they are now more accessible with the end of the Cold War. Equally, the information revolution, including the Internet, enables us to be a mouse-click away from learning about the most remote places in the former Soviet Union, as well as to be in communication with those who live there.

The interpretation of the past is also often regarded as unproblematic. It is assumed that we can somehow know the past simply through investigation.

By undertaking sufficient research we can step back in time and fully understand what the world was like one hundred, five hundred or a thousand years ago. This leaves aside questions such as: whose history are we interpreting? From whose perspective is this account of the world being presented? Places, processes and events are invariably subject to multiple or competing interpretations, yet rarely do interpretive sites present alternative versions of the past or of process. Rarely is an interpretation presented as precisely that – one among several possible interpretations .

Past, present and future are often treated in interpretation as disconnected periods and not part of a continuum subject to ongoing processes, causes and consequences (Wallace 1987). Marc Laenen (1986: 14) argues: 'Most museums present the past in isolation from the present, forgetting that the present is a continuation of the past, and that the present is tomorrow's past … One way to make the past relevant to the public is to trace the links with the present and to point up the strands of cultural continuity … The challenge lies in devising ways of bridging the gap between past and present.' But one can go further than this and argue that all historical moments should be seen as part of larger historical processes which are still in operation, and which often have wider spatial ramifications than are typically represented.

For example, the Cuban Missile Crisis may be interpreted as the focus of a major clash between the USA and the Soviet Union. If we set the Cuban Missile Crisis in a larger time frame, say between 1939 and 1989, we can see it as demonstrating how alliances and allegiances between states can change over time so that the Soviet Union and the USA can be allies against the Fascists in 1945 but in ideological conflict with each other less than twenty years later. If we take a still longer-term perspective, we might see the East–West conflict as the most recent manifestation of global geopolitics which extends back to the Greek and Roman empires and which may soon be replaced by a North–South conflict. Changing the temporal framework opens up the possibility of alternative social, economic, political and historical interpretations.

Interpretation is typically past-oriented. But what of the future? Very little interpretation, even when it is concerned with science and technology, looks to the future. This is not to make any claims for the prophetic skills of interpreters. Predicting the future is not the only option for a future-oriented perspective. With the extensive range of communication skills at our disposal, interpreters are well placed to raise the level of debate about alternative futures as exemplified by O'Riordan *et al.*'s innovative project in the North York Moors in England. (O'Riordan, Shadrake and Wood 1989) They used an interpretive exhibition to present alternative environmental options for the Moors under different agro-economic regimes. This was used as a starting point in a citizen participation exercise to involve local people in the planning of the environment. While not necessarily being prescriptive, interpretation could present alternative scenarios for the future direction of society and challenge people to consider and make informed choices about the sort of society in which they want to live.

Personal memories and collective representations

As elderly people walk through museums and interpretive centres which attempt to capture what life was like in our grandparents' day, images and artefacts serve to provide triggers for long-forgotten events and ways of life. But heritage sites and museums are not necessarily just places for the reconstruction of memories, but also settings where visitors come to negotiate cultural meaning. As Middleton and Edwards (1990) point out, the 'memory of individuals does not just act as a passive "storehouse" of past experience, but changes what is remembered in ways that enhance and transform it according to present circumstances'. Some, like Hewison (1987), go so far as to suggest that many museums do not provide an informative view of the past, but rather a symbolic representation. For young people, it is a world they have never known, yet having viewed the interpretive displays or with the aid of 'first-person interpretation' experienced life in a mine, a factory or the Napoleonic army, they can now be said to know the past. The re-presentation of the past becomes the memories of the future. This is well illustrated by a panel in the Australian War Memorial Museum in Canberra which is also used to advertise the museum (Plate 2.1).

The museum and interpretive centre can be seen as a place where people come to understand themselves. If museums and other heritage sites are to be socially meaningful then they will be about the visitor. Museums and art galleries are often criticised for being élitist and the domain of the middle classes. One reason for this is that it is suspected that working-class people feel they are being given a particular type of truth which has no meaning for them, largely because the representation of culture by museums and heritage sites through the interpretation of objects or places often implies that the visitor has a certain role and history in society. Gottesdiener (1993) suggests that museums must be places which put the citizen back in society.

This is fundamental because it lies at the heart of how we acquire knowledge and understanding of the world and of ourselves. There are at least two approaches that we can take to the acquisition of knowledge and meaning. The traditional approach suggests that meaning and significance is self-evident from the object itself. In a museum, it used to be conventional to label objects with minimal information, typically just the name and if that could be in Latin so much the better. We have now moved on, of course, to recognise that meaning is not always self-evident, which is why we need interpreters. Although this is a step forward we are only replacing one objectification and reification process by another. A subjective interpretation of the world continues to be presented as if it were objectively true. The individual's role is still one of correctly identifying the meaning of the object as re-presented by the interpreter. The assumption is still that the exhibition designer will have a direct influence on a totally passive audience. In a sense, interpretation becomes a form of manipulation and therapy.

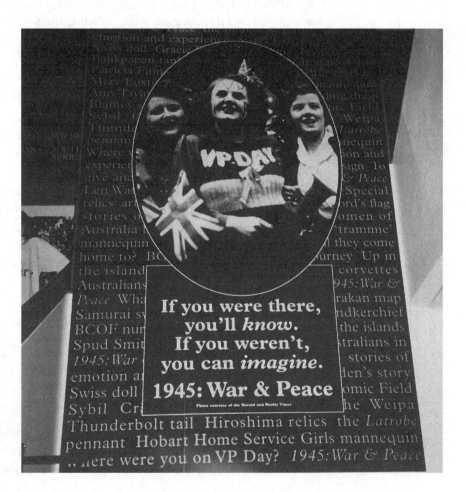

Plate 2.1
One war, many memories, Australian War Memorial Museum.
Source: David Uzzell

Alternatively, we can see knowledge as socially constructed. This perspective regards the audience as actively making sense out of the interpretation and relating it to their experience and world-view. The difference between these two positions is essentially one of meaning-taking versus meaning-making. Frameworks of meaning intervene between us and the object or place. It is these frameworks of meaning – the perceptions and attitudes of individuals and groups, and what events, practices and the environment mean to people – that have to be and should be interpreted.

The visit as a social experience

Visiting any interpretive site is a social experience for most people. In every survey we have undertaken, we have found that family and friendship groups make up at least 90 per cent of the visitors. The dynamic relationship between the interpretive content, the place, the visitor and the social group to which people belong ,and the meanings which are generated as a consequence of that interaction, are well illustrated by some research we undertook several years ago on the social nature of the experience and in particular the role of social interaction in the learning process (Blud 1990; Uzzell 1992).

Exhibition designers assume, perhaps not unreasonably, that visitors learn as a consequence of reading their exhibition panels. However, most research in museums has demonstrated that people do not learn very much from reading exhibition panels, generally because they spend only a fraction of the time necessary to read them, because, for example, they are too long or use complicated language and difficult concepts (see Chapter 13). We also know that exhibits with which visitors can physically interact are more effective for learning, providing that the interaction illustrates concepts central to the process being interpreted and it is not just a question of pulling levers and pressing buttons (Alt and Shaw 1984).

Research by Linda Blud (1990) has shown that the most effective exhibits for learning are those which encourage social interaction among visitors, i.e. exhibits which encourage visitors to talk to each other about the exhibits, what they mean and how they relate to their life. Not only does the social-interactive exhibit encourage much more discussion among family members, but this interaction is qualitatively different to that prompted by exhibits which do not encourage social interaction. Therefore, it is not the interpretation *per se* which leads to learning, but rather the discussion encouraged by the interpretation. What does this mean for practice? It suggests that interpretation which is designed to encourage social interaction will be more effective. The planning participation example referred to earlier (O'Riordan *et al*. 1989), where exhibition visitors are questioned as to their preferences and priorities for future environmental change, is one way in which this approach could be implemented. Elderly visitors recollecting life 'in the old days' is another (Gagnon 1996; Haight *et al*. 1995; Woods 1994).

For Gottesdiener (1993), the consequence of placing the visitor rather than the exhibition at the centre of the learning experience and treating knowledge as a social construction is that the visitor becomes the author of the exhibition. Each new visitor will bring to the museum a different reading or interpretation of the exhibits. The visitor starts psychologically to construct the exhibition. One consequence of this is that each exhibition becomes a mirror in which to reflect the visitor's own attitudes, values and beliefs. Perhaps this means that the visitor is unable to step back and take a wider perspective on society and culture. It does imply that the exhibition designers start to lose their autonomy – which challenges Hooper-Greenhill's (1991) idea that museums are simply agents of political and ideological propaganda and inculcation.

What are the consequences for the interpreter and the interpretive profession? I think that interpreters have a potentially exciting role to play in helping visitors to discover and come to a better understanding of past, place, society and ultimately themselves. To some this may be unsettling and threatening. but it does represent a challenge.

What are the implications of a meaning-making approach for interpretation, and in particular for the institutions responsible for interpretation? What should the institutional response be to this changed way of thinking? If we change our model of knowledge, then surely we have to change our model of the mechanisms by which institutions impart knowledge and make knowledge available (Gottesdiener 1993). It is questionable whether museums, interpretive centres and other agents of interpretation can be used in the way they are at present if we want environmental and heritage education to be effective in changing society and the environment. Since the museum or interpretive centre, like any other institution, is part of the environment, it too will have to be changed. In other words, a change in our understanding of the construction and development of knowledge will lead not only to structural changes in the way interpretive programmes are devised, but also in the way interpretive organisations see themselves and relate to the wider community. If museums and visitor centres are to have the desired effect as agents of conservation, then they will have to open themselves in new ways to visitors and the local community. They will come to be seen as active agents in the creation of change rather than as passive transmitters of information or values.

Heritage interpretation: divisive or unifying

There is something inherently divisive about heritage interpretation. Perhaps it is unavoidable because the rationale of heritage interpretation is to focus on specialness and uniqueness. The supposed virtue of interpretation lies in its propensity to draw attention to and stress the differences rather than the similarities between people, places, objects and events. While this may be a source of pride, it can also be an inciter of prejudice, with murderous effect, as Anterić (Chapter 11) has demonstrated in the former Yugoslavia. Here, the heritage of Bosnians, Serbs and Croatians is interpreted to emphasise ethnic differences in order to promote ethnic conflict and genocide.

Plate 2.2
Is heritage interpretation a force for division or unification? South Africa Museum, Cape Town, South Africa
Source: David Uzzell

When discussing with colleagues in South Africa a few years ago the possibility of interpreting the heritage of the Afrikaners, Cape Coloureds, Europeans, Indians, Xhosas and Zulus, I was told forcefully that to highlight such cultural differences, even under the laudable guise of promoting the rich heritage of these groups, was divisive and would only reinforce the apartheid mentality. It would stress the differences between peoples at a time when the nation was trying to pull together and to identify commonalities (Plate 2.2). What is and what should be the role of heritage interpretation in nation building? Throughout the world we are witnessing increased political and ethnic fragmentation, division, instability and conflict. This often arises out of ignorance, prejudice, insecurity and a lack of both individual and collective pride and confidence. Interpretation ought to be a force for the giving and getting of mutual understanding and empathy, thereby leading to the eradication of anachronistic and anti-democratic thinking.

What role can interpretation play in group identity? Tajfel's (1982) theory of inter-group conflict suggests that even the most arbitrary and meaningless groupings elicit aggression from its members. He concluded that this occurs because people need a positive social identity as part of their self-concept, which is derived from group membership. This drives them to maximise the differences between their group and others. Is there a danger that interpretation only serves to reinforce this process? Should not heritage interpretation encourage people to see similarities between themselves and their neighbours – to identify shared problems and struggles, and encourage empathy and co-operation in order to achieve shared solutions?

Interpretation leading to place and group identity does not, of course, have to be divisive. It is here that we can see the value of research and theory in suggesting prescriptive roles and functions for interpretation to aid the interpretive planner and designer.

Both the motivation to visit and the kind of benefits derived from heritage sites can be seen in terms of individuals seeking to identify with a place and, as a consequence, deriving from that identification a positive self-image. This can occur through the positive attributes of the place being perceived to 'rub off' onto the person. For example, individuals might see themselves as people who like and appreciate towns which are historical and cultural and, as a consequence, enquiring and educated types who enjoy culture. While this may not translate into formal group membership (although one can imagine a situation where it could lead, for example, to a person joining a national conservation body), it could lead to identification with more informal groupings of people (for example, making repeat visits to heritage sites).

It is often suggested in the rhetoric of interpretive philosophy that interpretation contributes to a person's sense of place. The absence of research in interpretation has meant that such an assertion has not been tested. I undertook some research in 1994 to find out to what degree museums or visitor centres contributed to the visitor's sense of place and place identity (Uzzell 1995).

Urban identity theories in environmental psychology stress the social value to be gained by people who perceive their town as being unique and special. This uniqueness serves to differentiate one town or place from another which in turn can lead to positive self-evaluations, such as a sense of pride. What are the defining characteristics of place that confer identity? Museums and heritage sites may not only serve to enhance a person's sense of historical or place identity. Consciously or unconsciously, they may instil gender, ethnic, class or generational identity.

A considerable amount of research has been undertaken in social psychology to determine the criteria which are central to the social identity process (Breakwell 1986; Tajfel 1982). Drawing on this research, the dimensions which serve to define social identity were applied to an investigation of place identity. Four dimensions of identity were taken from Breakwell's social identity process model as they seemed to have a particular affinity with the goals of heritage interpretation: distinctiveness, as this emphasises uniqueness; continuity, which emphasises stable links with the past; self-efficacy, which places emphasis on a sense of control and competence; and self-esteem, which engenders a sense of pride and self-respect.

In summary, it was found that the particular town museum used for the study was successful in communicating a sense of place and a sense of identity to its visitors. Furthermore, two of the original four dimensions of social identity (distinctiveness and self-efficacy) used in the study to measure place identity were reflected in respondents' assessment of place identity. The research also sought to ascertain which particular elements of the town (past and present) were most meaningful to respondents in terms of creating a sense of place: the people of the town, the natural and manmade spaces and buildings in the town, or the activities and industries within the town. It is noteworthy that of these three elements, the only one which did not emerge as a coherent scale was that concerned with spaces and buildings in the town. This suggests that the people and activities of the town, rather than the buildings or areas within it, contribute to its identity.

To my knowledge, this is the first piece of research which has attempted to assess the effectiveness of interpretation in creating place identity as measured by theoretically derived and validated variables. These results lend support to the argument that theory is not only essential for extending our understanding of the role, effects and benefits of heritage interpretation, but can also, as a consequence, drive practice.

Conclusion

Gore Vidal once said that if you see yourself on television and you think you have been bad, it turns out that you were not really that bad. Equally, if you see yourself on television and you think you have been good, it turns out that you were not really that good either; it's just television – here in a moment and gone the next. Interpretation is in danger of falling into the same trap – images which move before the eyes, without leaving much of an impression on the retina and even less on the brain. Interpretation should be a force for change. It needs to be as powerful as those forces which it has been designed to counter. It will only be a force for change when practice is built upon firm theoretical and research-based foundations.

References

Abramson, L., Seligman, M. and Teasdale, J. (1978) 'Learned helplessness in humans: critique and reformulation', *Journal of Abnormal Psychology*, 87: 49 –74.

Alt, M. B. and Shaw, K. M. (1984) 'Characteristics of ideal museum exhibits', *British Journal of Psychology*, 75: 25–36.

Bem, D. J. (1972) 'Self-perception theory', *Advances in Experimental Social Psychology*, 6: 2–62.

Blud, L. M. (1990) 'Sons and daughters: observations on the way families interact during a museum visit', *Museum Management and Curatorship*, (9)3: 257 –64.

Breakwell, G. M. (1986) *Coping with Threatened Identities*, London: Methuen.

Gagnon, D. L. (1996) 'A review of reality orientation (RO), validation therapy (VT), and reminiscence therapy (RT) with the Alzheimer's client', *Physical and Occupational Therapy in Geriatrics*, 14(2): 61–77.

Gottesdiener, H. (1993) *La Visite du Musée: Les interactions visiteur–environnement*, Note de Synthèse présentée pour l'habilitation à diriger des recherches, Université Paris X-Nanterre.

Haight, B. K., Webster, J. D. *et al.* (eds) (1995) *The Art and Science of Reminiscing: Theory, Research, Methods, and Applications*, Philadelphia PA: Taylor and Francis.

Herzlich, C. (1973) *Health and Illness: A Social Psychological Analysis*, London: Academic Press.

Hewison, R. (1987) *The Heritage Industry: Britain in a Climate of Decline*, London: Methuen.

Hooper-Greenhill, E. (1991) *Museum and Gallery Education*, Leicester: Leicester University Press.

Laenen, M. (1986) 'The integration of museums and theme parks: the example of Bokrijk', paper presented at 'White Knuckle Museum: The Converging Roles of Museums and Theme Parks', Ironbridge Gorge Museum, 15 May 1986, reproduced in D. L. Uzzell, L. Blud, B. O'Callaghan and P. Davies (eds) *Ironbridge Gorge Museum: Strategy for Interpretive and Educational Development*, report to the Leverhulme Trust, Ironbridge Gorge Museum Trust, February 1988.

Lowenthal, D. and Prince, D. C. (1965) 'English landscape tastes', *Geographical Review*, 55: 186–222.

Lowenthal, D. (1985) *The Past is a Foreign Country*, Cambridge: Cambridge University Press.

McGuire, W. J. (1985) 'Attitudes and attitude change', in G. Lindzey and E. Aronson (eds) *Handbook of Social Psychology*, 3rd edn, volume 2, New York: Random House, pp. 233–346.

Machlis, G. E. and Field, D. R. (1992) *On Interpretation: Sociology for Interpreters of Natural and Cultural History*, Oregon: Oregon State University Press.

Middleton, D. and Edwards, D. (1990) *Collective Remembering*, London: Sage.

O'Riordan, T., Shadrake, A. and Wood, C. (1989) 'Interpretation, participation and national park planning', in D. Uzzell (ed.) *Heritage Interpretation: Volume I: The Natural and Built Environment*, London: Belhaven, pp. 179–89.

Tajfel, H. (1982) *Social Identity and Inter-group Relations*, Cambridge: Cambridge University Press.

Tilden, F. (1957) *Interpreting Our Heritage*, Chapel Hill: University of North Carolina Press.

Uzzell, D. L. (1988) 'The Interpretative experience', in D. Canter, M. Krampen and D. Stea (eds) *Ethnoscapes, Volume II: Environmental Policy, Assessment and Communication*, Aldershot: Gower, pp. 248–63.

Uzzell, D. L. (1989) 'The hot interpretation of war and conflict', in D. L. Uzzell (ed.) *Heritage Interpretation: Volume I: The Natural and Built Environment*, London: Belhaven, pp. 33–47.

Uzzell, D. L. (1992) 'Les approches socio-cognitives de l'évaluation sommative des expositions', *Publics et Musées*, 1(1): 107–23. An abbreviated version in English is published in D. L.Uzzell (1993) 'Contrasting psychological perspectives on exhibition evaluation', in S. Bicknell and G. Farmelo (eds) *Museum Visitor Studies in the 1990's*, London: Science Museum, pp. 125–9.

Uzzell, D. L. and Blud, L. M. (1993) 'Vikings! Children's social representations of history', in G. M. Breakwell and D. Canter (eds) *Empirical Approaches to Social Representations*, Oxford: Oxford University Press, pp. 110–33.

Uzzell, D. L. (1995) 'Creating place identity through heritage interpretation', *International Journal of Heritage Studies*, 1(4): 219–28.

Uzzell, D. L. (forthcoming) 'The Psycho-spatial dimension to global environmental problems'.

Wallace, M. (1987) 'Industrial museums and the history of deindustrialisation', *Public Historian*, 9(1): 9–19.

Woods, B. (1994) 'Management of memory impairment in older people with dementia', *International Review of Psychiatry*, 6(2–3): 153–61.

3 Selfishness in heritage

DAVID LOWENTHAL

A famously sacred cow, heritage none the less needs frequent culling for lunacy. The gulf between good heritage intentions and malign behaviour seems abysmal. Why is so saintly a realm riven with squabbles over possession and control?

It is often taken for granted that heritage stewards are unselfish – disinterested guardians dedicated to protecting and exhibiting the sites and objects in their care. Yet self-serving motives suffuse the whole heritage enterprise. Heritage is mainly sought and treasured as our own; we strive to keep it out of the clutches of others we suspect, often with good reason, of aiming to steal it or spoil it. Indeed, stewardship requires selfishness. The good steward is one who cares intensely about what is in his custody; as in marriage, true devotion means excluding others. Whether on behalf of individuals or of empires, stewardship is intrinsically possessive .

But not for one's own sake. The traditional steward is not an owner but an agent, a keeper for another – the guardian of sacred mysteries, the manager of a landed estate. The steward keeps vigil for someone else. For some*one*, not *every*one else – a jealous god against His enemies, a landlord against poachers, a king against rival nobles, a nation against foreign foes. Only those pledged to their clients' exclusive cause can be relied on as stewards. An heir must be sure his trustee acts solely on his behalf; a nation that implacable custodians will yield no part of the domain. Generosity and charity may be laudable traits, but in our chosen stewards they spell betrayal if not treason. Stewards must be fierce watchdogs, not tame poodles.

Dog-in-the-manger zealotry is thus a hallmark of national heritage. Seeing Constable paintings overseas, a British connoisseur exclaims: 'Heritage never means more to us than when we see it inherited by someone else.' Only when the English spoke of shipping ruined Norman abbeys across the Channel did the French rescue them from neglect; only when the Victoria and Albert Museum bought a 17th-century Dutch church fitting did the Dutch rally round their legacy; only when Americans were about to ship Tattershall Castle overseas did Parliament act to protect Britain's built heritage (Lowenthal 1985: 394; Mandler 1997: 184–8). Outrage at J. P. Morgan's transatlantic shipment of a staircase from the Casa de Miranda in Burgos prodded the Spanish into heritage pride (*New York Times* 1910 quoted in Harris 1990: 274). The Tower of London sold off two Hanoverian state crowns in 1836; for decades no one knew or cared where they were. But in 1995 word that this 'purest national heritage of priceless importance' might be sold abroad roused huge dismay (Alberge 1995). A Brunei prince came forward to 'rescue' the crowns for Britain.

Medieval Christendom's most treasured relics were stolen ones; the act of theft attested to their transcendent value. To be sold or given away suggested that a relic had not been prized enough to keep; in order to enhance the fame of their treasures, some even pretended to have stolen what they had in fact bought (Geary 1990: 7–14). Displays of pillaged booty legitimated many a regime. Looted European treasure boosted the egos of Ottoman sultans; Napoleon's conquests of Italy and Egypt culminated in stripping them of their finest works of art and antiquity, which were hauled off to Paris in triumphal pomp.

Heritage that conquerors cannot appropriate is apt to be expunged. As the Romans had done with Carthage, so did the Nazis obliterate Old Warsaw as a font of Polish pride. The present decade has seen the archival, archaeological and architectural legacies of Croatia, Bosnia, Rwanda and Romania deliberately destroyed. As a heritage too eclectic to suit the fancy of Muslim fanatics, almost everything in Afghanistan's National Museum has since 1980 been stolen, sold or smashed (Thomas 1996).

Heritage rivalry is legion. Ongoing disputes over the Elgin Marbles and the Stone of Scone are the rule, not the exception. Jerusalem is indispensably and indissolubly hybrid, yet Jews, Muslims and Christians heatedly dispute tunnel access to the Wailing Wall and the Via Dolorosa near the Sacred Mount. French potholers dispute government take-over of Stone Age cave paintings in the Ardèche, on a site local peasants also claim as 'the land of our ancestors' for six centuries; potholers and peasants alike are bent on keeping some of the fruits of tourism for themselves (Macintyre 1996; Simons 1996).

Corporate avarice threatens the American national legacy. A full-page news advertisement on 1 April 1996 advised readers that the fast-food chain Taco

Bell had bought sole rights to Philadelphia's Liberty Bell, henceforth to be known as the 'Taco Liberty Bell', though it would 'still be accessible to the American public'. Irate callers jammed National Park Service lines until Taco 'explained' this was an April Fool's joke. But Taco did in fact pay $50,000 for an exclusive parks facilities franchise – part of a heritage sell-off that included a Coca-Cola concession (*New York Times*; Fahri 1996). Nor has British heritage stayed free from corporate sponsorship. It is hardly surprising to find a nation that privatises so many national assets likewise marketing its past. British Airways and Walker's Crisps, among other firms, have sponsored signs for street names in some English towns; plans were mooted for the management of Stonehenge under the aegis of Madame Tussaud's.

Only on rare occasions, notably when some beloved national icon is under threat, is public heritage safeguarded from exploitation by personal and commercial interests. Thus a federal Eagle Morgue near Denver, Colorado, protects the United States' feathered national heritage from Native American and other predators. In cold storage are hundreds of carcasses of United States endangered national bird, the bald eagle. Twenty years ago, when extinction loomed, eaglet restocking was launched with corporate support. Bald eagle numbers have since soared, but the bird remains at risk owing to burgeoning tribal use and the clandestine collectors' market – a feathered war bonnet can fetch up to $20,000. From the National Eagle Repository, bald and golden eagles hit by cars or downed by electric power lines are sent, packed in five pounds of dry ice, to bona fide customers who have filed a four-page Native American Religious Purposes Permit Application and Shipping Request. But tribal religious resurgence brings three times more requests than there are dead birds; the usual waiting time is now two and a half years. And eagle feathers are needed for initiation and burial rites at short notice (Brooke 1996).

Heritage angst in Britain now typically focuses on items held nationally sacred. Patriotic alarm bells rang with the imminent sale of the Thomas à Becket casket to the Getty Museum in Los Angeles. 'Six days from now,' thundered *The Times*, 'this treasure could be lost to the nation' (*The Times* leader, 23 June 1996), To *The Times* columnist Simon Jenkins, the claim of national talisman seemed sheer hypocrisy. 'The casket is not British. The French made it. It attracted no patriotic hordes at the British Museum, where it had been on loan for the past fifteen years.' Yet such was the outcry that the sale was stopped, export rules were bent and the casket was 'saved for the nation' (Jenkins 1996).

1. One correspondent, however, averred the casket would be safer in Norfolk than in a Los Angeles suburb at risk from forest fires and the earth tremors of the San Andreas fault (Claus Bulow, 'Getty complaint', *The Times*, 5 November 1996).

But was it? Measures to save heritage for the public often put it back into private hands; 'for the nation' is all too likely to mean 'on the walls of some country house in Norfolk', seen by only a small fraction of those who could view it in California (Letts 1996).[1] (Britain's stewards sometimes seem to prefer foreign products to foreign people: as a cartoon blimp reacts to the headline 'Velasquez set to leave country', 'Why did we let the foreigners in here in the first place!') But the tendency to cling to whatever one holds against all claimants, exemplified here in the Elgin Marbles, is anything but uniquely British; 'no' is the habitual response to any request even to share a heritage, as in Spain's recent refusal to lend Picasso's *Guernica* to France.

This is where sanctimony comes in. We become distressed that heritage watch-dogs so often become dogs-in-the-manger because we fail, in my view, to distinguish between venality and self-concern. The term 'selfish' properly applies only to the former. It was first used in the 1640s when Archbishop John Williams, striving to placate King and Parliament, was besieged in London by Presbyterians bent on root-and-branch reform. His hagiographer relates that Williams reasoned so sweetly that the Presbyterians begged him to become their own agent: 'they would buy him, if his Faith had been saleable, at any price, [until] they saw he was not Selfish . . . (a word of their own devising)' (Hacket 1692: 144). In short, self-ishness implied personal corruption, not zealous defence of a cause or a principle, even if undertaken on behalf of oneself, or one's family or state. By the same token, those who nowadays immortalise themselves in museum benefactions and academic chairs, like men who formerly endowed churches to save their souls, are at once generous *and* self-concerned.

Unable to divest self-concern from selfishness, heritage stewards eschew the latter for three reasons: it is morally wrong; it is all too likely to boomerang; and it cripples global heritage goals seen as more and more desirable, even essential. I discuss each of these in turn.

First, selfishness is unprincipled; it links us with the covetous and the miserly. Avid accumulators of art or antiquities commodify what should be sacred and debase people into things. Confucian precept in ancient China rebuked the possessive: to amass collections demeaned both object and owner. In a classic caveat, a 12th-century imperial official tells his wife what to do with his collection as Mongol invasion looms: 'Abandon the house-hold goods first, then the clothes, then the books and scrolls, then the old bronzes – but carry the sacrificial vessels for the ancestral temple yourself; live or die with *them*; don't give them up' (Ryckmans 1986: 79). So she learned her own place in the collection, to die gloriously with the sacrificial vessels. Modern collectors are similarly pilloried, notably by archaeologists, as anal-retentive monsters of selfish disregard for all others (Lowenthal 1997: 39–43, 245–7).

Second, selfishness is often self-defeating; rather than promoting, it is often a deterrent to stewardship. Buildings listed as historic are allowed to decay or are even razed by their owners on the eve of being legally 'saved' from development. Legacies are often destroyed to prevent anyone else from getting them. New England town chroniclers were foiled by a local hoarder who 'got all the oldest newspapers I could find, took down what I wanted and then burned them. It's all mine now. The history of the Town of Bethel is my own personal business' (Lowenthal 1977: 265). The possessor of a unique *incunabulum* is dismayed when a second copy turns up; he at once buys it and then burns it so that his will still be the only copy. Ian Fleming's billionaire *Goldfinger* (1959) sought to steal the gold in Fort Knox not to keep but to irradiate it, making his own hoard more valuable by reducing the world supply (O'Malley 1995: 79).

Squabbling over heritage tends to spoil its context and integrity for all claimants. In the centuries-old dispute between England and Scotland, the Stone of Scone was stolen from Westminster by Scottish Nationalists who copied it before returning it, so that no one now knows for sure which is the 'real' stone. In 1996 it was sundered from its accompanying Coronation chair to be 'returned' to Scotland (Binski 1996). Schubert's brother, after the composer's death, snipped his music scores into tiny pieces, giving favourite pupils a few bars each. Rivalry may result in some treasures being withdrawn from view entirely. Forbidden to export a Lucian Freud painting she had bought at auction, an American has locked it away in a London bank vault. 'If Britain's export laws could stop her hanging it in her collection, she would stop Britain's public galleries hanging it in theirs' (Alberge 1996).

Some legacies are destroyed to save them from abuse. Siegfried Lenz's novel *The Heritage* depicts a Masurian folk art museum subverted by chauvinists, first Russian, then German, then Polish. In the end the despairing curator sets fire to the lot, to 'bring the collected witnesses to the past into a final and irrevocable safety from which they could never again be exploited for this cause or that' (Lenz 1981: 458). This is no mere literary trope; millions of grave goods returned to Australian Aboriginal and Amerindian tribes have been 'purified' by being burnt or reburied.

Third, selfishness stymies global heritage crusades now seen as justified by social equity and environmental necessity (Lowenthal 1997: Chapter 10). In the past, heritage was restricted to princes and prelates, merchants and magnates; others had to be content with a legacy of an after-life. The 19th and 20th centuries democratised heritage. The poor inherited few personal goods but increasingly shared national legacies. The end of empire has made heritage a global right. Third World demands for the return of cultural property, tribal and indigenous demands to restore sacred goods and sites, are accepted in principle, at times even in practice. In the heyday of imperialism, the notion of global heritage was often deployed to rationalize or excuse the aggrandizement of tribal and colonial cultural goods by Western heritage stewards; the great bulk of global heritage still remains in Western collections. But more and more the human global heritage means just that: everyone is entitled to it.

Not only is heritage now seen as a global right, it becomes ever more global in character. When people were fewer and less mobile, cultures were more isolated, heritage diffusion slow and limited; modern communications make such diffusion swift and pervasive. Global heritage is often decried as blandly uniform or spiritually vacuous, but it is also valued for spreading cultures – the arts and skills of classical Greece, of Confucian China, of Enlightenment Europe and of Western science. Whatever its anxious corollaries, such a heritage has doubled or trebled life- spans and freed millions from incessant toil.

Beyond dispute is the global reach of environmental heritage. The interdependence of the whole world on the legacy of nature is a newly realised but immensely potent concern. Unlike most of our precursors, we have begun to view the living globe as a common resource requiring communal custody. Fresh water and fossil fuels, rain forests and gene pools are seen as legacies common to all – and needing all our care. Even more than culture, nature attracts concerted protection. Antarctica is a reserved continent, global outrage rescued Tasmania's temperate rain forest; global skills and resources combat marine pollution. Few now feel no concern about nuclear decay, global warming, ozone depletion, species loss, eco-diversity.

Yet these and other global agendas time and again succumb to narrow partisan ends. New Zealand museums where Maoris now mount their own displays are assailed by non-Maoris and by Maori women banned from exhibits sacred to Maori men. Aboriginal custodians of Uluru (Ayers Rock) in Australia bar tourists from much of this sacred site. Needs for privacy and secrecy may well justify excluding outsiders, but to proclaim a global heritage cause often inflames local and tribal possessiveness. The disinherited mistrust global pieties that may still mask acquisitive avarice or neo-colonial hegemonic bias, consciously or unconsciously pursued. Hence, Third World folk curtail outsider intrusion, denouncing as predators Western fossil hunters, archaeologists, and seekers of rare plants and human genes .

The restitution crusade makes states more, not less, retentive. Ex-colonial states that have endured actual or fancied deprivation mistake restitution as a panacea. Western museums fearing wholesale loss speak of transcendent obligations to conserve and study a dwindling global heritage. Heritage-rich lands ever more jealously cling to their patrimony, forbidding all exports. The less such diktats can be enforced, the more stridently they are voiced.

Every effort to curb private greed for global good aggravates chauvinism. Just as minorities claim sole rights to ritual sites and objects, so each state struts as the sole true steward of its heritage – especially if others contest their claim. As with martyrs' bodies and saints' relics in medieval times, heritage hoarding inflates market demand and promotes looting and smuggling. Classical sites are ransacked, Mayan temples sawn apart to evade export bans. The environment fares no better. Freon, a coolant used in refrigerators but banned from manufacture in the United States to protect the ozone layer, is now smuggled from Mexico – more lucrative and deadly than cocaine (Goldberg 1996).

The best-known example of a heritage uneasily shared between its native begetters and the global community is that of classical Greece. I have elsewhere shown how Greek pride and anxiety alike are bound up in the appreciative purloining of Greek tradition by the rest of the world, leaving modern Greece at once famed and deprived (Lowenthal 1988). Global fame inflates Greek pride in the classical legacy but makes it less their own. 'We're glad you all admire our heritage,' they say; 'now please give it back.' The Greek story is unique in its antiquity and in the global reach of its consequences. But other legacies are similarly buffeted back and forth among global, national and ethnic claimants.

I conclude with an episode of heritage rivalry unmatched for its complex marriage of stewardship and sanctimony. The Tutankhamen find in 1922 dazzled the world – and pitted private and imperial aims against national aspirations at the dawn of Egyptian independence. Archaeologist Howard Carter was the archetype of both personal selfishness and Western arrogance. He loved 'the great days of excavating, [when] anything to which a fancy was taken, from a scarab to an obelisk, was just appropriated, and if there was a difference with a brother excavator, one just laid for him with a gun' (Fagan 1977: 92–3). Carter's insistence that he (and his curse-laden patron, Lord Carnarvon) 'owned' Tut's tomb stiffened Egyptian resolve to keep it all in Cairo. Western experts strove to distribute the treasure among museums best equipped to look after what they said 'belonged not to Egypt alone but to the entire world'. Offended Egyptians rebuffed them. The Tut excavation ended one chapter of cultural imperialism: after Carter, the spoils of archaeology ceased to be automatically Western.

But a half century later, as Melani McAlister (1996) has shown, King Tut's triumphal tour through the United States revived Western hegemony cloaked as global heritage. Ostensibly Egypt's gift to the United States bicentenary, Tut's three-month visit in fact helped recoup American global stewardship after OPEC's Middle Eastern oil squeeze. The Tut tour was vital to the United States' Middle Eastern stance. President Nixon warned its major-domo, Metropolitan Museum head Thomas Hoving, that the tour's failure would 'disturb' the government – that is, cost the Metropolitan Museum federal grants.

Under Hoving, Tut toured the states not as dynastic history but as universal art 'too ennobling and precious to belong to any one people (Arabs) or nation (Egypt)'. Here was 'the common heritage of mankind', owned and operated by the United States in the whole world's interest. The mania for Tut's gold regalia mirrored obsession with Middle Eastern oil, 'black gold'. Indeed, the phrase 'common heritage of mankind' was first coined in the journal *Foreign Affairs* to refer to Middle Eastern oil. Global oil, like global art, must serve both producers and importers (collectors). Like art, oil needed Western, notably American, know-how. *Our* activity gave *their* resource its value; without Western oil users, Arabs would still be poor desert sheikhs; without Western art know-how, Tut would have stayed unsung, underground. Commandeering Tut as universal art stood for regaining control of world oil.

This analogy was undermined, not by Egypt or Arab sheikhs, but by Afro-Americans, who highjacked Tut as a symbol of their own heritage. In line with current Afrocentric myths, blacks claimed Tut for themselves. Tut was Egyptian; Egypt was African; Tut was black. When the show came to Los Angeles, the city council, under black mayor Tom Bradley, made 12 February 1978 'King Tut Day': 'Whereas, each of the rulers of the 28th dynasty was either black, "negroid" or of black ancestry; and Whereas it is particularly important to focus on positive black male images during Black History Month to instill self-esteem; the Council declares King Tut Day for the increased cultural and historical heritage which has enriched our black community.' Tut was *their* history, not *every*one's art. When museum gurus and art critics sought to reclaim Tut as a universal emblem, blacks denounced this as élite 'whitening'. King Tut had become as integral to black American roots as Alex Haley's West African griot, Kunta Kinte.

Steve Martin's comic rendition of King Tut in *Saturday Night Live* signalled further postmodern subversion. Tut now parodied mainstream appropriation of black culture, 'the Blues Brothers' posing as 'white guys pretending to be black guys making fun of white guys who pretend to be black guys'. Finally a feminist T-shirt warned all males, black and white, to 'Keep Your Hands Off My Tuts'. What had been sullied as common global heritage was restored first to ethnic and then to inviolable private possession.

Selfishness is crucial to identity – and to cherished difference. We must keep ourselves to ourselves or we cease to be ourselves. But to cosset our own heritage, need we keep the world so much at bay? Unless we welcome it in we become smug and sterile. While most heritage is private, it is also hybrid in origin. None of it was ever purely native or wholly endemic and today every heritage is utterly commingled. Purity is a chimera; we are all creoles.

Acclaiming the creative commingling of Caribbean cultures, Nobel laureate Derek Walcott refutes purists who despise bricolage as rootless, mongrelized, fragmented. 'Break a vase, and the love that reassembles the fragments is stronger than that love which took its symmetry for granted when it was whole. It is such a love that reassembles our African and Asiatic fragments, the cracked heirloom whose restoration shows its white scars. This shipwreck of fragments, these echoes, these shards of a huge tribal vocabulary, these partially remembered customs are not decayed but strong' in the polyglot babel of cities such as Port of Spain (Walcott 1993: 9).

Stewards should study how sharing can strengthen heritage. The Methodist chapel where Margaret Thatcher's father once preached was dismantled and shipped from Leicestershire to Kansas. Melton Mowbray's planning stewards were at first aghast. But in Sproxton the abandoned chapel had been mouldering; in Baldwin City it is restored to eloquence. A stained glass window above the vestibule now carries John Coy's verse commemorating the founder's daughter Mary (Bone 1996):

> *For thou must share if thou wouldst keep*
> *That good thing from above*
> *Ceasing to share we cease to have*
> *Such is the law of love.*

A statecraft for sharing calls for law as well as love.

References

Alberge, D. (1995) 'Kings' crowns fall into private hands', *The Times*, 4 December.

Alberge, D. (1996) 'Buyer frustrates art export laws', *The Times*, 5 March.

Binski, P. (1996) 'Even more English than Scottish', *Spectator*, 13 July: 11–16.

Bone, J. (1996) 'Final resting place', *The Times Magazine*, 26 October: 16–18.

Brooke, J. (1996) '"Eagle Morgue" near Denver slowly keeps Indian tribes in fine feather', *International Herald Tribune*, 26 November.

Fagan, B. M. (1977) *The Rape of the Nile*, London: Macdonald and Jane's.

Fahri, P. (1996) 'For whom the Taco Bells toll?' *International Herald Tribune*, 3 April.

Fleming, I. (1959) *Goldfinger*, New York: New American Library.

Geary, P. J. (1990) *Furta Sacra: Thefts of Relics in the Central Middle Ages*, rev. ed., Princeton NJ: Princeton University Press.

Goldberg, C. (1996) 'Lucrative new contraband', *International Herald Tribune*, 11 November.

Hacket, J. (1692) *Scrinia Reserata: A Memorial offer'd to the Great Deservings of John Williams, D.D.*, London.

Harris, N. (1990) *Cultural Excursions*, Chicago: University of Chicago Press.

Jenkins, S. (1996) 'Great art knows no borders', *The Times*, 29 June.

Lenz, S. (1981) *The Heritage*, New York: Hill and Wang.

Letts, Q. (1996) 'Getty boss attacks "bent" British rules', *The Times*, 29 October.

Lowenthal, D. (1977) 'The bicentennial landscape', *Geographical Review*, 67: 253–67.

Lowenthal, D. (1985) *The Past Is a Foreign Country*, Cambridge: Cambridge University Press.

Lowenthal, D. (1988) 'Classical antiquities as national and global heritage', *Antiquity*, 62: 726–35.

Lowenthal, D. (1997) *The Heritage Crusade and the Spoils of History*, London: Viking.

McAlister, M. (1996) '"Common heritage of mankind": race, nation, and masculinity in the King Tut exhibit', *Representations*, 54: 80–103.

Macintyre, B. (1996) 'Potholers lay claim to cave art', *The Times*, 15 November.

Mandler, P. (1997) *The Fall and Rise of the Stately Home*, New Haven: Yale University Press.

New York Times (1996) 'Taco Bell buys the Liberty Bell', 1 April: A5.

O'Malley, M. (1995) 'Fort Knox: memorial to the gold standard', in Jean Kempf (ed.) *Lieux de mémoire aux États-Unis* (*Annales de l'Université de Savoie*, 18), Chambéry, France: CREPLA: 65–80.

Ryckmans, P. (1986) *The Chinese Attitude towards the Past*, Canberra: Australian National University.

Simons, M. (1996) 'Red tape still sealing cave with ancient art', *International Herald Tribune*, 10 December.

Thomas, C. (1996) 'Lost forever: a nation's heritage looted by its own people', *The Times*, 22 October.

Walcott, D. (1993) *The Antilles: Fragments of Epic Memory*, London: Faber & Faber.

4 Gender and heritage interpretation

BRIAVEL HOLCOMB

Half of human experience has been female. However, if history is defined as what is known today about the past, then much less than half of history is about females. If heritage is defined as the material remnants, cultural customs and traditions which survive from the past to the present, then even less of heritage is about females. It could be argued, therefore, that the heritage which gets conserved and interpreted in most contemporary societies is overwhelmingly 'male' in the sense that it was built by men, commemorates men's actions, celebrates male heroes and mourns male suffering and loss.

This generalisation is neither new nor surprising. It has long been accepted that those occupations and professions which shape the cultural landscape – from farming and forestry to architecture and engineering – are primarily male. In many parts of the world, construction workers, sculptors, urban planners and landscape architects are usually men. This has not always been the case. In North America, 'Indian women were the architects of their communities … In fact, architecture was often considered women's work' (Cole 1973: 2), and recently the proportion of women in many of these occupations has been increasing. Nevertheless, it is not an exaggeration to say we live in a largely manmade world.

There is considerable contemporary controversy concerning the question of the extent to which gender matters, and how it is expressed, in the built environment. However, there is general agreement that, regardless of the motives of its designers, the built environment is experienced differently by men and women and that space is gendered. Much has been written about public (male) versus private (female/domestic) dichotomies and about issues of power and control played out in built environments. There have been proposals for more gender neutral and feminist designs (see, for example, Agrest *et al.* 1996; Betsky 1995; Boyer 1994; Coleman *et al.* 1996; Colomia 1992; Garber and Turner 1995; Greed 1994; Landes 1988; Massey 1994; Reed 1996; Ryan 1990; Sanders 1996; Spain 1992; Weisman 1992; Wilson 1991). There is ample evidence to support the view that built environments, both historical and contemporary, are supportive and reflective of male rather than female values and perspectives.

This chapter focuses on that part of the environment commonly recognised as 'heritage' and upon the ways in which heritage is understood and explained. Definitions of heritage are numerous (see Tunbridge and Ashworth 1996) and vary from the widely encompassing: 'those things – cultural traditions as well as artefacts – that are inherited from the past' (Hardy, 1988: 333) to narrower concepts which involve valuation and meaning. Not everything old is heritage. In a literal sense heritage means an inheritance passed on from one generation to another. 'In this sense cultural heritage is cultural *property*, and in extreme cases may be fought over or otherwise physically appropriated' (Prentice, 1994: 312). While heritage is understood to include both natural and built environments, and indeed most of the largest World Heritage Sites recognised by Unesco are 'natural' landscapes (such as Serengeti, Keoladeo or Yellowstone National Parks), this chapter focuses on cultural or built landscapes. Although much of the built landscape, even in rapidly changing places, was constructed by generations preceding the present inhabitants, what is considered by many, or officially labelled, 'heritage' is a very small part of the whole. Heritage which gets preserved, conserved, recognised, publicised and interpreted has qualities in addition to age (Lowenthal 1985). These qualities often have to do with aesthetics, rarity, extreme age or historical significance. But vital to the declaration of heritage is the contemporary recognition of the social significance of the site, a significance which is, of course, socially mediated.

As noted earlier, much of recorded and written history is *his story*, or the story of men's lives and deeds, although there has been much recent historical work which seeks to redress that imbalance. Women's history is one of the few growth fields in that discipline (see, for example, the journal *Gender and History* and the proliferation of books in the field). As discussed below, within the heritage 'community' too there is growing recognition of gender inequalities in what constitutes heritage and in efforts to make women's heritage more visible. Before turning to that, however, the questions of does it matter and why are addressed.

Women living in a manmade world

Women live today, as they have done for much of recorded history (though possibly not in prehistoric times), in a world designed and built by men, a world which accurately reflects power relationships between people. As Monk has argued:

> Often unspoken social and cultural beliefs, that is the ideologies which people hold about gender, are important in shaping landscapes. In turn, landscapes set the contexts within which men and women act and reproduce gender roles and relationships ... landscapes, both materially and symbolically, reflect power inequalities between men and women by embodying patriarchal cultural values. These values support the dominance of men and the subordination and oppression of women: they are often interpreted as being universal and historically pervasive, though they vary in expression and in the intensity of their impact in different times and places.
>
> *Monk 1992: 123–4*

Monk and others (cited previously) have discussed the many ways in which gender power relationships are, sometimes subtly, sometimes blatantly, imbued in landscape. Over a quarter of a century ago, Wagner (1972) envisaged the cultural landscape as a kind of memory bank for people. Humans have the advantage over other animals in that we have transformed landscapes in which records of common experiences are stored. 'The advantage of mankind [sic] rests in environments suffused with manmade [sic] symbolism, peerless and imperishable repertories of the past experience of the species' (Wagner 1972: xi). The landscape is thus a medium of communication between generations and peoples. It communicates the experience, values, customs and aspirations which comprise culture. The cultural landscape thus becomes not only the medium but the message. It is part of culture and may weaken or reinforce that culture. Landscape is a mirror into which its inhabitants peer to assess their own identity in the world.

The imprint of a strong, cohesive culture is clearly visible in the land. Members of that culture derive confidence from familiar patterns and artefacts and are able to function effectively and consolidate further cultural growth. It can be argued, however, that peoples (cultures, subcultures and other groups) who are not in a position to make their mark on the landscape, who, contrary to Walter Benjamin's dictum, have lived but left no traces, are deprived of this supportive environment. Since the environment does not reflect their shared experience, values and preferences, they are denied an identity-strengthening agent and their cultural efforts may be diffuse and forgotten in succeeding generations. I argue that women are one such group whose imprint on the landscape is less visible and more ephemeral, less clarifying and more ambiguous than their male peers.

While feminist architects, geographers, planners and others have begun to document and analyse the logistical and economic effects on women of living in 'patriarchal' cities and buildings, the psychic effects are more nebulous. What is clear, however, is that environmental 'texts' are polysemic. A built environment, including heritage sites, is 'read' differently by different people. In a postmodern sense, like Gertrude Stein's Oakland, there is no 'there' there other than what observers 'see'. Oppositional readings, in which the observer deconstructs the text and reads the silences, supplies meaning not intended by the 'author' and 'reads' into the text new meanings, are certainly one strategy by which women (whether consciously or not) are able to 'see' both sources of oppression and missing herstories. Oppositional readings, however, require knowledge, understanding and energy. It may be that one of the most useful roles a feminist heritage interpretation could now provide are such 'oppositional readings' to the contemporary cultural inheritance.

Feminist heritage: an oxymoron?

If indeed the history of women has largely been one of subordination, victimisation, struggle and frequent defeat and oppression, why remember it? Is it useful to try to resurrect a heritage which is antithetical to the preferred direction in which gender relationships are moving? Feminists of my generation who have experienced not only the gender wars of academia in the 1970s, but the critique of feminism by younger women scholars, might be excused for not wishing to reiterate the historical victimisation of women, despite the clichéd admonitions that she who knows her own generation remains always a child or that those who ignore history are doomed to repeat it. Perhaps a selective amnesia is justifiable, especially since, as Tunbridge and Ashworth (1996) note, heritage is a contemporary product intended for current and future consumption. Should we emulate the long tradition of mainstream, male heritage and look for heroines, matriarchs, and halcyon happenings to immortalise? Alternatively, would a feminist heritage lay bare the oppression of women but emphasise, as well, their resistance to that oppression? Or would it, perhaps with greater accuracy (authenticity?), but lesser marketability, simply attempt to represent the lives of quiet desperation which most women (and men) led? There are no easy answers to these and related questions. Responses may vary according to assumptions made about the purposes of heritage displays (education, entertainment, empowerment?), about the consumer (young girls, elderly women, affluent men, feminists or Fascists?), about the permanence or ephemerality of the exhibit, among others.

Women in contemporary mainstream heritage

That men are numerically over represented in heritage products, whether in monuments, sites, re-enactments or museums, is incontrovertible. In many parts of the world, public monuments depict male heroes, victims (of war, especially), and a panoply of Great Men. In the USA many heritage sites commemorate the Revolutionary or Civil Wars, both fought mainly by men. In Britain, the growing popularity of industrial heritage, while not exclusively male, is predominantly so. Even the growth industry of historical re-enactments – heritage in action – has more than its share of chaps dressed in period military costumes and playing with weird weapons, though there are, of course, serving wenches and dancing girls at medieval festivals.

Statuesque statuary?

The preponderance of monumental males has been noted by Gross and Rojas (1986), Inglis (1989), Johnson (1995), Monk (1992) and Warner (1985) among others. In a pilgrimage to New York City's Manhattan Island to photograph the only three statues of actual (rather than allegorical) women, this author too observed that the city, and especially its parks, are replete with statues of local, national and international Great Men ranging from General Sherman (Plate 4.1) to William Shakespeare. Central Park is generously sprinkled with statues of artists, musicians and poets. There is even one of the egregiously awful Scottish poet Robert Burns (Plate 4.2), but the only 'monument' to a female poet I could find was a tiny, derelict patch of inaccessible ground adjacent to a school near the park and dedicated as the Emily Dickenson Reading Garden (Plate 4.3). It was not until 1915 that the first statue of a 'real' woman, Joan of Arc, was erected in New York. On Riverside Drive, the relatively inconspicuous equestrian statue has a plaque which simply reads that she was born in 1412 and burned at the stake in 1431. What she did in between to 'deserve' that fate is a silence. The first public outdoor statue in New York City of an American woman was that of Gertrude Stein in Bryant Park. Although sculpted (by her friend Jo Davidson) in 1923, it was not cast and placed in the park until 1992. Stein's bust is close to, and overshadowed in scale by, a larger-than-life statue of William Bryant (a poet and newspaper editor).

Plate 4.1
General Sherman led
by Angel on foot
Source: Briavel Holcomb

Plate 4.2
Robert Burns in Central
Park (although he
never visited New York)
Source: Briavel Holcomb

Plate 4.3
The Emily Dickinson Reading Garden, Manhattan
Source: Briavel Holcomb

Plate 4.4
Eleanor Roosevelt statue in Riverside Park. One of only three statues of 'real' (as opposed to apocryphal) women in public spaces in Manhattan and the only one with a strong connection with New York
Source: Briavel Holcomb

While there are literally hundreds of statues of American presidents, including several in New York City, the first statue in a public place of an American First Lady is that of Eleanor Roosevelt in Riverside Park. Unlike Stein, who spent much of her life and was buried in Paris, Eleanor Roosevelt was born and died in New York and spent much of her life in the city. The statue, unveiled in 1996, was, like the other two statues discussed, sculpted by a woman (Penelope Jencks) and Mrs Roosevelt's granddaughter was one of her models (Plate 4.4). Hilary Clinton, who once talked about seeking solace in imaginary conversations with her predecessor, said at the statue's unveiling: 'When I last spoke to Mrs Roosevelt she wanted me to tell you how pleased she is by this great, great new statue' (*New York Times* 1996). Not coincidentally, the first First Lady to be honoured in a national memorial was also Eleanor Roosevelt in 1997 (Clines 1997).

While the ratio of statues of real men versus real women is very unequal, the balance may be reversed when allegorical statues are considered. In London, Paris, New York or Mexico City, liberty, truth, justice, mercy, peace and other virtues are routinely personified by semi-draped female forms. The messages, both intended and received, by these personifications are presumably numerous, but as Monk notes the 'associations of female figures with Liberty, whether the French Marianne or the American Miss Liberty, can only seem ironic given the history of restriction and political exclusion of real women in male-dominated democracies' (Monk 1992: 126). On the other hand, it is also ironic that a New York statue which personified Civic Virtue as male and included two female figures lying at his feet representing vice, provoked great controversy at its unveiling in 1922. Although the sculptor, Frederick MacMonnies, said that the women were intended to represent sirens and temptresses, others saw the statue as a man thrusting his toes on a woman's neck. Despite the controversy and its eventual removal from City Hall in Manhattan to Queens' Borough Hall in 1941, the statue remains part of the civic landscape (Bogart 1989). Smyth (1991) discussed how interpretations of a statue in Dublin of James Joyce's character, Anna Livia Plurabella, illustrate the ambiguities of women living in a patriarchal society.

In his fascinating analysis of French World War I monuments, which typically depict male soldiers, some with supporting female nurses, weeping women, or allegorical roles such as peace, Sherman argued that the 'monuments did not simply reflect gender roles … monuments helped create them' (1996: 82). During the absence of men on the battlefield, women took over roles and responsibilities usually assigned to men. After the war, its commemoration 'served to reinscribe gender codes that World War I had disrupted in France, but that commemoration itself played out, in gendered terms, a pervasive cultural unease in which nothing less than the masculine cast of politics and of national citizenship was at stake' (Sherman, 1996: 84). A measure of the effectiveness of such 'cultural work' of re-establishing traditional masculinity and gender relations is that French women did not attain suffrage until after World War II.

Public statuary in many cultures represents males in dominant, assertive and active stances while women are typically passive, recessive and subordinate. George Washington, Simon Bolivar, Benito Jaurez and Chiang Kai-shek are memorialised in heroic stance. In contrast, the two women whose graven images are perhaps most numerous are the Virgin Mary and Queen Victoria, the former usually with her hands together in prayer while the latter sits holding her orb. Although I have no supportive quantitative data, I would contend that women are generally depicted as victims with greater frequency than men (unless you count war memorials). From Mary Queen of Scots or Joan of Arc to Virginia Dare (the first English child to be born in the New World who mysteriously disappeared three years later) or We-no-nah (the Sioux maiden who legend has it drowned herself rather than marry the warrior chosen by her father), a disproportionate number of memorialised women seem to have had hard lives and bad ends (Sherr and Kazickas 1994). As others have noted, both real and allegorical women appear naked, bare breasted or revealingly draped while, with the exception of classical Greece, similarly disrobed male forms are unusual (Warner 1985). Historically, such sexualised depictions have sometimes met with disapproval, though usually on the basis of prudery rather than sexism. Today, even American towns with statutes banning topless garb in public (for living women), still have bare-breasted statues in public places.

An alternative strategy for memorialisation is evident in the new memorial, completed in 1997 at Arlington National Cemetery, to women who served in the armed forces. Its design includes no statues but rather quotations from women who served which are inscribed in glass, casting legible shadows and representing 'collective memories' (Weiss, 1996).

Heritage sites

As noted earlier, the great majority of the heritage sites which are preserved, recognised and interpreted were both built by, and commemorate the actions of, men, although obviously women lived in and are integral to the history of virtually all such sites (with a few possible exceptions such as the Cistercian Abbey of Fontenay or the Monastery of Batalha; but then the Convent of Christ in Tomar was presumably all female). The Unesco World Heritage site of Valletta, Malta, has had female inhabitants throughout its existence, but few are visible in its interpreted heritage. A souvenir programme of a 1996 Valletta History and Elegance festival contains the image of only one historical female figure – Queen Victoria – whose statue is also the only 'real' woman in the town, unless you count the Virgin Mary. A multimedia show of the island's history similarly mentions only one woman by name – Queen Elizabeth I. Even a brochure produced by the National Tourism Organisation recommending a tour of Valletta for children asserts: 'Boys will enjoy a visit to the Armoury with its many swords and cannons and suits of armour and parents can then relax in one of the many colourful outdoor cafes.' Meanwhile, the girls are not mentioned. The multimedia show of Malta's World War II experience has many depictions of heroic fighter pilots and sailors (all male) while women are seen as the victims of bombs and blockades. While the photographs and film footage are authentic, the narrative suggests that women were helpless victims rather than assertive in their resistance and resilience.

Valletta is used here as an illustration not because its heritage interpretation is more gender biased than other sites, but because of the author's familiarity with it. As a contrast, it is instructive to consider one of the 'most feminist' heritage sites – the Women's Rights National Park in Seneca Falls, New York. The first women's rights convention was held in 1848 in a Wesleyan chapel in Seneca Falls as the start of a movement which culminated in women's suffrage in 1920. The landmark significance of the site was not recognised by the Federal Government until the park's establishment in 1980 and restoration of the remains of the chapel and their integration into a small park, that includes a granite wall inscribed with the Declaration of Sentiments, the (wo)manifesto of the convention, which was not completed until over a decade later. Adjacent to the park is a visitor centre which houses exhibits related to women's rights and across the street there is another tiny park named for Elizabeth Cady Stanton, although it includes no statue or explanatory plaque. Overall, the park is modestly scaled and inconspicuous, but Hayden argues that because 'it is physically integrated with the urban fabric of Seneca Falls, it can engage the life of the town in a way that many larger, more expensive projects do not' (Hayden 1996: 57). There is not a little irony to the fact that the Women's Rights National Historical Park is one of several projects designed to revive a 19th-century industrial town into a late 20th- century tourist destination. Its role in resuscitating women's heritage may be a quite secondary motive. As a local businessman is reported to have observed, 'local merchants "don't give a hoot" about feminism but they see the money opportunity. I mean, if you've got Old Faithful in your town, you are in favour of geysers' (Hayden 1996: 59).

Nearby, on the same street, is the National Women's Hall of Fame, housed in a former bank building and also rather inconspicuous. Established in 1969, it contains exhibits related to the lives of the inductees of the Hall of Fame – an eclectic group as illustrated by the three whose last names begin with 'O' – Annie Oakley (a sharpshooter of the Wild West Show), Sandra Day O'Conner (Supreme Court Justice) and Georgia O'Keefe (artist). The Women's Hall of Fame is dwarfed in comparison with the Baseball Hall of Fame (Cooperstown, New York), the Football Hall of Fame (Canton,

Ohio) or the Rock and Roll Hall of Fame (Cleveland, Ohio) whose honourees are mostly male.

Heritage museums

Museums are relatively recent institutions, many having been established in the 19th century with a wide variety of motivations ranging from the desire to preserve cultural treasures, the promotion of civic and national pride, to the demonstration of 'progress' (the present is superior to the past), and that 'Western society was more civilised than so-called primitive cultures' (Knibb 1994: 35). Although women have long been involved in museum work, it was often as volunteers and usually low in the museum hierarchy. Many museums include in their collections numerous items related to women's history, but it was not until the 1980s that feminist critiques of museum acquisition, display and interpretation appeared. In Britain, WHAM (Women, Heritage and Museums) was formed in 1984 largely by museum workers and raised debates concerning not only sexism but the racism inherent in many museum representations of the past. More recently, others have provided both feminist critiques and suggestions for improving women's representation in museums.

Porter (1991), among others, has discussed how the conventional domestic tableaux representing women's domain, whether the kitchen, parlour or boudoir, usually display a static, tidy, orderly space quite different from the noisy, vibrant, chaotic scenes of factory, mill or mine. As in other aspects of heritage discussed earlier, women's history is typically portrayed more passively than men's. The considerable physical exertion of washing and mangling sheets, stoking bread ovens or coping with infants and toddlers simultaneously – all tasks familiar to my grandmother – are perhaps more mundane than rolling steel, stoking coke ovens or leading labour unions, but required similar effort and skill. While it is true that men's lives historically often did involve greater physical exertion and public action, and sometimes a 'chapter of history' was led mostly by men, it is often perceived that while they were 'making history', women were living in it. Sometimes, as in 19th-century migration from Ireland to London, women were more numerous than men, but because their work as domestic servants is less well documented than that of male construction labourers, their heritage is less visible.

Knibb asserts that while museum collections may often include much related to women's history, only a fraction of that may be displayed and 'many collections are artefact poor on such topics as pregnancy, childbirth and child rearing ... [and] ... fail to address the lives and histories of specific groups of women such as the poor, the working class, the homeless, immigrants, women of colour, lesbian and aboriginal women' (1994: 34). Knibb does concede, however, that these omissions may have more to do with those women's lack of material surplus and alienation from the traditional museum idea than with any museo-conspiracy.

In the USA, comparisons between one of the most popular museum exhibitions depicting women's history, the First Ladies Hall of the Smithsonian Institution which opened in 1964, and subsequent more 'feminist' exhibits illustrate increased sensitivity, despite a 1984–5 exhibit – 25 Years of Barbie Dolls – that inadequately problematised that sexist icon (which my daughter loved) (Melosh and Simmons 1986).

Assessing the state of house museums in Scotland, Nenadic wrote that while there are plenty that 'commemorate male achievement ... [there is] ... not a single one devoted to celebrating in her own right the life of an eminent woman of the past three hundred years ... At the most basic level, there are many "great" men in Scotland's past, but no "great" women' (Nenadic 1994: 426). Nenadic, like Edensor and Kothari (1994) in their analysis of the masculinisation of Stirling's heritage, attributes much of the Scottish emphasis on male heritage to the association of men with the nation and the need to define a national identity separate from England.

Natural history, archaeological and ethnographic museums seem to have been particularly egregious in associating women (and 'primitive' peoples) with nature and men (and 'civilised' European races) with culture (Shoemaker 1994: 324). Ever since Linnaeus used the male to represent the species, the female has been depicted as the variant. Writing on the presentation of gender in French ethnographic museums, Segalen asserts 'without exaggerating it can be stated that there is a near total absence of feminist perspectives in such public presentations' (1994: 334). Jones and Pay provide, depressingly, many examples of gender bias in British museums. In an archaeological museum in Leicester:

> Figures in the nuclear family tableaux spanning the historic and prehistoric past are firmly moulded into their respective gender roles. Each male clutches his symbol of power or authority; each female watches anxiously over a small child. Ironically, despite years of criticism from within the profession, the museum's reluctance to dispose of the figures is largely a response to public

demand. These families are what visitors expect: the images are easy to understand, comfortable, and unchallenging.

Jones and Pay 1990:162

The all-too-familiar role of woman as victim is played out once again in the Jorvik Viking Centre in York where visitors 'are presumably correct in thinking that all Viking men are tall, fair, and incredibly good looking, while women exist mainly as victims. The woman-as-victim imagery is vividly confirmed by the last scene of the time tunnel, where a woman in tattered garb flees from a Norman soldier' (Jones and Pay 1990: 162).

There is, of course, controversy concerning the appropriate role of contemporary museums as guardians of the past versus commentators and reformers for the future. Are exhibitions justified which alienate, irritate or bore significant portions of the population? Should the curatorial goal be one of gender equity or should specifically feminist collections and interpretations redress historical imbalances? Probably either goal is reasonable and Hasted (1994), Knibb (1994) and Melosh and Simmons (1986) are among those with helpful suggestions including greater attention to oral and archival sources, better documentation of objects at the time of accession, collaboration with women's groups, regional collaborations to facilitate specialisation and sharing of resources, greater effort in primary research and active collecting rather than reliance on what is already in the collection.

There are indications that the representation of women in museums is improving and that feminism seems also to encourage exhibits more inclusive of varied classes and ethnicities (Grant 1994; Graves and Green Devens 1994; Miller and Digan Lanning 1994; West 1994). The exhibition at the visitor centre of the Women's Rights National Historic Park includes not only memorabilia (such as the bloomers worn by early suffragists and campaign buttons for progressive candidates) but interactive displays which present contemporary scenarios such as one relating to affirmative action which enables the viewer to register her 'vote' on the issue and to see how other visitors have 'voted.' (Not surprisingly, the majority of visitors respond in favour of affirmative action, women's rights and gender equity.)

Gender and heritage in the future

The latter part of the 20th century has witnessed the beginning of the effort to reclaim women's history and heritage, but work remains to be done. Much of women's past remains unknown, obscure or uncovered, but consciousness of that memory loss is growing. Feminist heritage interpretation requires research in both content of the past and presentation in the present. An interesting example of the former is Bell's (1990) work which showed that while the 18th-century garden is virtually always presented as a male creation (whether of the landscape architects such as Henry Wise, John Vanburgh or Capability Brown or their patrons such as Lord Burlington, the Earl of Carlisle or the Duke of Marlborough), in fact women were quite active as gardeners and in supervising gardening work. Likewise, an example of innovative presentation is Davey and Chamber's (1994) account of how a woman interpreter dressed in period costume in an 18th-century Canadian fort was able to raise questions about, and awareness of, women's roles in a setting conventionally assumed to have been exclusively male. Kavanagh (1994) points both to exhibits that are particularly central to female experience (such as the 1993 Glasgow exhibition on childbirth, 'From Here to Maternity') and those that make particular effort to include both sexes (such as 'The Story of Hull' and the 1993 'People, History and Change in Birmingham's Heartlands').

The growing inclusion of women's heritage is far from unproblematic. 'Backlash' so familiar to early feminism is likely as heritage becomes more feminised, and even academics resort to 'labelling': 'in North America, where the gender issue originated and is most *stridently* developed' and, in pointing out that influential women, such as Octavia Hill, principal founder of the National Trust, in fact defended 'patriarchal heritage', but that 'this is a matter on which *protagonists of gender* [of which, I assume, I am one] have little to say' (Tunbridge and Ashworth 1996: 81–2) [my emphasis]. Similarly controversial is the question addressed earlier of whether the depiction of women as victims, however historically accurate, may reinforce contemporary feelings of vulnerability and, equally, alienate male heritage visitors who do not wish to be reminded of the sins of the father. Tunbridge and Ashworth argue that 'the "victimist" position that human society is a vast machine built by men to oppress women, and that all men are collectively guilty for male crimes against women, has become powerful in official and academic pronouncements in Canada … "victimism" would essentially invalidate all heritage in female eyes except as heritage of oppression' (1996: 195). While I know of nobody who holds these extreme views attributed by those authors to some radical feminists, the 'victim question' in heritage is sensitive and unresolved. Indeed, representations of women as the opposite of victims – as daring, dominant, sexy and strong – may also provoke accusations of celebrating women with 'male' qualities, as in the Cowgirl Hall of Fame in Fort Worth, Texas (Moore 1994).

While it can be argued that feminist heritage is more class/race/sexual orientation sensitive than mainstream heritage has been, it certainly is not without controversies, as witnessed by the recent protest by the National Political Congress of Black Women concerning the campaign to move a statue of women suffragists to a conspicuous site in the Capitol Rotunda. The sculpture honouring Susan B. Anthony, Lucretia Mott and Elizabeth Cady Stanton was presented by the National Woman's Party to Congress in 1921, but was soon removed from the Rotunda to a storeroom while women's groups tried for decades to have it returned. The Black Women's Group argued that Sojouner Truth should be chiselled into an unfinished part of the sculpture. As a member of that group remarked: 'For it to represent suffragists, it would have to have Sojourner Truth. History has been distorted enough. We don't need it distorted again' (*New York Times* 1997: 28). However, the sculpture was replaced without modification in the Rotunda in 1997.

In summary, there is growing recognition of the need to redress gender imbalance in heritage interpretation but much remains to be done. A 1986 volume intended to introduce the US heritage to the public has a foreword which mentions over a dozen men and no women, by name, an omission less likely to occur a decade later (Bennett 1986). The 'add-women-and-stir' recipe is a start, but inadequate in the long run. Jones and Pay are among those calling for fundamental changes:

> existing structures and disciplinary divisions within museums need to be changed radically...Unless research strategies are devised to examine the dimensions of gender more fully, curators will continue to present a past devoid of women. Since the past reflects and reinforces the present, a re-evaluation of gender is also critical for change today. To that end, a feminist perspective is indispensable. It is also not remedial, because it questions what has long been labelled important, and is a political protest against making the past solely one of men.
>
> *Jones and Pay 1990: 169*

Since 1990 such radical reinterpretations have been assayed with varying success, but in a field which is intrinsically conservative, it will probably take decades to achieve gender equity.

References

Agrest, D., Conway, P. and Weisman, L. K. (eds) (1996) *The Sex of Architecture*, New York: Harry N. Abrams.

Bell, S. G. (1990) 'Women create gardens in male landscapes: a revisionist approach to eighteenth century English garden history', *Feminist Studie*s, 16(3): 471–91.

Bennett, R. (ed.) (1986.) *Visiting the Past: America's Historylands*, Washington DC.: National Geographic Society.

Betsky, A. (1995) *Building Sex: Men, Women, Architecture, and the Construction of Sexuality*, New York: William Morrow.

Bogart, M. (1989) *Public Sculpture and the Civic Ideal in New York City, 1890–1930*, Chicago: University of Chicago Press.

Boyer, C. (1994) *The City as Collective Memory: Its Historical Imagery and Architectural Entertainments*, Cambridge MA: MIT Press.

Clines, F. X. (1997) 'Clinton Hails FDR at memorial's opening', *The New York Times*, 3 May.

Cole, D. (1973) *From Tipi to Skyscraper: A History of Women in Architecture*, Boston: i press.

Coleman, D., Danze, E. and Henderson, C. (eds) (1996) *Architecture and Feminism*, New York: Yale Publications on Architecture and Princeton Architectural Press.

Colomia, B. (ed.) (1992) *Sexuality and Space*, New York: Princeton Architectural Press.

Davey, F. and Chambers, T. A. (1994) '"A woman? At the fort?": A shock tactic for integrating women's history in historical interpretation', *Gender and History*, 6(3): 468–73.

Edensor, T. and Kothari, U. (1994) 'The masculinisation of Stirling's heritage', in V. Kinnaird and D. Hall (eds) *Tourism: A Gender Analysis*, Chichester: John Wiley. pp. 164–87.

Garber, J. and Turner, R. (1995) *Gender in Urban Research*, Urban Affairs Annual Reviews 42, Thousand Oaks CA: Sage.

Grant, L. (1994) '"Her Stories": Working with a community advisory board on a women's history exhibition at a Canadian municipal museum', *Gender and History*, 6(3): 410–18.

Graves, D.C. and Green Devens, C. (1994) 'Subject as audience: the politics of public exhibits on women', *Gender and History*, 6(3): 419–25.

Greed, C.H. (1994) *Women and Planning: Creating Gendered Identities*, London: Routledge.

Gross, S. H. and Rojas M. H. (1986) *But women have no history! Images of women in the public history of Washington DC*. St. Louis Park MI: Genhurst Publications.

Hasted, R. (1994) 'Tales of the city: women in a community history exhibition', *Gender and History*, 6(3): 397–409.

Hayden, D. (1996) *The Power of Place: Urban Landscapes as Public History*, Cambridge MA: MIT Press.

Inglis, K. (1989) 'Men, women and war memorials: Anzac, Australia' in J. K. Conway, S. C. Bourque and J. W. Scott (eds) *Learning about Women: Gender Politics and Power*, Ann Arbor: University of Michigan Press, pp. 35–59.

Johnson, N. (1995) 'Cast in stone: monuments, geography and nationalism', *Environment and Planning B: Society and Space*, 13: 51–65.

Jones, S. and Pay, S. (1990) 'The legacy of Eve', in P. Gathercole and D. Lowenthal (eds) *The Politics of the Past*, London: Unwin Hyman.

Kavanagh, G. (1994) 'Looking for ourselves, inside and outside museums', *Gender and History*, 6(3): 370–75.

Knibb, H. (1994) '"Present but not visible": searching for women's history in museum collections', *Gender and History*, 6(3): 352–69.

Landes, J. B. (1988) *Women and the Public Sphere in the Age of the French Revolution*, Ithaca NY: Cornell University Press.

Lowenthal, D. (1985) *The Past as a Foreign Country*, Cambridge: Cambridge University Press.

Massey, D. (1994) *Space, Place and Gender*, Minneapolis: University of Minnesota Press.

Melosh, B. and Simmons, C. (1986) 'Exhibiting women's history' in S. P. Benson, S. Brier and R. Rosenzweig (eds) *Presenting the Past: Essays on History and the Public*, Philadelphia: Temple University Press, pp. 203–21.

Miller, M. and Digan Lanning, A. (1994) '"Common parlors": women and the re-creation of community identity in Deerfield, Massachusetts, 1870–1920', *Gender and History*, 6(3): 435–55.

Monk, J. (1992) 'Gender in the landscape: expressions of power and meaning', in K. Anderson and F. Yale (eds) *Inventing Places: Studies in Cultural Geography*, Melbourne: Longman Cheshire.

Moore, L. J. (1994) '"She's my hero": women's history at the Cowgirl Hall of Fame', *Gender and History*, 6(3): 474–80.

Nenadic, S. (1994) 'Museums, gender and cultural identity in Scotland', *Gender and History*, 6(3): 426–34.

New York Times (1997) 'A black group assails statue of suffragists.' 7 March.

New York Times (1996) 'One first lady salutes another at statue's unveiling', 6 October.

Porter, G. (1991) 'How are women represented in British history museums?', *Museum*, 43: 159–62.

Prentice, R. (1994) 'Heritage: a key sector of the "new" tourism', in C. Cooper and A. Lockwood (eds) *Progress in Tourism, Recreation and Hospitality Management*, volume 5, Chichester: Wiley, pp. 309–24.

Reed, C. (ed.) (1996) *Not at Home: The Suppression of Domesticity in Modern Art and Architecture*, London: Thames and Hudson.

Ryan, M. P. (1990) *Women in Public: Between Banners and Ballots, 1825–1880*, Baltimore: Johns Hopkins Press.

Sanders, J. (ed.) (1996) *Stud: Architectures of Masculinity*, New York: Princeton Architectural Press.

Segalen, M. (1994) 'Here but invisible: the presentation of women in French ethnography museums', *Gender and History*, 6(3): 320–33.

Sherr, L. and Kazickas, J. (1994) *Susan B. Anthony Slept Here: a Guide to American Women's Landmarks*, New York: Random House.

Sherman, D. (1996) 'Monuments, mourning and masculinity in France after World War I', *Gender and History*, 8(1): 82–107.

Shoemaker, N. (1994) 'The natural history of gender', *Gender and History*, 6(3): 320–33.

Smyth, A. (1991) 'The floozie in the jacuzzi', *Feminist Studies*, 17(1): 6–28.

Spain, D. (1992) *Gendered Spaces*, Chapel Hill: University of North Carolina Press.

Tunbridge, J. E. and Ashworth, G. J. (1996) *Dissonant Heritage: the Management of the Past as a Resource in Conflict*, Chichester: John Wiley.

Wagner, P. (1972) *Environments and Peoples*, Englewood Cliffs NJ: Prentice-Hall.

Warner, M. (1985) *Monuments and Maidens: the Allegory of the Female Form*, London: Weidenfeld and Nicolson.

Weisman, L. K. (1992) *Discrimination by Design: a Feminist Critique of the Man-Made Environment*, Urbana: University of Illinois Press.

Weiss, M. (1996) 'The politics of underestimation', in D. Agrest, P. Conway and L. K. Weisman (eds) *The Sex of Architecture*, New York: Henry N. Abrams, pp.251–62.

West, P. (1994) 'Gender politics and the "invention of tradition": The museumization of Louisa May Alcott's Orchard House', *Gender and History*, 6(3): 456–67.

Wilson, E. (1991) *The Sphinx in the City: Urban Life, the Control of Disorder, and Women*, Berkeley: University of California Press.

5 Interpretation as a social experience

LYNN D. DIERKING

Introduction

Millions of people worldwide, visit museums and heritage settings every year. The majority of these people visit in social groups and even if they visit alone they are quickly immersed in the social setting of other visitors, staff and volunteers. Why do people visit these social settings? What do they do while there? What meaning do they make of these settings, what do they remember afterwards and what role does the social nature of the experience play in this meaning-making process? In order to explore these questions, this chapter will document the social nature of these experiences, review relevant social science theories within the domains of social psychology, anthropology and communications theory, and explore the implications of these theories for practice.

The visit as leisure-time activity

In order to understand the social nature of interpretive experiences, one must first take a visitor-centred perspective, remembering that for most people a visit to a nature centre, environmental park or historic home is an enjoyable way to spend leisure time: one involving family or friends on weekends, holidays or free time during the week. People come individually, in small groups, or as part of an organised group participating in a pre-planned visit. The notion of visitation as leisure-time activity is clear to staff of most parks, historic sites and other heritage settings because often it is quite obvious that visitors have come intending not only to visit, but to combine it with a weekend camping trip or other outing. Many of these sites are popular holiday destinations or stops along the way to somewhere else.

Many common strands run through visitor experiences, regardless of the type of setting visited or the type of visitor. These patterns are influenced by a number of variables, including the frequency with which visitors attend such settings, the expectations they might have and the background and experience they bring. In an effort to present a coherent picture of the visitor experience, Falk and Dierking (1992) created a framework for making sense of both the common strands and unique complexities of these experiences. This framework, the 'Interactive Experience Model', suggests that a visitor-centred perspective and all experience and subsequent meaning-making is contextual. It is suggested that a visitor's Interactive Experience is dictated by the interplay of three contexts:

- the Personal Context of the visitor: that is, personal characteristics, such as reasons for visiting, learning style, prior knowledge, experience, attitudes, interests and cultural background;

- the Physical Context they encounter: that is, the physical characteristics of the site including where it is located, what it looks like, its interpretive features and the 'feel' or site ambience;

- the Social Context of the experience: including people with whom they attend as well as the staff, volunteers and other visitors encountered during the experience. Another important influence in this context is cultural factors.

Due to the constraints of space, this chapter will focus on a discussion of the social context dimension of this framework, recognising that there is a great deal of interaction between each of the three contexts above. Social interaction includes the questions and discussions generated by looking at the offerings of a site and reading labels and trail markers, as well as conversations, glances and touches totally unrelated to the site.

The social context: groups and the visitor experience

Given that so many people find interpretive settings enjoyable places to spend leisure time, few dispute that such settings are first and foremost social environments (Falk and Dierking 1992; Rosenfeld 1979). Because most people choose to visit these settings as part of a social group, a large part of their attention is devoted to the people with whom they arrive. Studies indicate that a great deal of the time and energy which families and other social groups expend during a visit is invested in social dynamics. Unfortunately, although research has been undertaken on the influence of groups on the interpretive experience, there is essentially no research on social interactions between all-adult groups or lone visitors, although anecdotal evidence suggests that some visitors go to interpretive settings specifically to meet others. Many interpretive settings have built popular and profitable programming around the single adult's desire to meet someone interesting.

It is clear from research that groups come to 'do a site' and consequently they read some of the interpretive pamphlets and, if available, watch the introductory film and participate in some activities, enjoying 'learning' something new. Research data also indicate that groups are trying to be model visitors, but they are frequently disoriented, overwhelmed by the quantity and level of material presented and desperately trying to personalise the experience, all within the context of the social interaction of their group.

Families

In the case of families, research indicates that a typical family spends a consistent 15 to 20 per cent of its visit interacting as a group, plus an additional 2 to 5 per cent attending to people outside their social group. Collectively, these interactions make up what is termed the social context. It is clear from such data that the family visitor experience is a social one and that social interaction plays a major role in shaping the visitor experience.

Several studies support the idea that families use such settings as socially 'mediated' meaning-making environments (Chase 1975; Dierking 1987, 1989; Hilke and Balling 1985; Lakota 1975; Rosenfeld 1979; Taylor 1986). Families spend the majority of their time in conversation, asking questions, either about the exhibits in general or about specific content contained within exhibits. Parents ask children questions; children ask parents questions; both point to particularly interesting things and occasionally read labels or trail markers. Minda Borun and a group of researchers in the Philadelphia/Camden Informal Science Education Collaborative (PISEC) found that the learning observed in their study was related to specific observed behaviours which included asking and answering questions, commenting on the exhibit and reading the labels aloud – all social behaviours (Borun, Chambers and Cleghorn 1996). Even the lone behaviour, reading labels silently, was observed by these researchers in the context of a social group.

In addition to questions, families also talk about what they know from previous experiences, discussing what they see in terms of these experiences and memories. As researchers have observed, these discussions provide opportunities for parents and children to reinforce past events and family history and to develop a shared understanding among family members. During many of these conversations one also observes people's efforts to negotiate personal and cultural meaning, actively making sense of the interpretation presented and attempting to relate it to their own experience and world view.

Because such settings are social, one of the things that visitors also like to do is to 'people watch'. In interviews, they often state that watching other visitors is something they do frequently during a visit and that it is important to their sense of satisfaction with the outing. Watching other visitors seems to be a natural thing to do in these settings and visitors enjoy it. Beyond mere curiosity, they observe other visitors to gain information or knowledge. They watch other people to see what they are doing and where they are going in the museum.

Modelling, a socially mediated form of learning stemming from 'people watching', is also a frequently observed social interaction in interpretive settings. In the case of families, members observe one another, other groups and staff to figure out how to manipulate interactives and behave appropriately in the setting. Modelling also plays an important role in the types of learning observed among families. In a study by Dierking (1989), a continuum of social learning styles was identified among families, ranging from 'collaborative learning' to 'independent learning'. Analysis of the data suggests that teaching and learning is taking place over the whole continuum and that modelling plays a critical role in the process.

Other groups

The overwhelming majority of social interaction research has focused on families, probably because visitor demographics over the years have consistently shown that family groups constitute a majority of all visitors to these settings and because these groups are so obviously social in composition. However, people visit museums in other social configurations including all-adult groups and school parties. A few studies that have examined all-adult groups suggest that, as with families, social interaction plays an important role in influencing the way people relate to exhibits and share the experience with companions (Lakota 1975; McManus 1987; Silverman 1990). However, except for the Silverman study which will be discussed later, these studies did not analyse in depth how social interaction among all-adult group members influenced the meaning-making process.

School groups

Very little research has been conducted on the social context of school field trips, after family groups, the next largest portion of most museum's visitors. Much as educational researchers neglected the important role that social mediation plays in the learning process in classrooms until recent interest in co-operative learning, research about field trips also neglected the role it plays in student learning in museums. Studies that have been conducted were for the most part experimental, focusing on variables such as the advance preparation of students or docent teaching styles, assessing their effects on primarily cognitive outcomes. The social nature of the field trip experience was at best disregarded and at worst considered a confounding variable.

Preliminary work suggests that social interaction is an important aspect of field trips for children which supports their ability to find personal meaning in the event (Birney 1986; Falk and Dierking 1992; Griffin and Symington 1997; Tuckey 1992; Tunnicliffe 1995; Wolins *et al.* 1992). Supporting research has found that the most effective orientation, even more effective than conceptual orientation, was one that accommodated the child's social agenda. In another study, where children were able to talk about their learning, it was found that social mediation played an important role in the learning process. In this study, children indicated:

1. They enjoyed acquiring new information and perceived the museum as a place to do this.

2. They preferred to share the information with others, particularly peers, rather than listen to docents.

3. They were able to define specific places and conditions in which they could best share this information.

4. They felt that there were optimum conditions under which to visit the museum by expressing dislike for certain negative aspects of museums, such as crowding, that hindered their ability to look at exhibits.

Children also seem to remember the most about visits to interpretive settings when they can interact socially with one another, talk about what they are seeing and engage in related co-operative learning activities back at school. In a Scottish study (Tuckey 1992), children who were allowed freely to explore a science centre recalled more about the exhibits where they interacted with friends. These interactions seemed to stimulate label reading and increased positive attitudes about the science centre and its contents.

Notwithstanding the studies above, few researchers have actually observed and documented the social aspects of children's field trip experiences. The role of important social processes such as conversations or modelling is barely documented and any role they might play in promoting meaning-making is barely understood. It is highly likely that just as these processes play an important role in the casual visitor experience, they also play a similarly important role in the school field trip experience.

Between group interactions

All of the studies focusing on social interaction reinforce the notion that the museum experience is a social one for visiting groups and plays a critical role in mediating and influencing group experience. What role does social interaction play between groups? The influence of social interaction with other people, either as an individual or as part of a group is not well documented. There are, however, preliminary data from two studies conducted at the Florida Museum of Natural History suggesting that museum visitors attend to other visitors and, beyond mere curiosity, seem to be observing one another to gain information or knowledge (Koran *et al.* 1988). These studies demonstrate the role that modelling or social learning plays in influencing the visitor experience between groups. The first preliminary observation of an exhibit on the geology of Florida that included a hands-on rock cycle interactive indicated that visitors were not touching it at all. When a person was used to 'model' the appropriate touching behaviour the researcher consistently recorded groups, including children and adults, touching the rocks, a behaviour infrequently observed before modelling. Similar results were observed in the second study, conducted in a 'Mesic Hammock' exhibit, with headphone stations. Visitors did not listen to the commentary on one phone for long and mistakenly assumed that all headphones had the same message. The use of people modelling the appropriate listening behaviours and verbalising that the messages were different, significantly increased visitor attention to individual phones and the number of phones to which they listened. Both of these studies demonstrate that visitors do pay attention to what other visitors in the museum are doing.

Interactions with staff and volunteers

The social context of a visit also includes the staff whom visitors encounter. Research suggests that personal interaction with staff increases the likelihood that a museum experience will be memorable. In recollection studies (Falk and Dierking 1992) it is not uncommon for individuals to remember the qualities of docents and staff years after the experience. The few studies conducted with the casual visitor indicate that staff and volunteers can positively influence the experience. When a staff member or docent was available to answer questions informally, the time spent at individual exhibits increased. Researchers consistently observed that families spent more time at exhibits involving interaction between visitors and the exhibit, or between visitors, docents or staff.

Theatre and performance

Another form of social mediation increasingly common in interpretive settings is the use of theatre and performance. It is surprising, therefore, that there are no current studies that focus on the influence of this interpretive style on the visitor experience. A pilot project at the National Zoo, however, suggests that it could be a powerful educative medium (Dierking 1990).

In summary, although the data indicate that social interactions constitute only 20 per cent of visitors' time, this chapter has attempted to indicate that their significance is much greater than the figure suggests. Data on what visitors recall from their visit many years later consistently indicate that the social aspects of visits are rarely forgotten, and sometimes what a visitor recollects are primarily the social aspects of the visit.

Before leaving this topic, it is important to recognise that social interaction with other visitors is not always positive. Crowding is often a major problem in exhibits and, as even the children in Birney's study (1986) were able to suggest, such crowding does not result in pleasant experiences that facilitate personal meaning-making. Families tend to walk past exhibits when other visitors are blocking their view – families stop only when they find an empty space. Taylor (1986) found that in a museum layout with a one-way traffic pattern, a new family group arriving at an exhibit would 'bump' the current family on to a new exhibit, limiting their time at the display. Negative aspects aside, however, there is much to learn about how social interactions between visitor groups and others in the museum influence the interpretive experience.

Relevant social science theories

Obviously, social interaction is an important dimension of interpretive settings. However, what that means in terms of the meaning-making process and how best to utilise this knowledge to create meaningful experiences for visitors is poorly understood. In my opinion, this lack of understanding has left a tremendous gap in the field's ability to understand the meaning-making process for it is largely through the social and cultural context that individuals are able to construct personal meaning. From the earliest moments of conception, humans are immersed in a rich physical and social context that envelops and nurtures the foetus. Research suggests that beyond the expected exchange of nutrients, waste products and gases, there is a great deal of social exchange between the foetus and the mother. *In utero* infants hear music and conversations and their development is strongly influenced by the emotional and social milieu of the mother (Gallagher 1993).

In interpretive settings, as the previous section of this chapter documented, social interaction is an important way in which visitors share what they know or find out more. There are opportunities for group members to share, watch one another, have a new and novel experience or reinforce something they already know. There are opportunities for social, kinaesthetic, aesthetic and affective learning. By looking at objects together, reading labels, manipulating interactives, watching others and talking with friends or family, there is an opportunity to accommodate new ideas and to have a highly personal experience, all important if successful meaning-making is to occur. Even when meaning-making seems not to be directly influenced by social interaction, there is indirect interaction. The books one reads alone, the exhibits one views alone, have all been created by other humans with the intention of communicating, that is 'conversing' with the reader or viewer, and all have been put together within some sociocultural context of their own. As the solitary person reads and interacts she brings her own experience, emotions and values to the fore, all mediated by her own social and cultural background. As suggested, successful meaning-making results when a person is able actively to construct and find personal meaning within the situation or experience. Virtually all such meaning-making is either directly or indirectly socially mediated. To optimise the social nature of the experience, this interaction must be recognised as an important and non-trivial ingredient that plays an essential role in making interpretive settings meaningful to people by personalising the experience for them. If such understandings can be developed, interpretive staff will be in a much better position to design meaningful experiences for visitors that facilitate the meaning-making which occurs there, enhancing connections between people's prior and subsequent experience.

Although literature discussing the role of social mediation in meaning-making is limited, there are three areas of social science research that provide some insights:

- social psychology theory including Vygotsky's theory of cognitive development and social modelling theory;

- communications and mass media theory;

- theory focusing on sociocultural influences on meaning-making.

Social psychology theory

Although the notion of the importance of the social dimension in cognition seems to be no surprising revelation, there has actually been little focus on understanding the role that social and cultural mediation plays in the meaning-making process. Research in the fields of social psychology for years was primarily focused on group functioning and interpersonal influence, particularly in the areas of social pathology. Asch (1952) and others within the social psychology's Gestalt tradition long ago emphasised the subject's active role in 'defining the situation', that is, in actively interpreting, rather than passively registering the events that unfold in the laboratory as well in everyday experience. However, it was only in the late 1960s and 1970s that social cognition as a discipline was truly born. Although it was encouraging that efforts were focused on social context, much of this early research was preoccupied with the cognitive responses of the individual to the social milieu, attempting to understand people's efforts to interpret information about their social environment, rather than an effort to understand how the social and cultural environment influences individual perception and the active interpretation of events, ideas and objects (Ross 1981).

Beyond these conceptual shortcomings, much of this research also had methodological flaws. Despite the fact that research focused on the social milieu was the prevailing research paradigm, much of it was conducted with individuals in laboratory settings, situations in which people were interviewed individually or given paper and pencil tests that probed their understanding of social context. There were few ecologically valid field-based studies.

A notable exception was the work of L. S. Vygotsky, a Russian social psychologist. Vygotsky felt that communication, along with culture and social life, has a profound effect on the way people think and learn. Central to his theory of cognitive development was the notion of mediation (Vygotsky 1978). He believed that people use language not only for social communication but also to guide, plan and monitor their own activity in a self-regulatory manner. Vygotsky referred to such self-regulatory language as private speech, feeling that people, particularly children, use this language as a tool in their thinking: in other words, the same language that mediates social interaction between individuals is used to mediate cognitive activity within individuals. Children take the language of everyday interactions, make it part of their private speech and use this speech to organise their own independent cognitive efforts (Berk 1986; Wertsch 1985). Vygotsky stressed the central role of social communication in the development of children's thinking by conceiving of children's learning as taking place within the 'zone of proximal development'. Tasks within a child's zone of proximal development were those too difficult to be done alone, but which could be accomplished with the verbal guidance and assistance of adults or more skilled children (Vygotsky 1978). The type of social process on which Vygotsky focused involved small groups (frequently dyads) of individuals engaged in concrete social interaction, similar to the groups one might observe in an interpretive setting such as a heritage park or historic home.

Vygotsky's notion of mediation was extremely rich, emphasising meaning and verbal and non-verbal language. He took a biological and evolutionary approach to trying to understand cognition, feeling that the emergence and transformation of forms of mediation had benefited humans and increased their survival as a species over the course of evolutionary history. Like another social psychologist, G. H. Mead, he felt that one could not analyse individual processes to understand social processes (Mead 1924–5, 1934). In fact, Vygotsky really saw it the other way around entirely: in order to understand the individual, he felt one must first understand the social relations in which the individual exists (Vygotsky 1979, 1981). He believed that all higher mental functions have social origins and appear, at first on an interpersonal plane, between individuals, before they exist on an intrapsychic plane, within the individual (Vygotsky 1978).

Although Vygotsky's research primarily focused on children and this research has great relevance for interpretive settings for children, his ideas have broader application as well. His interest in the nature of interactions between skilled and less skilled people in small groups is an important model for the field, since such interactions are frequently observed in interpretive settings.

Another social psychology theory of great relevance because it is so frequently observed in interpretive settings is social modelling theory.

Modelling, that is learning through observation and imitation, also often called social learning or observational learning, has long been studied in both animal behaviour and human learning (Bandura 1964; Bandura 1977; Bandura and Walters 1963). Many of the social, emotional and even intellectual abilities of humans are learned by modelling the behaviour of others, rather than by more formal instruction. For example, it is easier to learn how to dance a new dance step by watching someone who does it well than by reading a book about it. Social types of learning are extremely important; these are powerful tools for childhood (and adult) socialisation and evidence suggests that the results are extremely long term.

An extensive line of laboratory investigations by Albert Bandura (1964) demonstrated that modelling is the basis for a wide variety of children's learned behaviours, such as aggression, prosocial behaviour and sex stereotyping. Bandura recognised that from an early age children acquire many of their responses simply by watching and listening to others around them, without direct rewards and punishments.

Bandura was particularly interested in what would motivate children to imitate the behaviour of certain models. Research by him and his followers has shown that children are drawn to models who are warm and powerful and possess desirable objects and other characteristics. Modelling has also been used as an effective tool to modify behaviour. For example, Bandura showed that watching a peer play comfortably and pleasurably with a dog can help children who are afraid of dogs to overcome their fears (Bandura 1967).

Reinforcement and modelling have also been used to teach social skills to children who have few friends because they lack effective social behaviours (Asher *et al.* 1976). Modelling can also affect attitude and emotions. Laboratory evidence indicates that exposure to models who behave in a helpful or generous fashion is very effective in encouraging children to act more prosocially themselves (Bryan and London 1970; Canale 1977; Elliot and Vasta 1970; Gray and Pirot 1984).

Since modelling is such a frequently observed social interaction in interpretive settings, research in this area is extremely important (Dierking 1987, 1989). Obviously it is also a mechanism that can be used effectively to modify visitor behaviour, as the Koran *et al.* (1988) study described earlier demonstrates. Although much of the research to date has been conducted with children in laboratories, there is a tremendous need to understand the modelling that occurs in public settings between children, between children and other adults, and between adults, including other visitors, staff and volunteers. Only then will the field be able to optimise the use of this powerful but poorly understood social learning mechanism.

Communications and mass media theory

Silverman (1990) utilised mass media research and communications theory to understand how visitors make meaning in a museum. Although 'mass media' are typically thought of as the symbolic products of television, radio and print, Silverman suggested that museums share many of the same purposes, including the provision of opportunities for people to gain information, enjoy recreation and arrive at shared cultural meaning. Silverman suggests that museums facilitate these processes by housing many of the symbolic objects important to such communication.

Several researchers have explored the behaviour of visitors as it occurs within different social contexts, noting visitors' verbal behaviour and comments to each other as data which support Silverman's ideas (Birney 1982; Draper 1984; Hilke and Balling 1985; McManus 1987). In these studies, researchers found that although group members tended to look at, read and manipulate exhibits individually, they were directing others to look or naming or identifying objects for the benefits of others; a significant percentage of information was transferred within groups through the spontaneous and unsolicited sharing of salient aspects of an individual's experience. The presence of companions, particularly family members or close friends, significantly contributed to an individual's personal meaning-making.

In Silverman's (1990) study, visitor talk was analysed and found to consist of five major components, with visitors filtering the experience through the context of their relationship, constructing and reflecting on the meaning of the objects and the relationship to themselves. By recasting the museum in this mass media framework along with other free choice media such as television, radio and print, Silverman's findings suggest that interpretation in such arenas should take into consideration the following:

- the view of interpretation as an interactive creative process which takes place in the social context of interaction with one's companions;

- that a number of possible meanings of a particular message are possible (Iser 1978; Katz and Liebes 1986);

- that social interaction not only results in the transmission of new information but also serves to maintain social relationships and forge new social bonds, often through the communication and shared reinforcement of known or shared information, such as memories and experiences (Thelen 1989).

Sociocultural influences on meaning-making

A visitor-centred approach to interpretive centres recognises the visitors' active role in creating meaning through the contexts they bring to the setting. However, merely to focus on personal, physical and social contexts, without recognising the important overlay that culture contributes is to miss a great deal. Visitors find personal significance within these settings in a range of patterned ways that reflect basic human needs, such as the need for individuality and community, and which are also influenced greatly by the factors of self-identity, companions and leisure motivations. The meanings visitors derive are influenced by social and cultural norms, attitudes and values, as well as their own needs for self-identity (Silverman 1995). Depending upon the person, self-identity might centre around learning so-called 'expert information' about artefacts and history, or being able to identify personally with an artefact or some aspect of history.

The field of cultural psychology attempts to examine and understand how people's perceptions of customary practices, traditional institutions, symbolic and material resources and inherited conceptions of things influence their identity, sense of self and life space (Stigler *et al.* 1990). In terms of interpretive settings, this means that the researcher must understand what these settings mean to people socially and culturally in order fully to understand their motivation for visiting or not visiting and their subsequent behaviour within these settings should they decide to visit.

Ogbu (1990, 1995) describes what he calls a person's cultural model, that is, the understanding people have of their universe, including the social and physical components, as well as their understanding of how to behave in that universe. Following LeVine (1973), Ogbu suggests that a person's cultural world has five components:

- customary ways of behaving (e.g. making a living and eating);

- codes or assumptions, expectations and emotions underlying these customary behaviours;

- artefacts – things which members of the population make or have made – that have meanings for them (e.g. homes, clothing and other possessions);

- institutions – economic, political, religious and social – which form a recognisable pattern requiring knowledge, beliefs, competencies or skills and customary behaviours (e.g. museums, schools, hospitals and libraries);

- patterns of social relations.

Interpretive settings such as museums, historic homes and parks may or may not be part of a person's cultural world. For example, the differences between frequent visitors to interpretive settings and those people who do not visit at all can be explained in terms of differences in the cultural models and worlds of these two groups. Americans in general do not frequently visit museums; 60 per cent do not visit an interpretive setting in any given year and half of these, 30 per cent, never go unless they go involuntarily, for example, on a school field trip. Only 20 per cent of visitors to interpretive settings are frequent visitors (Falk 1993). Ogbu would argue that such differences can be accounted for by a number of variables, but are primarily a function of differences in the history of these groups. The primary variable that seems to influence this behaviour is a history of museum going, particularly a history of visiting such cultural institutions as a child with one's family. Falk (1993, 1995) in a study of African-American leisure time utilisation of museums also found that a history of museum going and a family history of participation in cultural and family activities emerged as the most important determiners of African-American museum visitation.

The above synthesis of the sociocultural influences on meaning-making would suggest that they operate at a number of levels and all contribute in some way to people's perceptions of interpretive settings. At the society level, one can analyse the place which these institutions have within society and how they are perceived by the larger society in general (i.e. as cultural institutions harbouring precious artefacts or as public educational institutions). The perception of the institution at the group–tribe level is another important level focusing on the question of whether interpretive settings meet the needs of or appeal to certain groups (i.e. do I perceive interpretive settings as friendly, useful or alien places as a function of my group?). The next level at which sociocultural influences operate is at the friend–family level. This is where family history, sense of community and companions so strongly influence one's perception of and subsequent behaviour in interpretive settings. The final level, that of the individual, is where personal values, self-identity and motivation are the focus. Museum researchers have focused on the individual and family levels to the exclusion of the greater society and group–tribe. The individual and family levels are not static, discrete entities, but dynamic, constantly shaping and reshaping one another, suggesting that the only way truly to understand the complexity of the meaning of interpretive settings to people is actually to understand these processes in the context of the greater society and group.

Implications

In this chapter I have suggested that fostering meaningful social interaction within interpretive settings will result in more satisfying opportunities for visitors to find their own personal meaning in these settings. I also suggested that such personal meaning is just that, exceedingly personal. One visitor might marvel at certain information provided by interpreters, while another visitor is quite satisfied to look carefully at objects without reading any of the interpretive material at all. In order to be successful, interpretive staff need to understand the role that social mediation plays in the meaning-making process and they need to be open to the variety of ways that visitors can personally connect and relate to the material contained within their settings.

How does one design exhibitions, interpretative materials and programmes that foster social interaction? How can social science theories be used to improve these practices? Answers to such questions need to be considered for families, all-adult groups and school groups, as well as for the social interaction occurring between visitor groups, interpretive staff and volunteers.

Obviously, physical spaces need to be designed that encourage social interaction. Creating comfortable sitting areas, inviting work tables and group-oriented interpretive materials are some simple ways to promote social interaction, but there are endless possibilities with which to experiment. In two articles summarising PISEC action research (Borun and Dritsas 1997; Borun et al. 1998) a set of exhibition characteristics is shared which can facilitate family learning, including making exhibits multi-sided and multi-modal.

Social interaction issues also need to be taken into account as programmes are planned for particular audiences. For example, why not design school programmes that allow small groups of students to interact together as they look at a specific interpretive area or to engage together in a problem-solving activity? This requires rethinking a new role for interpretive staff, one of facilitator, rather than disseminator. By integrating the school group's desire socially to interact with the actual programme, interpretive staff may find that both the child's agenda, as well as their own, can be fulfilled.

Involving families, school groups and all-adult groups on advisory committees providing input for exhibits, interpretive materials and programmes is another way to help to ensure that such groups' needs and desires are known. At the National Museum of American History, Smithsonian Institution, Washington, DC, staff recently assembled a family-based advisory committee to provide input for their educational programmes and they are pleased with the results thus far.

Obviously, sociocultural influences must be considered much more carefully when designing exhibits, interpretive materials and programmes. Respecting the diversity of backgrounds and experience that visitors bring and their own need to find connections of personal meaning is critical. In order to create successful interpretive experiences, care must be taken to understand the value of these settings to people's lives within a cultural context that makes sense to them. Interpretive staff should be thinking about what they need to know about visitors' cultures and backgrounds in order to understand them better and best support their ability to find personal meaning in the experiences provided. Frames of references used to guide exhibition and programme development should be informed by visitors' world-views, not by the world views of staff, board members, administrators and/or frequent visitors (Falk and Dierking 1995).

There is still much to be understood about social interaction. In a study by Rosenfeld (1979), families did not listen to the commentary by the trained guides on the zoo train, nor did they ask questions, a seeming contradiction of much of what has been discussed in this chapter. Perhaps it was an issue of training and knowledge. Taylor (1986) found that volunteer interpreters frequently did not have enough content background or training to respond effectively to visitor questions and perceived their role as policemen rather than explainer. Obviously there is a need to do more focused action research that will actually provide some additional insights into factors influencing social interaction. One creative example of such action research is the PISEC project (Borun, *et al.* 1996), which in its next stage is focusing on modelling. Working closely with staff at the Philadelphia Zoo, they are experimenting with 'model' families, trained to engage in conversations and activities designed to model positive social interactions. Research efforts are documenting this activity and attempting to understand its usefulness as a potential programme element for other institutions.

More basic research is also needed. Research designs for such studies need to be more sensitive to social interaction and should employ longitudinal research methodologies, when possible. Social interactions continue long after visitors have left the museum; preliminary work by McManus suggests that learning may occur long after the visit, as family members discuss and reinforce the experience with one another (McManus 1995). Utilising theories such as Vygotsky's theory of cognitive development and communications and mass media theory as guiding research paradigms should ensure more sensitivity to group interactions. Research designs also need to be guided by frames of reference that represent visitor world views and do not bypass fundamental questions about interpretive settings as cultural institutions to which people relate in very different and personal ways.

My hope is that with further experimentation and research, both basic and applied, we will further strengthen our understanding of the role that social interaction plays in the meaning-making process. Armed with this knowledge, interpretive staff should be in a position to foster interactive visitor experiences that provide a variety of opportunities for visitors to find their own personal meaning.

References

Asch, S. (1952) *Social Psychology*, Englewood Cliffs NJ: Prentice-Hall.

Asher, S. R., Odden, S. L. and Gottman, J. M. (1976) 'Children's friendships in school settings', in L. G. Katz (ed.) *Current Topics in Early Childhood Education*, vol. 1, New York: Erlbaum, pp. 38–61.

Bandura, A. (1964) 'Behaviour modification through modelling procedure', in L. Krasner and L. P. Ullman (eds) *Research in Behaviour Modification*, New York: Holt, Rinehart and Winston.

Bandura, A. (1967) 'Behavioral psychotherapy', *Scientific American*, 216(9): 78–86.

Bandura, A. (1977) *Social Learning*, Englewood Cliffs NJ: Prentice-Hall.

Bandura, A. and Walters, R. (1963) *Social Learning and Personality Development*, New York: Holt, Rinehart and Winston.

Berk, L. E. (1986) 'Private speech: learning out loud', *Psychology Today*, 20(5): 34–42.

Birney, B. (1986) 'A comparative study of children's perceptions and knowledge of wildlife and conservation as they relate to field trip experiences at the Los Angeles County Museum of Natural History and the Los Angeles Zoo', unpublished doctoral dissertation, University of California, Los Angeles.

Birney, R. (1982) 'An evaluation of visitors' experiences at the Governor's Palace, Colonial Williamsburg, VA', *Academic Psychology Bulletin*, 4: 135–41.

Borun, M., Chambers, M. and Cleghorn, A. (1996) 'Families are learning in science museums', *Curator*, 39(2): 123–38.

Borun, M., Chambers, M., Dritsas, J. and Johnson, J. (1998) 'Enhancing family learning through exhibits', *Curator*, 40(4): 279–93.

Borun, M. and Dritsas, J. (1997) 'Developing family-friendly exhibits', *Curator*, 40,(3): 178–96.

Bryan, J. H. and London, P. (1970) 'Altruistic behaviour by children'. *Psychological Bulletin*, 73: 200–211.

Canale, J. R. (1977) 'The effect of modelling and length of ownership on sharing behaviour of children', *Social Behaviour and Personality*, 5: 187–91.

Chase, R. A. (1975) 'Museums as learning environments', *Museum News*, Sept.–Oct.: 36–43.

Damon, W. (1981) 'Exploring children's social cognition on two fronts', in J. H. Flavell and L. Ross (eds) *Social Cognitive Development: Frontiers and Possible Futures*, Cambridge: Cambridge University Press.

Dierking, L. D. (1987) 'Parent–child interactions in a free choice learning setting: an examination of attention-directing behaviours', unpublished doctoral dissertation, University of Florida.

Dierking, L. D. (1989) 'What research says to museum educators about the family museum experience', *Journal of Museum Education*, Spring–Summer.

Dierking, L. D. (1990) *Evaluation of the Super Week Program*, (final report), Annapolis MD: Science Learning.

Draper, L. (1984) 'Friendship and the museum experience: the interrelationship of social ties and learning', unpublished doctoral dissertation, University of California, Berkeley.

Elliot, R. and Vasta, R. (1970) 'The modelling of sharing: effects associated with vicarious reinforcement, symbolization, age and generalization', *Journal of Experimental Child Psychology*, 10: 8–15.

Falk, J. H. (1993) *Leisure Decisions Influencing African American Use of Museums*, Washington DC: American Association of Museums.

Falk, J. H. (1995) 'Factors influencing African American leisure time utilisation of museums', *Journal of Leisure Research*, 27(1): 41–60.

Falk, J.H. and Dierking, L.D. (1992) *The Museum Experience*, Washington DC: Whalesback Books.

Falk, J. H. and Dierking, L. D. (1995) *Public Institutions for Personal Learning: Establishing a Research Agenda*, Washington DC: American Association of Museums.

Falk, J. H., Phillips, K. E. and Johnson Boxer, J. (1992) 'Invisible forces exhibition: using evaluation to improve exhibitions', paper presented at the Annual Meeting of the Visitor Studies Conference, St. Louis MO, 23–7 June.

Gallagher, W. (1993) *The Power of Place: How Our Surroundings Shape Our Thoughts, Emotions and Actions*, New York: Poseidon Press.

Goffman, E. (1959) *The Presentation of Self in Everyday Life*, Garden City NY: Anchor Books.

Gray, R. and Pirot, M. (1984) 'The effects of prosocial modelling on young children's nurturing of a "sick" child', *Psychology and Human Development*, 1: 41–6.

Griffin, J. and Symington, D. (1997) 'Moving from task-oriented to learning-oriented strategies on school excursions to museums', *Science Education*, 81(6): 763–79.

Hilke, D. D. and Balling, J. B. (1985) 'The family as a learning system: an observational study of families in museums', unpublished paper, Washington DC: Smithsonian Institution.

Iser, W. (1978) *The Act of Reading: A Theory of Aesthetic Response*, Baltimore: Johns Hopkins University Press.

Katz, E. and Liebes, T. (1986) 'Mutual aid in the decoding of "Dallas": preliminary notes from a cross-cultural study', in P. Drummond and R. Patterson (eds) *Television in Transition*, London: British Film Institute, pp. 187–98.

Koran, J. J., Koran, M. L., Dierking, L. D. and Foster, J. (1988) 'Using modelling to direct attention in a natural history museum', *Curator*, 31(1): 36–42.

Lakota, R. A. (1975) 'The National Museum of Natural History as a behavioral environment', unpublished manuscript, Washington DC: Smithsonian Institution.

LeVine, R. A. (1973) *Culture, Behaviour and Personality*, Chicago: Aldine.

McManus, P. (1987) 'It's the company you keep…The social determination of learning-related behaviour in a science museum', *International Journal of Museum Management and Curatorship*, 53: 43–50.

McManus, P. (1995) 'The social nature of museum experiences', keynote address at Visitor Studies Conference, Minneapolis MN, 19–22 July.

Mead, G. H. (1924–5) 'The genesis of the self and social control', *International Journal of Ethnoscience*, 35: 251–77.

Mead, G.H. (1934) *Mind, Self and Society from the Standpoint of a Social Behaviorist*, Chicago: University of Chicago Press.

Mead, G.H. (1962) *Mind, Self and Society*, Chicago: University of Chicago Press.

Nelson, K. (1981) 'Social cognition in a script framework', in J.H Flavell and L. Ross (eds) *Social Cognitive Development: Frontiers and Possible Futures*, Cambridge: Cambridge University Press.

Ogbu, J. U. (1990) 'Cultural model, identity and literacy', in J. W. Stigler, R. A. Schweder and G. Herdt (eds) *Cultural Psychology: Essays on Comparative Buman Development*, Cambridge: Cambridge University Press.

Ogbu, J. U. (1995) 'The influence of culture on learning and behaviour', in J. H. Falk, and L. D. Dierking, (eds) *Public Institutions for Personal Learning: Establishing a Research Agenda*, Washington DC: American Association of Museums.

Rosenfeld, S. (1979) 'The context of informal learning in zoos', *Roundtable Reports*, 4: 3–5.

Ross, L. (1981) 'The "intuitive scientist" formulation and its developmental implications', in J. H. Flavell and L. Ross (eds) *Social Cognitive Development: Frontiers and Possible Futures*, Cambridge: Cambridge University Press.

Silverman, L. H. (1990) 'Of us and other "things": the content and function of talk by adult visitor pairs in an art and history museum', unpublished doctoral dissertation, University of Pennsylvania.

Silverman, L. H. (1995) 'Visitor meaning-making in museums for a new age', *Curator*, 38(3): 161–70.

Stigler, J. W., Schweder, R. A and Herdt, G. (1990) *Cultural Psychology: Essays on Comparative Human Development*, Cambridge: Cambridge University Press.

Taylor, S. (1986) 'Family behaviour at the Steinhart Aquarium', unpublished doctoral dissertation, University of California, Berkeley.

Thelen, D. (1989) 'Memory and American history', *Journal of American History*, 75 (4):1117–29.

Tuckey, C.J. (1992) 'Schoolchildren's reactions to an interactive science centre', *Curator*, 35(1): 28–38.

Tunnicliffe, S. D. (1995) 'Talking about animals: studies of young children visiting zoos, a museum and a farm', unpublished doctoral dissertation, King's College, London.

Vygotsky, L. S. (1978) *Mind in Society: The Development of Higher Mental Processes*, Cambridge MA: Harvard University Press.

Vygotsky, L. S. (1979) 'Consciousness as a problem in the psychology of behaviour', *Soviet Psychology*, 17(4): 3–35.

Vygotsky, L. S. (1981) 'The genesis of higher mental functions', in J. V. Wertsch, (ed.) *The Concept of Activity in Soviet Psychology*, Armonk, NY: M.E. Sharpe, p. 164.

Wertsch, J. V. (1985). *Vygotsky and the Social Formation of the Mind*, Cambridge, MA: Harvard University Press.

Wolins, I.S., Jensen, N. and Ulzheimer, R. (1992) 'Children's memories of museum field trips: a qualitative study', *Journal of Museum Education*, 17(2):17–27.

6 Interpreting 'visions': addressing environmental education goals through interpretation

ROY BALLANTYNE

The field of environmental education is internationally recognised as being of major importance in preparing future citizens to address a range of environmental issues facing the global community. From tentative beginnings in the 1970s the approach has increasingly been adopted and promoted by school educators within a cross-curriculum framework. This focus on environmental issues by school planners, curriculum decision-makers and teachers has been fuelled and sustained by a general concern about, and search for solutions to, intractable environmental problems facing individuals in the world today. Environmental educators are thus in the vanguard of those attempting to bring about a re-evaluation of society's goals and practices and the adoption of sustainable lifestyles. What role can interpreters play in this process and how can they support and extend the aims of environmental education through the design of informal learning experiences?

The role of interpretation and informal learning in environmental education

Formal school environmental education programmes have much to gain by incorporating visits to environmental centres, displays and sites (Rennie and McClafferty 1995). Visits to interpretive sites allow students to apply theoretical knowledge 'in the field', discover real-life examples of principles, problems and issues, and undertake problem-solving and decision-making within a real world setting (Ballantyne and Uzzell 1994). Modern zoos, aquaria, museums and environmental centres typically provide realistic simulations and examples of environments which are inaccessible in classroom settings (Hauenschild 1996). Students reportedly enjoy visiting such settings in which they have an opportunity to handle materials, engage in activities and observe animals and objects (Price and Hein 1991).

Despite the potential of informal experiences to contribute to student environmental learning, evaluation studies suggest that visitors to interpretive centres may not actually learn a great deal (Uzzell 1993). Interpretive displays and experiences are not often designed for use by school groups but rather for visitors from a range of different age and educational backgrounds, who are there by choice, have time constraints and are motivated by a desire for relaxation, enjoyment and entertainment rather than a learning experience (Borun 1977; Markwell 1996; Miles 1988). Informal learning experiences are generally unstructured and self-directed, designed to attract and engage visitors while delivering their messages quickly and succinctly (Ballantyne and Uzzell 1994). It is not surprising, therefore, that environmental educators often question the value of interpretive exhibits and experiences in addressing environmental education goals (Knapp 1997).

Accordingly, if interpretation is to contribute to the achievement of environmental education goals, interpreters need to understand and incorporate some of the aims and principles of the approach in their planning and design of exhibits and experiences. It is hoped that interpreters will join with environmental educators and extend their vision to include the development of an environmentally literate society. Why don't interpreters use the opportunities they have to pursue an environmental education agenda? Perhaps a major reason for this is a lack of understanding regarding the common aspects of the aims, nature and practice of environmental education and interpretation.

Aims of interpretation and environmental education

What then are the aims of environmental education and how compatible are they with the aims of interpretation? Often there is a perceived lack of consensus on the part of environmental educators regarding the goals of the subject. Disagreements in this regard generally revolve around the emphasis placed upon developing student environmental knowledge, attitudes/values or behaviour (Ballantyne and Packer 1996) and the relative importance of a concern with content or process (Gough 1997). Personal philosophies and ideologies have a large impact, both on perceptions of the goals of environmental education and on choice of teaching approach and techniques. For instance, those holding the view that environmental education should predominantly aim to develop environmental knowledge may emphasise a 'directive' approach and use techniques suitable for the transmission of information. Those mainly concerned with developing attitudes/values may emphasise a learner-centred approach and use techniques which actively involve students in a values clarification or decision-making role. Those emphasising consideration of environmental behaviour may adopt a 'critical' approach and use techniques which engage students in the critique of environmental knowledge, attitudes and behaviour. Although these brief characterisations are over-generalised, each approach has both supporters and critics regarding its importance and effectiveness in developing environmentally literate students.

It is, of course, impossible to teach environmental education which is knowledge or attitude/value free or which does not have implications for student behaviour. In isolation, none of the above approaches can adequately fulfil the aims of environmental education (Ballantyne and Packer 1996). Although educators may differ regarding the emphases they place on the relative importance of developing students' environmental knowledge base, attitudes/values and behaviour, there is an appreciation that environmental education should include aspects of each. Ultimately, environmental education aims to develop responsible environmental behaviour which is informed by accurate knowledge and supporting attitudes and values. However, educators dispute the best approach and methods to be used to achieve this goal (Ballantyne and Packer 1996; Howe and Disinger 1991; Hungerford and Volk 1990).

Although less consideration has been given in the literature to articulating the aims of environmental interpretation, it is clear that there is much overlap between the two fields. Knapp *et al.* (1997) have done extensive work in establishing a framework within which the goals of environmental interpretation might be discussed. After reviewing a collection of textbooks, journal articles, agency guidelines and official memos which contained principles, goals and objectives for interpretation, they concluded that behaviour change outcomes were of major importance for a significant portion of the interpretive field, thus confirming the close relationship between environmental interpretation and environmental education. These behaviour change outcomes included community participation, resource preservation, energy conservation, park preservation and park protection.

Knapp *et al.* (1997) then proceeded to synthesise the interpretation goals derived in this way with Hungerford and Volk's (1990) environmental behaviour change model which was developed in the context of environmental education. This model (Figure 6.1) considers citizenship behaviour to be influenced by three categories of variables:

- entry-level variables (such as environmental sensitivity, knowledge of ecology, attitudes toward pollution, technology and economics);

- ownership variables (such as in-depth knowledge of issues, personal investment in and commitment to issues and the environment, knowledge of the consequences of behaviour);

- empowerment variables (such as knowledge and skills in using environmental action strategies, locus of control and intention to act.

Their findings indicated that the majority of interpretation goals, as perceived within the literature and by major agencies in the field, fell within the entry-level category, reflecting basic awareness aspects of environmental education.

Figure 6.1 Major and minor variables involved in environmental citizenship behaviour
Source: Hungerford and Volk (1990)

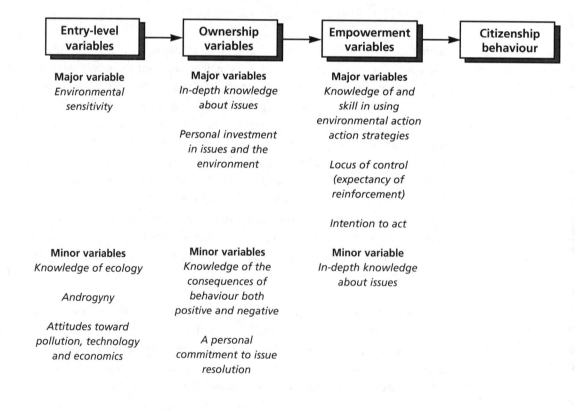

The ownership category was particularly poorly represented among interpretation goals, indicating an area in need of further attention if environmental interpretation is to impact significantly on visitor environmental behaviour. According to Knapp *et al.* (1997), goals in this area might include developing visitors' awareness of how their activities influence the site and its environment and how environmental problems and issues can occur through these interactions. Interpretation might also aim to develop visitors' skills in identifying, analysing, investigating and evaluating these issues. Similarly, empowerment goals might aim to develop visitors' knowledge and skills in identifying, evaluating and applying solutions to environmental issues.

Knapp *et al.* (1997) report that this framework of goals was generally supported by a panel of nationally (USA) recognised experts in environmental interpretation, although the entry-level goals received more consistent approval than the environmental issue investigation and evaluation goals contained within the ownership and empowerment categories. These findings indicate that, although the aims of environmental education and interpretation are generally compatible in theory, there is still some reluctance on the part of environmental interpreters to embrace a concern for environmental behaviour change which goes beyond site-specific and short-term target behaviours.

In practice, interpreters traditionally adopt a directive or expository approach towards the interpretation of environmental objects or issues, reflecting an emphasis on the cognitive rather than the affective or behaviour-change aspects of interpretive practice (Meredith *et al.* 1995). Rarely does interpretive material deliberately attempt to address visitor environmental attitudes/values or behaviour. There is little or no attempt to raise awareness of differing attitudes and values towards objects or issues and these are few the examples of interpretation aimed at actively engaging visitors in critiquing their environmental knowledge, attitudes/values and behaviour.

The literature suggests, however, that the field of environmental interpretation is gradually beginning to broaden its horizons. Ham and Krumpe (1996), for example, in their identification of audiences and messages for environmental interpreters, consider on-site and off-site, short-term and long-term behavioural outcomes, as well as extending the target audience beyond on-site visitors to local communities and remote audiences. Ballantyne and Uzzell (1993) urge interpreters to extend their focus beyond the conservation movement and to actively address specific social, environmental and moral issues, with the aim of engaging the public's attention, challenging them to examine their attitudes and actions with respect to these issues. If interpreters wish to promote environmental education goals through the design of informal learning experiences, they will need to consider selecting material and adopting practices which actively engage the visitor in a consideration of the impacts of their own and others' behaviour in the environment.

It is clear, therefore, that the potential of environmental interpretation's as a contribution to the development of an environmentally literate citizenry is only just beginning to emerge. In order to actualise this potential, it will be necessary for a new partnership to be forged between environmental educators and interpreters.

Developing environmental education and interpretation partnerships

There is a perception that school teachers 'do' environmental education while park managers, recreation, tourist, museum, science centre and eco-tourist specialists 'do' interpretation. This is unfortunate as practitioners in both fields would benefit from a closer partnership (Knapp 1997). Although it is possible to pinpoint differences between environmental education and interpretation in relation to, among others, target audiences, audience motivation, purpose of activities, time spent in activities, formal/informal educational approaches and methods, there remains a lot in common (Aldridge 1989; Ballantyne and Uzzell 1994).

An emphasis on the differences rather than the similarities between the two fields has done little to promote co-operation between environmental educators and interpreters or discussion and critique of ideas and practice affecting each. What are the benefits which could accrue to practitioners from both sides if they were to perceive and act on their commonalities rather than their differences? There is little doubt that collaboration with environmental educators would be beneficial to interpreters in attracting and meeting the needs of the school market, as well as improving the effectiveness of their exhibits and facilitating visitor environmental learning. Similarly, an active partnership with interpreters would be of benefit to educators who are increasingly seeking to expose their students to appropriate informal and lifelong environmental learning experiences.

An active partnership between environmental education and environmental interpretation could begin to address the weaknesses of both.

Environmental interpretation is limited in its ability to bring about lasting behavioural change because of the time frame within which messages must be communicated. Environmental education is limited by its formal nature and dependence on school curricula and classroom learning environments. By working in partnership, interpreters can provide enjoyable and motivating field experiences which will be valuable in stimulating students' interest and involvement in environmental learning, while environmental educators can act to reinforce and extend their students' learning from the interpretive setting to the classroom and beyond.

Such a partnership will have implications not only for environmental education in schools, but also in the wider community. School students who experience interpretive exhibits as part of their school environmental education programme may well return to the interpretive centre or site with their parents. Even if they do no more than discuss their experience at home, their potential to act as catalysts of environmental change is powerful (Ballantyne *et al.* 1998a, 1998b; Uzzell *et al.* 1994; Uzzell and Rutland 1993). Further, as interpreters use some of the approaches and techniques employed in environmental education, the effectiveness of interpretive experiences in encouraging individuals to reflect on their environmental behaviour will gradually increase. In these ways, the partnership between formal environmental education and environmental interpretation will have a flow-on effect in influencing wider audiences toward the adoption of environmentally responsible behaviour.

Interpreters who wish to design experiences or exhibits which contribute to environmental education goals will need to develop their understanding of some of the pedagogical principles which have been found to be effective in environmental education practice. As indicated in the preceding sections, environmental educators are by no means united in their allegiance to one model of teaching. As it is impossible within the limits of this chapter to deal fully with all possible approaches, the following discussion will focus on one theory – the constructivist approach – which it is felt has much potential for facilitating the integration of personal environmental knowledge, attitudes/values and behaviour.

Constructivism and the design of interpretive learning experiences

According to the constructivist viewpoint, learners are active participants in the learning situation; they construct their own meanings from, and for, the ideas, objects and events they experience (Australian Education

Council 1991). Learners come to a learning activity with different purposes and conceptions, may learn different things from the same event and apply their understanding in different ways (Ballantyne and Packer 1996; Driver 1984). This process is influenced by the individuals' prior knowledge, their interpretation of the learning context and by opportunities for discussion and the refinement of understandings (Ballantyne and Bain 1995; Roschelle 1992).

Applying a constructivist approach to learning in interpretive centres extends the focus from the exhibition or experience itself to include the visitor who interprets, understands and imposes meaning on the displays, often within a social context and perhaps with an educational purpose derived from elsewhere. Meaning is not necessarily evident within the exhibition material itself. Rather it acquires meaning when visitors relate it to aspects of their own experience and reasons for being there. Learning is not only the accretion of bits of information, but the development and elaboration of a person's understandings and knowledge organisation (Uzzell 1993). Social interaction has been found to facilitate this kind of learning, particularly when there is an opportunity to question and explore ideas and derive their implications (Ballantyne and Bain 1995). This interpretation of learning is supported by the cognitive conflict theories of Piaget (1965) which have been elaborated into socio-cognitive conflict theory by Doise *et al.* (1975) and applied in a museum context by Blud (1988).

When environmental interpreters design an exhibit or trail they traditionally organise the learning activities and experiences around a framework of themes, stories and messages. Although such a planning approach is 'good' in that it ties learning to what is relevant to the visitor experience, it often fails to consider what the visitors bring to the site in terms of prior learning and does not help them to extend their learning to the world 'outside'. To promote the goals of environmental education, learning experiences should be planned in the light of likely visitor prior knowledge and should use information about objects or issues as a springboard to engage visitors in a consideration of environmental attitudes/values and behaviour which are not purely site specific. Interpreters wishing to promote environmental education goals should expand their vision of their role to include the development of visitor environmental conceptions.

Visitor environmental conceptions consist of the integration of their knowledge, attitudes/values and behavioural orientations towards a specific object or issue (Figure 6.2). A full discussion of the nature of environmental conceptions is presented in Ballantyne and Packer (1996). To illustrate, an individual's conception of an ecosystem includes the integration of knowledge about ecosystems (ecological balances, food chains, feedback loops and energy flows), attitudes/values towards ecosystems (people should manage ecosystems so as to minimise human impact upon other species) and behavioural orientations in relation to ecosystems (government planning laws should demand that developers undertake environmental impact studies and use an integrated environmental planning approach). Conceptions are thus constructed from thoughts, feelings and actions associated with different phenomena. Due to the selective nature of the process of perception and cognition no two individuals' conceptions are identical.

Individuals' conceptions are continually being constructed and reconstructed as they interact with the environment. The process of learning occurs when information input through the senses interacts with past learning and experience. According to Cheung and Taylor (1991), learning is a

---

Figure 6.2 Conceptions as a constructive integration of knowledge (K), attitudes/values (A) and behavioural orientations (B), relating to a phenomenon
Source: Ballantyne and Packer (1996)

Conception of phenomenon

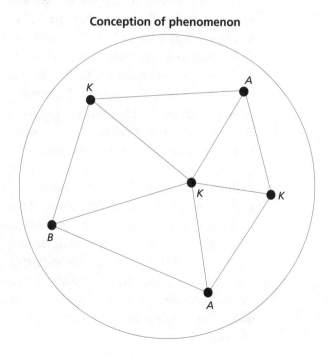

process of meaning construction, or as Novak (1987: 357) suggests, 'the constructive integration of thinking, feeling and acting'. Individuals often display inconsistencies within their conceptions, for example, their behavioural orientations may be inconsistent with their attitudes/values. In some cases, the knowledge component may be inadequate or inaccurate, leading to conceptions which are based on an incorrect view of the world.

In order to have a meaningful impact on the development of environmental conceptions, interpreters must consider visitors' prior learning, possible inconsistencies within conceptions and potential misconceptions when they plan interpretive learning experiences. Interpreters designing an environmental learning experience need more than knowledge of the site and interpretive techniques (allowing the creation and communication of appropriate themes, stories and messages). It is essential that they also have an understanding of likely conceptions that a visitor brings to the site (prior knowledge, attitudes/values and behavioural orientations), as well as knowledge of educational strategies designed to challenge and develop them.

Different visitors are likely to hold differing environmental conceptions depending on their age, gender, culture, education level and past experience. Individuals' conceptions of the world vary according to their past experience. These in turn shape the ways in which they respond to and assimilate new information. No one has a 'virgin' mind when it comes to reacting to new information. We cannot consider a new experience without attempting to make sense of it in terms of our past learning. Conceptions are, however, largely shared by people from similar backgrounds and it is therefore possible to generalise about the range of conceptions held by target visitor groups in relation to environmental knowledge, attitudes/values and behavioural orientations. From a constructivist standpoint, it is important for interpreters to have knowledge of the general conceptions that visitor groups are likely to hold towards objects and issues that they are wishing to interpret. It is inappropriate to act as if the visitors are an empty vessel to be filled with new insights and information. The visitor is 'active' in the learning situation so it is vital to understand what they generally know, feel and how they behave in relation to the environmental issues to be interpreted. It is unacceptable to 'forget' about the visitor until reviewing the learning experience as part of the exhibit evaluation process. How can an interpreter access general information about visitor expectations and understandings in relation to environmental concepts, attitudes/values and behaviours?

Determining target audience environmental conceptions and prior learning

Environmental and science educators have been involved for a number of years in exploring the range of conceptions or understandings people hold in relation to environmental issues, knowledge and concepts (Ballantyne 1995a,b; Ballantyne and Bain 1995; Ballantyne and Gerber 1994; Ballantyne and Witney 1996; Robertson 1993, 1994; Wals 1992). Similarly, there are a number of methods that interpreters can use to gauge common conceptions held by target visitor audiences. Such methods include personal interviews, focus group interviews, questionnaires and personal journals. The method which would seem to be most convenient, in terms of cost and time effectiveness, for interpreters to use in determining visitors' general prior conceptions would be focus group interviews with a representative visitor sample. Focus group interviews enable in-depth probing of visitor understandings of specific information, attitudes/values and behavioural orientations towards environmental issues and aid the design of learning experiences and materials. It would also be possible to test understandings of proposed information panels and responses to learning materials using this format.

Interpreters at the Two Oceans Aquarium in Cape Town are presently using focus groups in the manner suggested to identify the range of conceptions that senior primary students from differing cultural backgrounds hold in relation to the marine environment, prior to the development of interpretive learning materials. In this case, student groups have been asked to respond to an open-ended question, 'What do you know about the sea?' Follow-up questions are then asked in order to probe more deeply students' responses and understanding of elements of the marine environment. Focus group discussions are audio-taped, transcribed and analysed using a phenomenographic approach (Marton 1992; Saljo 1988; Svensson 1994) to establish the range of conceptions which the target group holds. Once interpreters have this information, how can they use it to inform interpretive practice designed to challenge and develop visitor environmental conceptions?

Developing environmental conceptions through interpretive practice

From a constructivist perspective, interpreters should use information about a target audience's environmental knowledge, attitudes/values and behavioural orientations to design learning experiences which help visitors become aware of inconsistencies within and consequences of their own conceptions as well as the relevance and relative merits of alternative conceptions (Ballantyne and Packer 1996). Learning experiences initially proceed from an awareness of visitors' possible understandings (or misunderstandings) and provide experiences which engage them in altering or expanding these (Ballantyne and Bain 1995). As environmental conceptions comprise the integration of knowledge, attitudes/values and behavioural orientations (Figure 6.2), to bring about change, the interpreter needs to engage the visitor in a re-evaluation of presently held understandings, feelings or behaviour towards an issue or object. Any alteration in the visitor's knowledge, attitudes/values or behavioural orientations as a result of the learning experience should lead to a restructuring of the interrelationships among the conceptual elements resulting in conceptual change. Conceptual change in this instance may involve a shift in or extension of current conceptions. Learning, therefore, does not always require a major alteration in conception as new understandings may just extend initially held viewpoints.

Strategies found to be effective in developing environmental conceptions are those that induce a state of cognitive conflict in the learner (Ballantyne *et al.* 1994). Cognitive conflict occurs when a visitor is presented with new knowledge, attitudes/values or behaviours which are incompatible with their present understandings and therefore need to be reconciled. This conflict motivates individuals to resolve the resulting cognitive dissonance by seeking new information or by reorganising the elements of existing conceptions. According to Watts and Bentley (1987), those wishing to generate cognitive conflict should use methods which help visitors to articulate and explore ideas they hold regarding a topic, examine the consequences of these ideas and become aware of and evaluate other viewpoints which challenge their own understandings.

Once interpreters have an idea of visitor conceptions regarding environmental issues or objects they wish to interpret, it is a relatively simple step to use this information to develop learning experiences which present a range of conflicting knowledge, attitudes/values and behavioural orientations. Designing successful interpretive experiences to engage visitors in conceptual change or enhancement requires the presentation of knowledge, attitudes/values or behaviour which is incompatible with their present understanding or actions. Visitors should have to 'wrestle' inwardly with the dissonance engendered by the learning experience. Ideally, a good interpreter should be able to put visitors in a state of mental unease similar to that felt by the character in Bob Dylan's song, *The Ballad of a Thin Man*, who knows something's happening but doesn't know what it is.

When designing learning experiences which stimulate cognitive conflict, care must be taken to ensure that learning materials do not alienate visitors by imposing inappropriate ideas and inducing counterproductive ideological confrontation (Negra and Manning 1997). Indoctrination of specific ideas, attitudes/values and behaviours should not be the aim of any learning experiences designed to develop environmental conceptions. Although it is suggested that visitors should examine their environmental actions, this does not imply that learning experiences should be designed to develop 'specific' attitudes and behaviour. Rather, individuals should be provided with information and alternative viewpoints allowing them to make informed choices in relation to their personal environmental conceptions.

The process above can be illustrated by the example of an interpreter wishing to develop a learning experience for school students around the theme of the 'greenhouse' effect and global warming. Research indicates that students may hold variations on one of three conceptions regarding the greenhouse effect: it results from air pollution; it causes global warming; or it is a natural process essential for life (Ballantyne and Witney 1996). Knowing this, the interpreter needs to select environmental knowledge, attitudes/values or behaviours to incorporate into messages and stories to extend students' conceptual understanding and address misconceptions. For instance, as students often incorrectly believe that the greenhouse effect causes global warming they assume that the process is 'bad'. To address this misconception, the interpreter could devise a learning experience which confronts the notion of a world without a greenhouse effect. Is a world without a greenhouse effect really a good thing? How will it affect students' lives? How then does global warming occur? What can individuals do about it? What attitudes/values do people hold which could conflict with solving the global warming problem? In attempting to answer these questions, interpreters' learning experiences should challenge students:

- to integrate their knowledge of the process of incoming and outgoing solar radiation, the energy cycle and the composition of the atmosphere;

- to explore and evaluate their own and others' viewpoints and attitudes regarding the greenhouse effect and solutions to the problem of global warming;

- to consider the consequences of their own and society's actions in relation to the problem of global warming;

- to adopt responsible actions, based upon their understanding of the greenhouse effect and global warming which contribute to sustainable and steady state practice.

Matching interpretive experiences to formal environmental education aims

Interpreters wishing to facilitate the achievement of environmental education goals through interpretive practice need to do more than just alter the way in which they design and present learning experiences for school students. They need to put themselves in the place of the student group and consider the 'holistic' experience of a visit from a formal education perspective. In essence, they need to view the exhibit through a school educator's 'spectacles'. What are some of the key factors that interpreters need to consider when viewing school teachers and students as a target audience? How can they improve the learning context to promote the aims of formal environmental education?

According to Ballantyne and Uzzell (1994) there are four areas that interpreters need to keep in mind when planning interpretive experiences for school students. These are: matching interpretive methodologies to the aims of formal environmental education; matching interpretive experiences to the age of the student group; matching facilities and services to the needs of teachers/students; and matching interpretive resources to constraints of national curricula.

With regard to matching interpretive methodologies to the aims of formal environmental education, much has already been written in this chapter about how interpreters can design learning experiences and choose methodologies which are consistent with the aims of environmental education. However, in addition to the points made in relation to developing environmental conceptions, interpreters should be aware that school students are not used to learning in informal or recreational settings and thus it is a novel situation for them. Research in museums and science centres indicates that the less novel the learning environment, the greater the student learning (Anderson and Lucus 1997). Accordingly, a pre-visit programme can positively influence the quality of student learning by decreasing the novelty of the visit, orientating students to what they will see and do and introducing them to cognitive structures upon which new learning can be built.

Interpretive learning experiences need to be organised into a sequence which facilitates student learning by enabling new information and experiences to be incorporated into cognitive frameworks developed in the classroom. An exhibition might be organised around a different theme to that needed by a student group. In such cases, interpreters and teachers will greatly increase potential student learning by being prepared to reorganise the exhibit or change the sequencing of activities according to school curriculum needs.

Multimedia presentations and other modern interpretive methods may be helpful in engaging the student, but often this is not at the level needed for the development of environmental conceptions. It might be necessary to design worksheet activities or group interactive sessions based upon multimedia presentations in order to engage students in higher order learning activities. Post-visit follow-up activities can also play an important role in reinforcing and extending student understanding and learning.

In relation to matching interpretive experiences to the age of the student group, it is also important to remember that most interpretive displays are not designed for a student audience but rather for the general public which incorporates a wide age range (Ballantyne and Uzzell 1994). As psychologists like Piaget and Bruner have demonstrated, young people do not perceive the world in the same way as adults. Accordingly, as pointed out by Tilden (1957), interpretation for students (particularly those in primary schools) needs to be different from that designed for adults. As the research of Uzzell *et al.* (1984a,b) indicates, although viewing the same displays, children and adults 'see' different exhibitions.

Furthermore, interpreters and teachers need to consult prior to school visits to ensure that the activities to be undertaken by, particularly, primary students, are pitched at an appropriate level. If young students are being taken on a guided trail, for instance, interpreters might need to change the examples and stories they normally use with older visitors to ensure that they 'connect' with young minds. The key to successful interpretation for young students is, as far as possible, to see the world from their perspective and then to design learning experiences starting from this viewpoint.

Matching the facilities and services of an interpretive centre or experience to the needs of teachers and students requires interpreters to appreciate that this visitor group has different requirements from tourists and recreationalists. Research by Uzzell and Parkin (1987) into teachers' perceptions of the strengths and weaknesses of interpretive facilities from a school perspective highlights the following points which interpreters should consider:

- Teachers appreciate the provision of learning experiences which involve students in investigatory and practical work, provide more than a content loaded 'look and listen' experience and involve students in a variety of indoor and outdoor activities.

- The availability of skilled interpreters with teaching experience, the provision of good teacher and student material and a well-equipped room for student work is also highly valued.

- Teachers do not appreciate 'shoddy' outdated student materials, untrained or inexperienced staff, overcrowded facilities, oppressive restrictions on student activities, lack of wet-weather facilities and workrooms and inappropriate 'messages' from staff and displays relating to multicultural and ethnic issues.

Involving teachers in the design of pre-visit and follow-up activities in relation to the exhibits or interpretive experiences will help to maintain the continuity between formal and informal learning environments. In some cases, it may be helpful to establish ongoing relationships with particular teachers who return regularly to the site or centre, enabling them to develop both their familiarity with the exhibits and their repertoire of resources for facilitating student learning.

The importance of providing interpretive experiences for school groups which match the demands of the school curriculum varies depending on the educational system in place. The less freedom teachers have in determining the learning programme for their students, the more important it will be for interpreters to provide experiences which are closely linked to curriculum aims. Interpreters wishing to attract student groups would do well to make the following provisions:

- access subject curriculum guides relevant to the areas they interpret in order to design learning experiences for school groups which promote the achievement of school curriculum aims;

- provide materials for both students and teachers which are specifically targeted at, and are clearly compatible with, formal education goals; and

- work with teachers prior to the visit in order to provide a programme which is seen to support their curriculum needs.

Conclusion

Environmental educators would like to invite interpreters to join them in promoting the vision of an environmentally sustainable future. To accept this challenge will involve interpreters in extending their own vision of their role beyond the confines of site specific concerns. There would appear to be mutual benefits for all concerned if environmental educators and interpreters formed active partnerships in order to expand the provision and improve the quality of informal learning experiences designed to develop student environmental conceptions. While some may feel that the time limits involved with student visits to interpretive centres and exhibits constrain the development of such conceptions, this can be addressed by establishing partnerships between teachers and interpreters which enable the interpretive experience to be clearly situated within the formal education programme. The collaborative development of materials and activities to be used before, during and after school visits to interpretive sites would extend and increase the impact of the interpretive experience as well as improving the student learning experience.

Acknowledgement

The author wishes to thank Ms Jan Packer for her helpful comments and suggestions in relation to drafts of this chapter.

References

Aldridge, D. (1989) 'How the ship of interpretation was blown off course in the tempest: some philosophical thoughts', in D. Uzzell (ed.) *Heritage Interpretation Volume 1: The Natural and Built Environment*, London: Belhaven.

Anderson, D. and Lucus, K. (1997) 'The effectiveness of orienting students to the physical features of a science museum prior to visitation', *Research in Science Education*, 27(4): 485–95.

Australian Education Council (1991) *A National Statement on Mathematics for Australian Schools*, Carlton: Australian Education Council and Curriculum Corporation.

Ballantyne, R. (1995a) 'Interpreters' conceptions of Australian Aboriginal culture and heritage: Implications for interpretive practice', *Journal of Environmental Education*, 26(4): 11–17.

Ballantyne, R. (1995b) 'Evaluating the impact of teaching/learning experiences during an environmental teacher education course', *International Research in Geographical and Environmental Education*, 4(1): 29–46.

Ballantyne, R. and Bain, J. (1995) 'Enhancing environmental conceptions: an evaluation of structured controversy learning units', *Studies in Higher Education*, 20(3): 293–303.

Ballantyne, R., Connell, S. and Fien, J. (1998a) 'Students as catalysts of environmental change: a framework for researching intergenerational influence through environmental education', *Environmental Education Research*, 4(3): 285–98.

Ballantyne, R., Connell, S. and Fien, J. (1998b) 'The impact of environmental education programmes: an investigation of factors influencing intergenerational communication', *Australian Journal of Environmental Education*, 14.

Ballantyne, R., Furtado, M. and Hoepper, B. (1994) *Cognitive Conflict and Structured Controversy: Environmental Teacher Education Units*, Monograph 94.2, Centre for Applied Environmental and Social Education Research, Queensland University of Technology.

Ballantyne, R. and Gerber, R. (1994) 'Managers' conceptions of environmental responsibility', *The Environmentalist*, 14(1): 1–10.

Ballantyne, R. and Packer, J. (1996) 'Teaching and learning in environmental education: developing environmental conceptions', *The Journal of Environmental Education*, 27(2): 25–32.

Ballantyne, R. and Uzzell, D. (1993) 'Environmental mediation and hot interpretation – a case study of District Six, Cape Town', *Journal of Environmental Education*, 24(3): 4–7.

Ballantyne, R. and Uzzell, D. (1994) 'A checklist for the critical evaluation of informal environmental learning experiences', *International Journal of Environmental Education and Information*, 13(2): 111–24.

Ballantyne, R. and Witney, E. (1996) 'Using a phenomenographic approach to determine students' conceptions of environmental issues', in R. Gerber and M. Williams (eds) *Qualitative Research in Geographical Education*, International Geographical Union, Commission on Geographical Education, pp: 73–83.

Blud, L. M. (1988) 'The role of social interaction in informal learning environments', unpublished doctoral dissertation, University of Surrey.

Borun, M. (1977) *Measuring the Immeasurable: A Pilot Study of Museum Effectiveness*, Washington DC: Association of Science-Technology Centres.

Cheung, K. C. and Taylor, R. (1991) 'Towards a humanistic constructivist model of science learning: changing perspectives and research implications', *Journal of Curriculum Studies*, 23(1): 21–40.

Doise, W., Mugny, G. and Perret-Clermont, A. N. (1975) 'Social interaction and the development of cognitive operations', *European Journal of Social Psychology*, 5: 367–83.

Driver, R. (1984) 'A review of research into children's thinking and learning in science', in B. Bell, D. M. Watts and K. Ellington (eds) *Learning, Doing and Understanding in Science: The Proceedings of a Conference*, London: SSCR.

Gough, A. (1997) 'Education and the environment: policy, trends and the problems of marginalisation', *Australian Education Review*, no. 39, Melbourne: ACER.

Ham, S. H. and Krumpe, E. E. (1996) 'Identifying audiences and messages for nonformal environmental education – a theoretical framework for interpreters', *Journal of Interpretation Research*, 1(1): 11–23.

Hauenschild, P. E. (1996) 'Research focus and methodology in environmental interpretation centres: a critical review', unpublished report, Queensland University of Technology.

Howe, R. W. and Disinger, J. F. (1991) 'Environmental education research news', *The Environmentalist*, 11(1): 5–8.

Hungerford, H. R. and Volk, T. L. (1990) 'Changing learner behavior through environmental education', *The Journal of Environmental Education*, 21(3): 8–21.

Knapp, D. (1997) 'The relationship between environmental interpretation and environmental education', *Legacy*, 8(3): 10–13.

Knapp, D., Volk, T. L. and Hungerford, H. R. (1997) 'The identification of empirically derived goals for program development in environmental interpretation', *The Journal of Environmental Education*, 28(3): 24–34.

Markwell, K. (1996) 'Challenging the pedagogical basis of contemporary environmental interpretation', *Australian Journal of Environmental Education*, 12: 9–14.

Marton, F. (1992) 'Phenomenography', unpublished manuscript.

Meredith, J. E., Mullins, G. W. and Fortner, R. W. (1995) 'Interpretation and the affective learning domain', *Legacy*, 6(4): 24–31.

Miles, R. S. (ed.) (1988) *The Design of Educational Exhibits*, 2nd edn, London: Unwin Hyman.

Negra, C. and Manning, R. E. (1997) 'Incorporating environmental behavior, ethics, and values into nonformal environmental education programs', *The Journal of Environmental Education*, 28(2): 10–21.

Novak, J. D. (1987) 'Human constructivism: towards a unity of psychological and epistemological meaning making', in J. D. Novak (ed.) *Misconceptions and Educational Strategies in Science and Mathematics: Proceedings of the Second International Seminar*, Ithaca, NY: Cornell University.

Piaget, J. (1965) *Etudes Sociologiques*, Paris: Droz.

Price, S. and Hein, G. E. (1991) 'More than a field trip: science programmes for elementary school groups at museums', *International Journal of Science Education*, 13(5): 505–19.

Rennie, L. J. and McClafferty, T. (1995) 'Using visits to interactive science and technology centres, museums, aquaria, and zoos to promote learning in science', *Journal of Science Teacher Education*, 6(4): 175–85.

Robertson, A. (1993) 'Eliciting students' understandings: necessary steps in environmental education', *Australian Journal of Environmental Education*, 9: 95–114.

Robertson, A. (1994) 'Toward constructivist research in environmental education', *Journal of Environmental Education*, 25(2): 21–31.

Roschelle, J. (1992) 'Learning by collaborating: convergent conceptual change', *Journal of the Learning Sciences*, 2: 235–76.

Saljo, R. (1988) 'Learning in educational settings: methods of enquiry', in P. Ramsden (ed.) *Improving Learning: New Perspectives*, London: Kogan Page.

Svensson, L. (1994) 'Theoretical foundations of phenomenography', in R. Ballantyne and C. Bruce (eds) *Phenomenography: Philosophy and Practice*, Brisbane: Queensland University of Technology, pp. 9–20.

Tilden, F. (1957) *Interpreting Our Heritage*, Chapel Hill NC: University of North Carolina Press.

Uzzell, D. (1993) 'Contrasting psychological perspectives on exhibition evaluation', in S. Bicknell and G. Farmelo (eds) *Museum Visitor Studies in the 1990s*, London: Science Museum.

Uzzell, D. L., Davallon, J., Bruun Jensen, B., Gottesdiener, H., Fontes, J., Kofoed, J., Uhrenholdt, G. and Vognsen, C. (1994) *Children as Catalysts of Environmental Change*, report to DGXII/D-5 Research on Economic and Social Aspects of the Environment (SEER), European Commission, Brussels.

Uzzell, D. L., Lee, T. R. and Henderson, J. (1984a) *Interpretive Provision in Forestry Commission Visitor Centres: Strathyre Visitor Centre*, report to the Forestry Commission, University of Surrey.

Uzzell, D. L., Lee, T. R. and Henderson, J. (1984b) *Children at the Strathyre Visitor Centre*, report to the Forestry Commission, University of Surrey.

Uzzell, D. and Parkin, I. C. A. (1987) 'Bedgebury National Pinetum and Forest: Interpretive Plan', unpublished report for the Forestry Commission, Edinburgh.

Uzzell, D. and Rutland, A. (1993) 'Inter-generational social influence: changing environmental competence and performance in children and adults', discussion paper for the Second International Workshop on Children as Catalysts of Global Environmental Change, CEFOPE, University of Braga, Portugal.

Wals, A. (1992) 'Young adolescents' perceptions of environmental issues: implications for environmental education in urban settings', *Australian Journal of Environmental Education*, 8: 45–58.

Watts, M. and Bentley, D. (1987) 'Constructivism in the classroom: enabling conceptual change by words and deeds', *British Educational Research Journal*, 13(2): 121–35.

7 Ecotourism and interpretation

KEVIN MARKWELL AND BETTY WEILER

One characteristic which modern tourism continues to share with earlier forms is the importance of the natural environment as an attraction in its own right and as a setting in which tourism experiences take place. It has been, and continues to be, an important component of the attractiveness of many destinations. It has been variously viewed in tourism as landscape, setting, backdrop, challenge, relaxation and recuperation, as therapy, and as a place of learning. Over the last decade a new concept, ecotourism, has emerged that has the potential to challenge some of the preconceived ways in which we think about and 'do' tourism. This chapter examines the place of interpretation within ecotourism and in particular presents a set of arguments which underline the importance of quality interpretation within ecotourism.

According to Buckley (1994), there are four main links between tourism and the environment: components of the natural environment as the basis for a marketable tourism attraction or product; management of tourism operations so as to minimise or reduce their environmental impacts; economic or material contribution of tourism to conservation, either directly or indirectly; and attitudes of tourists towards the environment and environmental education of clients by tourist operators. It is this last linkage between nature and the tourism industry which is to be explored here, and in particular the place of interpretation in ecotourism. The chapter begins by mapping out the main conceptual directions in our theoretical understanding of tourism generally, before briefly describing the development of the ecotourism concept. We then discuss the place of 'guides' in ecotourism, drawing upon the theoretical and conceptual understandings of tourism and, in particular, ecotourism in order better to understand the potential for, and limitations of, interpretation. Finally a number of issues relating to ecotourism interpretation are identified and discussed.

Conceptualising tourism

Ham (1992) makes a plea to professional interpreters to 'embrace the tourist'. He argues that traditionally tourists have been something of a problem to cultural and environmental interpreters, who perceive them as superficial sightseers. Apart from admonishing interpreters for being elitist and discriminatory and suggesting that the environmental awareness of the average tourist no doubt reflects broader society's increased awareness of environmental issues, Ham also makes the point that tourists as a group are likely to include people of considerable political power and decision-making responsibilities. However, Ham neglects to examine the ways in which tourism (and the tourist) have been conceptualised and theorised and the ramifications of these conceptual understandings for interpretation. Indeed, most writing on interpretation and tourism fails to locate interpretation within the broader theoretical perspectives on tourism which have been developed over the last three decades. It is for this reason that the following overview has been provided which contextualises the place of interpretation within tourism theory.

A number of authors have criticised modern tourism because of its apparent preoccupation with the trivial, the artificial, the contrived. Boorstin (1964) in his analysis of tourism coined the concept of 'pseudo-event', an event specifically contrived for consumption by the tourist. Tourists, according to Boorstin, are satisfied with inauthentic and superficial events and experiences. Eco (1986) extends Boorstin's thesis by arguing that tourists not only enjoy the contrivances offered to them by the tourism industry, but they actually expect copies and fakes rather than the original itself, a phenomenon which he terms 'travel[ling] in hyper-reality'. The notion of truth then is not an issue and indeed Feifer (1985, cited in Urry 1990: 10) has proposed the concept of 'post-tourist' to describe those who 'almost delight in the inauthenticity of the normal tourist experience. [They] find pleasure in the multiplicity of tourist games.'

In contrast, MacCannell (1989) argues that tourism occurs because people do not find meaning in the course of their everyday experience, but rather search for meaning and authenticity in other (usually more primitive) societies, or in the past. For MacCannell, the tourist is almost a pilgrim, searching for the truth, only to be thwarted in the attempt by the 'staged authenticity' offered by the tourism industry. MacCannell contends that the attractions which form the basis of the sights which tourists seek, need to be marked in some way in order to signify their importance for viewing.

These markers then become one of the ways that such sights are mediated (or interpreted) for tourists by the tourism industry and associated agencies. We would suggest that the notion of the ecotourist is conceptualised along the lines of MacCannell's conception of the tourist.

More recently McKercher (1993) maintains that it is unrealistic to think of tourists as anything more than consumers, and the tourist experience as anything more than entertainment. Bruner (1991) also critically examined the notion in much tourism advocacy literature that the nature of these experiences leads to the personal transformations of tourists. He concludes that such claims are exaggerated and suggests that rather than having their world views and values challenged by their experiences, mediated as they were by various forms of interpretation, tourists are just as likely to return from their tour with their pre-existing prejudices and misunderstandings reinforced and reconfirmed.

The degree to which the tourism industry regulates and controls the gaze of the tourist is developed in the work of John Urry (1990, 1992). Urry argues that the tourist gaze is a socially constructed and systematised one in which the industry sanctions certain sights, objects and events as worthy of being viewed and experienced by tourists. MacCannell (1989: 42) refers to this as 'sight sacralization', when he writes: 'The tourist has no difficulty deciding the sights he [sic] ought to see. His only problem is getting around to all of them. Even under conditions where there is no end of things to see, some mysterious institutional force operates on the totality in advance of the arrival of the tourists, separating out the specific sights which are the attractions' (MacCannell 1989: 42). The practice of sightseeing does not occur within a social vacuum, however, and the anticipation for and much of the pleasure derived from such sights are constructed and influenced by a wide array of popular culture, such as television programmes, music, films, books and, of course, the marketing attempts of the tourism industry. These are the forces that MacCannell (1989) would argue help develop a 'ritual attitude' which is necessary for sight sacralization to occur. Like MacCannell, Urry also emphasises the important role that signs have in validating the legitimacy of the tourist gaze. He says that 'the gaze is constructed through signs, and tourism involves the collection of signs' (Urry 1990: 3).

Alexander Wilson, in his book *The Culture of Nature* (1992), examines the ways by which nature has been constructed for us through such things as popular culture and the tourism industry, where documentaries or sightseeing have constructed nature as entertainment or scenery. Tourists bring to

Plate 7.1
The pressures of ecotourism: turtle laying eggs on Mon Repos Beach, Queensland, Australia
Source: David Uzzell

their touristic experiences, ideas about and attitudes towards nature which have themselves been strongly influenced by the images created and transmitted by popular culture. Television documentaries in particular have been an important medium through which people have experienced (however vicariously) what we know as nature. Wilson (1992), for example, discusses the role that television programmes such as the Disney nature films, series such as *Wild Kingdom* and magazines such as *National Geographic* have played in the construction of nature perceptions in North American society. He argues that the narratives contained within these texts are both culturally and historically defined and that they 'express deeply contradictory ideas about nature and its relation to human culture' (Wilson 1992: 118). Interpreters working in the ecotourism industry are thus faced with a considerable challenge: to overcome powerful cultural expectations, and to contextualise particularly popular or notable wildlife species within ecosystems and habitats (Plate 7.1).

Ecotourism: development and characteristics

In recent times a nature-based tourism industry has developed which enables and facilitates (but simultaneously may detract from or compromise) the nature tourism experience. During the last decade or so, the term 'ecotourism' has emerged as a concept which, depending on the way it is defined and operationalised, is either a new market niche or product, or alternatively a challenge to conventional forms of tourism representing a new, more ecologically sustainable form in which interpretation is seen as fundamental, rather than incidental. Although first mentioned by Romeril (1985), 'ecotourism' was first defined by Ceballos-Lascurain as:

> Tourism that consists in travelling to relatively undisturbed or uncontaminated areas with the specific objective of studying, admiring, and enjoying the scenery and its wild plants and animals, as well as any existing cultural manifestations (both past and present) found in these areas. In these terms, nature-oriented tourism implies a scientific, aesthetic or philosophical approach to travel, although the ecological tourist need not be a professional scientist, artist or philosopher. The main point is that the person who practices ecotourism has the opportunity of immersing him or herself in nature in a way that most people cannot enjoy in their routine, urban existence. This person should eventually acquire a consciousness and knowledge of the natural environment, together with its cultural aspects, that will convert him/her into somebody keenly involved in conservation issues.
>
> *Ceballos-Lascurain 1987, cited in Boo 1990: 2*

In the decade that followed Ceballos-Lascurain's definition, much has been written about ecotourism and the tourism industry has embraced the name, at least, with gusto. Ambiguities in the numerous definitions of ecotourism have led to considerable debate about the exemplifying characteristics of this form creating concerns over the misuse of the term by unscrupulous tour operators (Wight 1993). Much debate centres on whether ecotourism is best regarded as another form of special interest tourism (analogous with nature-based tourism), thus appealing to a certain (and limited) market, or whether it is regarded as the basis of an alternative, and competing, conceptualisation of tourism (Figgis 1993). Ceballos-Lascurain's definition, however, clearly articulated the need for ecotourism to be a learning, self-transformatory experience in which the tourist is 'immersed in nature'. A consequence of this immersion, according to Ceballos-Lascurain will be the development of a 'consciousness and knowledge of the natural environment ... that will convert him [sic] into someone keenly involved in conservation issues' (1987, cited in Boo 1990: 2).

Plate 7.2
The pressures of ecotourism: bus tours around Fraser Island, Queensland, a World Heritage Site
Source: David Uzzell

While a number of variations of the Ceballos-Lascurain definition have appeared in the ecotourism literature (see, for example, Boo 1990; Keenan 1989; Kutay 1989), the exemplifying characteristics are that ecotourism activities should minimise negative environmental and socio-cultural impacts on the host destination; that they should be ecologically sustainable; and that they should involve the active promotion of a conservation ethic. Ecotourism, therefore, is a particular form of tourism dependent upon high quality experiences in the natural environment during which the tourist is provided with opportunities (through an appropriate interpretation programme) to learn about the natural environment and as a result become more committed to environmental conservation. The experience must be both intellectually challenging and emotionally stimulating in order to influence tourists' attitudes and perhaps behaviour relating to environmental conservation and protection, in the destination region and/or in the tourists' home environment. Just as importantly, ecotourism and the ecotourists it attracts actively seek to minimise their impacts on the environments which they visit. In this way, ecotourism incorporates 'both a strong commitment to nature and a sense of social responsibility' (Western 1993: 8). As Orams (1995: 5) contends, ecotourists should be moved 'beyond mere enjoyment to incorporate learning and to facilitate attitude and behaviour change'.

Ecotourism can be seen as an agent for personal and social change. Such 'agency' is seen as fundamental to the ecotourism concept; it is not incidental to it. This necessary characteristic of ecotourism would seem to challenge one of the dominant ways of conceptualising tourism (that is, tourism as entertainment and diversion) in that a necessary outcome of ecotourism is personal change leading to social change. However, the personal transformations which are considered to be critical to a true ecotourism experience have not generally been treated as problematic. The assumption inherent in much of the literature on ecotourism is that as long as people are provided with high quality, appropriate learning experiences within their ecotourism experience, they will not only change their attitudes towards nature, but also change their behaviour. For those people already committed to ecotourism ideals, attitudes and behaviour will be strengthened by such an experience. Unfortunately, there is a very large body of literature on the relationship between knowledge, attitudes and behaviour which does not support such a linear and rather simplistic account of attitude and behaviour change (Ballantyne and Packer 1996; Newhouse 1990).

According to the World Resources Institute (1992), if ecotourism is to contribute seriously to conservation and development, certain basic guidelines should be followed. These are that ecotourism should:

- provide significant benefits for local residents;

- contribute to the sustainable management of natural resources;

- incorporate environmental education for tourists and residents;

- be developed and managed to minimise negative impacts on the environment and local culture.

From the above, it is noted that the concept of ecotourism is problematic, particularly in terms of being able to operationalise its key components. The World Resources Institute (1992) highlights this by noting that while ecotourism can in theory increase the value of ecosystems by maintaining them in their natural state and thereby provide governments and local communities with incentives for conservation, in practice the benefits accruing to local communities have not been great. Furthermore, the negative impacts on local ecosystems and culture have often been high – a combination that discourages conservation. Typically, the ecotourism industry employs personnel from outside a region or country for all but the lowest paid positions (as is the case with tourism generally) and any government entrance and concession fees charged go to the government, not to the community. In many cases, local residents pay the price of ecotourism.

Plate 7.3
Treetop walk in a
Queensland
rainforest
Source: David Uzzell

Ecotourism, more than any other form of tourism, implies the notion of reciprocal exchange between tourists, the places they visit and the communities who live in them. Unlike other forms of tourism where the tourists are essentially consumers of experiences and products, ecotourists by definition have to be involved in reciprocal exchange. This exchange can take a number of forms but might include a greater personal commitment to actions supporting nature conservation. In this way, ecotourism does to some extent challenge the accepted primacy of the dominant forms of tourism which define the tourist as consumer only. Effective interpretation is regarded as being essential in developing or reinforcing an appropriate conservation ethic in the ecotourist (Plate 7.3).

Place of the interpretive guide in ecotourism

Returning to the exemplifying characteristic of ecotourism as 'actively promoting a conservation ethic', this section examines the role of interpretation, and in particular ecotour guides, in educating visitors about the environment and thereby inspiring them to behave more responsibly, both during the tour and back home. According to Orams (1995) such education needs to be both intellectually and emotionally challenging. It is not surprising that the degree to which a nature-based tour can be credited with meeting the aims of ecotourism rests largely with the quality of the guide. Whether on a guided bushwalk, four-wheel drive tour, wetland boat cruise, or underwater snorkel tour, the role of the guide is critical in facilitating environmental and cultural awareness, understanding, and where appropriate, attitudinal and behavioural change.

Interpretation provides an important set of tools on which an ecotour guide can draw to deliver a quality product to visitors. Of course, the guide's responsibilities extend far beyond the use of interpretation: the guide is also often expected to plan the itinerary, develop and deliver a 'script', organise equipment and transportation, ensure the safety of tour clients, entertain, administer first aid, troubleshoot, facilitate social interaction and mediate between the tour clients and host populations (Cohen 1985). However, it is the application of the principles of interpretation which distinguishes the true ecotour guide from the traditional tour guide. Most mainstream tour guides have a sound knowledge of the destination, site and/or attraction and most can provide volumes of facts and figures. In addition, some guides can give considerable detail about the historical, socio-cultural, political and economic contexts of the destination. But the use of interpretation, that is the art of engaging and involving the visitor in the delivery of this information, is what makes the tour meaningful and therefore memorable to visitors. In short, it is the 'how' (or process) rather than the 'what' (or content) of the tour that is the first distinguishing feature of the true ecotour.

All tour guides, not just nature guides and ecotour guides, are expected to be able to speak clearly and with confidence, use appropriate vocabulary and pace, and make effective use of body language, eye contact, pauses and silences. These are all elements of effective public speaking, as are the use of good attention-getting devices to begin an interpretive session, systematic organisation and a strong conclusion. Good guides are also a good storytellers, use interesting anecdotes and weave humour into their talks where appropriate (Lingle Pond 1993).

Unfortunately, many tour guides are often just good talkers and not good listeners. Guides who are unfamiliar with the principles of interpretation seldom delve into the background and interests of their clients, let alone make use of visitors' knowledge and skills to give meaning and relevance to what is being experienced. The notable feature of good ecotour guiding is the involvement of visitors in the learning process, using techniques such as questioning, providing opportunities for visitor questions and feedback, the use of the senses (touching, smelling, tasting) and active participation by visitors. The guide must be willing to concede the position of 'expert' and replace it with the role of 'facilitator'.

The second feature of ecotour guides that distinguishes them from nature or mainstream guides relates to the outcomes that they are able to achieve. The presumed objective of the typical tourist experience, whether guided or independent, is visitor satisfaction, usually achieved by conforming to the visitors' existing set of values, attitudes and behaviours. A good guide is one who is able to provide an enjoyable and satisfying experience, presumably by not challenging the visitors' preconceptions. In contrast, the ecotour guide uses interpretation as a means to 'provoke, reveal and relate' (to use Tilden's words) information and experiences to challenge visitors' knowledge, values, attitudes and behaviours. The intended outcome is a better understanding of the impacts of one's own attitudes and behaviours and a commitment to act responsibly toward the natural and cultural environment, both while travelling and at home.

Achieving such outcomes requires that ecotour guides encourage and demonstrate environmentally responsible behaviour throughout their tours, discuss the impacts of their own behaviours (as guides and as tour operators), and encourage reflection by visitors on their own. It is not surprising that few ecotour operators, let alone mainstream operators, are comfortable with such objectives. Most do not know whether their tours achieve such outcomes and many do not train or reward their guides for doing so.

Issues in ecotourism interpretation

If ecotourism is to achieve the aims and objectives it has set for itself, then high quality interpretive experiences need to play a crucial role. However, there is a range of substantial issues which the ecotourism industry and the interpretation profession need seriously to address. These relate to many of the assumptions underpinning interpretation as well as to the ways by which interpretation can be located within the broader theoretical understanding of the tourist. Perhaps one of the most important issues concerns the educational framework or paradigm in which interpretation is located.

If decision-making and problem-solving are identified as key characteristics of an environmentally literate citizen, the educational framework in which visitors learn (regardless of whether the learning environment is formal or non-formal) must provide real opportunities for these skills to be developed and refined if they are to move to higher levels of environmental literacy. The traditional pedagogical model, in which the teacher or expert interpreter, assumes much of the responsibility for decision-making and to a large extent problem-solving, does not seem to be adequate. An educational paradigm for interpretation which enables visitors to be more self-directed and free to choose learning pathways seems more in keeping with the aims of environmental education and ecotourism (Schwass 1986). Uzzell (1989) has put forward the view that interpreters should be aiming to reduce the dependence of visitors on the interpreter and to assist them in the development of perception techniques allowing them to better interpret and understand environments for themselves. In the specific context of ecotourism, the challenge for the interpreters, and the agencies/ businesses for whom they work will be whether they are willing to 'hand over' to the tourists some of the responsibility for learning while still providing the necessary educational support required for the individual to make this transition successfully.

Tilden (1977) was quite clear that interpretation is not synonymous with information transmission; to be truly effective, interpretation needs to provoke an emotional response as well as making a personal connection with the visitor. Rather than phasing out the use of people as interpreters and increasing the reliance on relatively impersonal methods such as signage, audiovisuals and interactive exhibits, agencies responsible for interpretation might consider exploring ways of making greater use of appropriately trained people as key interpretive tools and not necessarily importing wholesale techniques which may be appropriate in one part of the world but inappropriate in another. Given that increasing amounts of ecotourism occur in Third World countries, the introduction of people-based interpretation relying on locally trained interpreters would have many beneficial effects. It would raise levels of environmental awareness in the local community, it would bring economic gains to the community and would allow local people to take ownership of the issues. This is not to deny the place of a wide range of effective interpretive techniques, but it is an argument for making the decision about using particular techniques on a sound educational basis.

Increasingly, agencies such as national parks and forest reserves have limited (if any) resources for face-to-face interpretation, so that messages about environmentally responsible behaviour in the 1980s and 1990s are largely left to commercial operators and not-for-profit organisations operating both within and outside protected areas. Those operating in protected areas are to some extent regulated through licensing systems, but the vast majority are held accountable only by the demands of the marketplace and voluntary accreditation schemes within the industry. If the promotion of a conservation ethic through interpretation is an appropriate and necessary role for commercial ecotour operators and their guides, it is imperative that quality interpretation is a requirement of such operations.

There are a number of implications from the above. First is the need to revisit the education and training of ecotour guides. Many ecotour operations are in fact owner–operator businesses and while the owners may well be excellent business people, their interpretive skills may be limited. Alternatively, guide staff employed by tour operators are often engaged for their content knowledge and understanding rather than for their understanding of the principles of interpretation. Culturally appropriate interpretive training is clearly important to ensure high quality of interpretation in ecotourism. Second is the consideration of minimum standards for operators and tours seeking to use the label 'ecotourism' to ensure that they aim to create a conservation ethic among clients. As a number of commentators have pointed out (for example, Wight 1993; Bottrill and Pearce 1995), a large proportion of firms promoting themselves as ecotour operators do not in fact meet even minimum criteria which define ecotourism. Third is the use of rewards and incentives for guides who embrace the principles of ecotourism and interpretation in their day-to-day practice. At present there is no real career structure for ecotour guides and many are comparatively poorly paid.

Finally, there is a need to evaluate, through objective research, the extent to which ecotour operators and their tours are actually achieving the outcomes espoused by ecotourism philosophy. This is a particular challenge for industry, governments and academies to overcome successfully and will require a commitment to fund and otherwise support research. Academic (and other) researchers will also need to do a better job in making the findings of their research accessible to industry stakeholders and governments.

Their findings should aim to inform interpretive training programmes, thus leading to improvements in the quality and standards of ecotourism interpretation.

Conclusion

High quality interpretation is regarded as an essential and integral component of all ecotourism experiences. Interpretation is one of the main vehicles through which greater understanding and awareness of the places being visited by ecotours is achieved. It is hoped that greater empathy with those places will result from the interpreted experiences offered to the tourist participating in such ecotours. Indeed, it is the ecotourists' commitment to act in an environmentally and ecologically appropriate way that sets ecotourism apart from other more mainstream forms. However, the ecotourism industry still has some way to go before high quality interpretation is an industry benchmark. Considerable misunderstandings still exist both within and outside the industry as to just what ecotourism is. Many ecotour operators and guides lack an understanding of the principles and philosophies of interpretation, or do not have well-developed interpretive skills. It is suggested that efforts must be made by stakeholders in the industry, in government and in the interpretation profession to overcome these problems and limitations through appropriate interpretive training programmes, accreditation schemes and ongoing research and monitoring.

References

Ballantyne, R. and Packer, J. (1996) 'Teaching and learning in environmental education: developing environmental conceptions', *Journal of Environmental Education*, 27(2): 25–32.

Boo, E. (1990) *Ecotourism: The Potentials and Pitfalls, Volumes 1 and 2*, Washington DC: World Wildlife Fund.

Boorstin, D. (1964) *The Image: a Guide to Pseudo-Events in America*, New York: Harper.

Bottrill, C. G and Pearce, D. G (1995) 'Ecotourism: towards a key elements approach to operationalising the concept', *Journal of Sustainable Tourism*, 3(1): 45–53.

Bruner, E. M. (1991) 'Transformation of self in tourism', *Annals of Tourism Research*, 18: 238–50.

Buckley, R. (1994) 'A framework for ecotourism', *Annals of Tourism Research*, 21: 16–20.

Ceballos-Lascurain, H. (1987) *Estudio de Prefactibildad Socioeconomica del Turismo Ecologica y Anteproyecto Arquitectonico y Urbanistico del Centro de Turismo Ecologico de Sian Ka'an, Quintana Roo*, cited in E. Boo, (1990) *Ecotourism: The Potentials and Pitfalls, Volumes 1 and 2*, Washington DC: World Wildlife Fund.

Cohen, E. (1985) 'The tourist guide, the origins, structure and dynamics of a role', *Annals of Tourism Research*, 12: 5–29.

Eco, U. (1986) *Travels in Hyper-Reality*, London: Picador.

Figgis, P. (1993) 'Eco-tourism, special interest or major direction', *Habitat*, 21(1): 8–10.

Ham, S. (1992) 'Embrace the tourist', *Legacy*, 3(6): 6–7.

Keenan, J. (1989) 'Ecotourism, where capitalism and conservation meet', *Mexico Journal*, 22 May:16–24.

Kutay, K. (1989) 'The new ethic in adventure travel', *Buzzworm: The Environmental Journal*, 1(4): 31–6.

Lingle Pond, K. (1993) *The Professional Guide, Dynamics of Tour Guiding*, New York: Van Nostrand Reinhold.

MacCannell, D. (1989) *The Tourist, a New Theory of the Leisure Class*, New York: Van Nostrand.

McKercher, B. (1993) 'Some fundamental truths about tourism: understanding tourism's social and environmental impacts', *Journal of Sustainable Tourism*, 1(1): 6–16.

Newhouse, N. (1990) 'Implications of attitude and behavior research for environmental conservation', *Journal of Environmental Education*, 22(1): 26–32.

Orams, M. B. (1995) 'Towards a more desirable form of ecotourism', *Tourism Management*, 16(1): 3–8.

Romeril, M. (1985) 'Tourism and the environment – towards a symbiotic relationship', *International Journal of Environmental Studies*, 25: 215–18.

Schwass, R. (1986) 'The university and the concept of environmental education', in *Universities and Environmental Education*, Paris: UNESCO and the International Association of Universities, pp. 33–40.

Tilden, F. (1977) *Interpreting Our Heritage*, 2nd edn, Chapel Hill: University of North Carolina Press.

Urry, J. (1990) *The Tourist Gaze, Leisure and Travel in Contemporary Societies*, London: Sage.

Urry, J. (1992) 'The tourist gaze and the "environment"', *Theory, Culture and Society*, 9: 1–22.

Uzzell, D. L. (1989) 'Introduction: the natural and built environment', in D. Uzzell (ed.) *Heritage Interpretation, Vol. 1: the Natural and Built Environment*, London: Belhaven, pp. 1–14.

Western, D. (1993) 'Defining ecotourism', in K. Lindberg and D. E. Hawkins (eds) *Ecotourism: a Guide for Planners and Managers*, Vermont: The Ecotourism Society, pp. 7–11.

Wight, P. (1993) 'Ecotourism: ethics or eco–sell?', *Journal of Travel Research*, 31(3): 3–9.

Wilson, A. (1992) *The Culture of Nature, North American Landscape from Disney to the Exxon Valdez*, Cambridge MA: Blackwell.

World Resources Institute (1992) *Global Biodiversity Strategy*, Washington DC: World Conservation Union and United Nations Environment Programme.

8 Heritage, identity and interpreting a European sense of place

GREGORY ASHWORTH

This chapter explores the existence of a distinctive European interpretation of heritage and its related issues of identity, identification and the identifier. To proceed four questions need answers. First, what is meant by the term 'European heritage', as opposed to the heritage of someone else? Second, what is or could be the content of such a heritage? Third, who could, or might, create, manage and interpret this? Fourth, what repercussions ensue from the dissonance that exists between the various but simultaneously present scales, meanings and interpretations of such a heritage? The establishment of the EU 'Socrates' consortium, 'European Heritage Planning and Management', has of necessity focused thinking (Ashworth 1998; Ashworth and Graham 1997; Ashworth and Larkham 1994; Graham 1998; Graham and Murray 1997) on the questions pursued here. However, first the relationships of three much used and overlapping ideas, namely, heritage, place identity and sense of place will be considered.

Heritage, identity and a sense of place

This chapter begins with a single assertion, namely that heritage interpretation has an important spatial dimension. Simply, individuals and social groups endow their local environments with meanings that are not intrinsic to the physical forms themselves but are ascribed to them by people. Places thus both receive and convey identities. This is the sense of place which is a powerful instrument in shaping and reinforcing feelings of identification with specific areas in individuals, who in turn, by their reaction, further strengthen such identities. These meanings are both expressed through the medium of heritage and become the perceived collective heritage of individuals and groups. Such a point hardly needs mentioning when those studying, governing or selling places have a long tradition of creating distinctive localities and regions by endowing spaces with a personality, thereby rendering them understandable, examinable and memorable. Thus what Anderson (1991) called 'imagined communities' can be related here to a much older idea of 'imagined places'. Such collective imagination, it should be stressed, does not just exist as a result of some natural intrinsic human need for a native land, it can be created by deliberate external intervention, whether the goal is the economic commodification of places for sale on particular markets or for the facilitating of social or political cohesion of groups within areas. However, this simple idea has three major complicating corollaries, namely displacement, multilayering and spatial scale.

Place, non-place, displacement

First, it is by no means inevitable that people identify with their places nor that places reflect the identity of their populations. Two other conditions are possible. 'Placelessness' (Relph 1976) is the opposite of a sense of place, meaning a location that lacks distinctiveness, conveying only a sense of being anywhere and thus nowhere in particular. There is, however, a third possible circumstance, namely a sense of 'displacement'. This is when it is not 'anywhere' that is communicated but the wrong 'somewhere'. A sense of place exists and is experienced, but it does not accord with the identity needs of the recipient who therefore feels 'out of place' and consequently suffers a degree of psychological or even, in extreme cases, physical displacement.

Multilayering

Because people differ in their social and cultural attributes, different people can imagine different places in the same locations and ascribe different meanings to the same places. Thus 'landscapes are multivocal', as Graham (1997: 3) has expressed it for the Irish case, where a landscape, taken here to include built as well as the natural physical features, is inevitably speaking with the many different voices that have ascribed meanings to it over time. The sense of place is thus polysemic in conveying different messages, including different identities, to different recipients either sequentially or synchronously. This is not a particularly alarming condition, although it is often exemplified in those extreme cases where physical conflict for the control of place identities has resulted. It is in fact an almost universal condition of heritage: almost all heritage is multilayered in the sense that places are endowed with different identities by different groups for different purposes in the same locations. Such a statement is not particularly remarkable, nor indeed in most circumstances controversial, but it does, however, have many implications, not least for heritage management which must contend not only with the multi-use of space but the instability of these uses through time.

At the very least, for those concerned with analysing the interpretation of heritage, this idea cautions against a too simplistic application of what has now become the conventional wisdom of the so-called 'dominant ideology thesis'. This, together with its related concepts of political legitimation, culturally dominant and subordinate groups, and the accumulation and exploitation of the cultural capital, is usually drawn loosely and selectively from Abercrombie *et al.* (1980), Habermas (1973) and Bourdieu (1977) respectively. However, places rarely inevitably convey a simple master narrative of the imposition of a single coherent dominant ideology for the establishment of legitimacy by a hegemonic authority or social group. More usually the multilayering of identities allows for a much more volatile, pluralist situation where different senses of place, at different times and for different motives, among which the economic or the aesthetic are often as important as the political, may coexist, supplement each other and even incorporate each other rather than simply conflict, dominate or displace.

Identity and scale

An inherent characteristic of places is that they exist within a hierarchy of spatial scales and thus different senses of place exist simultaneously at different levels in such a hierarchy. This raises questions about the relationships between messages about place identities expressed at different spatial scales or at different points in a spatial hierarchy. Local, regional, national, continental and global place identities may all receive the identification of individuals (the 'Russian doll' model), but with strengths of allegiance that vary between groups and through time, leading to a spectrum of interscale relations ranging from a mutually reinforcing complementarity, through coexistence to competition and conflict. This interplay between local and global cultures may lead, as Schimany (1997) has argued, to the globalisation of local attributes, but also to the localisation of global cultures resulting in many types of 'creolisation' of cultural identities.

This is not just a theoretical possibility; it has numerous practical implications in heritage interpretation. The long-running argument about who 'owns' the past, its relict objects and associations has a distinct spatial dimension. Consider the case of misplaced heritage, that is objects whose physical locations are different from the locations of the people who are ascribing values to them: they are for one reason or another out of place. One of the most publicised cases, taken here to represent countless more, would be the so-called 'Elgin Marbles' (which is so archetypical as to have coined the term 'Elginism' to describe the general condition and 'de-Elginisation' as its corrective). They can be regarded as Athenian (contributing to the urban identifying 'signature' structure), Greek national (providing historical legitimacy to the current nation-state), European (representing the classical origins of Western humanist civic democracy), or indeed a world heritage (demonstrating the artistic and political achievements of humanity). The point is that they are important in the sense of place at a variety of scales which raises the practical questions, for which there are no obviously correct answers, of who should therefore own, maintain, house, interpret and experience them.

At a prosaic level practitioners of place marketing are acutely aware of the possibility of scale shadowing, that is where the established place image at one spatial scale permeates the image at another, despite the character of the places involved, or the objective of the marketing, being quite different (Ashworth and Voogd 1990). This may be a beneficial possibility to be exploited in promotion, as trivially exemplified in the regional geographical nomenclature of real estate agents (Gold and Ward 1994); a threat to be mitigated (as when the image of an individual tourism resort is polluted by unattractive elements of the wider regional image); or a combination of the two. Places seek through marketing policies either to associate themselves with positive shadows or to distance themselves from negative ones at various levels in the hierarchy of spatial scales.

The specific argument

The specific argument developed from these general points about heritage, identity and senses of place accepts three limitations on an otherwise unwieldy field.

1. The attention here is upon heritage as a deliberately managed process with official structures, formal organisations and legislative procedures and their results in designated monuments and areas, spatial planning and place management practices.
2. Although place identities and the heritage used to create and project them have many uses, one in particular is considered here, namely the identification of people in specific areas with jurisdictional territorial units and their governments. Heritage has historically fulfilled this purpose and although it has since acquired other purposes, not least the economic, these, however profitable, remain incidental and do not determine to any significant degree what, where or how heritage is created.
3   Although heritage and its role in place identities is a worldwide phenomenon, this chapter will focus upon a single continent, and the attempt of a part of that continent to shape a new sense of place, popular identification and legitimacy in support of a new political entity.

A further restriction is needed because heritage, defined here simply as the contemporary uses of the past, can include an exceptionally wide variety of possible elements, drawn from history, memory or physical survivals. In practice, it is the built environment that has been used most extensively as the visible, publicly accessible and readable vehicle for the transmission of heritage place identities through the creation of heritage places.

We now arrive at the central proposition, namely that the stumbling progress of the states of Europe, over the last half of the 20th century, towards forms of economic, social and ultimately political union has resulted in intergovernmental agreements and bureaucratic structures but lacks popular identification and thus legitimacy. The successful integration of Europe, as other than an organisational convenience, requires a validating identity vested in place and, as has occurred in the past and with jurisdictions at other spatial scales, it is the management of heritage that can superimpose an additional layer of meaning to the existing multilayered heritage sandwich to achieve this goal. Whether this is a desirable political goal is not argued here, only that if it is desired then the important question is the instrumental one of how to do it.

Heritage and European continentality

A commonsense reaction to the above proposition is that the argument is unnecessary because a sense of Europe has existed for at least two millennia. The classical mythology of the birth of Europa recognised the existence of a distinctive continent on what otherwise is no more than a group of sea-indented peninsulas in Western Asia. The physical area has long been endowed with cultural attributes whether described as European or some other, more or less synonymous term, such as Christendom or just Western civilisation. But different Europes were imagined for purposes different from those considered here.

Before considering the continental scale it is essential to examine the context of other scales of place identity. Although there has long been a sense of Europe, this has been subordinated, through a particular historical circumstance in the past few centuries, to a sense of national identity. Heritage was in practice so used as a major instrument in the creation and maintenance of the nation-state that it became effectively synonymous with national heritage. Most current concepts, institutions, legislative instruments and practices of heritage were developed synchronously with the political idea of the nation-state. Heritage was created by and largely for the nation-state, which is thus almost everywhere the dominant scale of interpretation (Featherstone 1990). Whether the invention of national heritage was a necessary precondition for the invention of the nation or whether nationalism created national heritage as an instrument of its legitimation is immaterial here: the past was effectively nationalised in national ministries, museums, histories, monuments and the like (see Horne's (1984) detailed study of European national museums), so that these national heritages form the context within which a European heritage would be shaped.

The dominance of the national scale, and thus nation legitimating interpretation, has not however gone unchallenged by two other scales, namely the subnational (whether regional, local or urban) and, at the other extreme, the supranational (continental or even global). The first is easier to recognise and relate back to the arguments about local identity raised above. The 'localisation' of the past stems from the perceived needs of localities to express their distinctiveness to themselves and to others. At a mundane level the conserved past is currently so widely used in the shaping of local place images as part of the competition of the 'Europe of the regions' or the 'Europe of the cities' (Masser *et al.* 1992) that further elaboration is unnecessary. The degree to which this occurs may often relate as much to such administrative matters as the spatial hierarchical organisation of decision-making in heritage planning and, in particular, the division of official responsibilities for the selection, financing and interpretation of sites and artefacts, as to existing perceived local differences in cultural identity. In short, 'who does it' determines what is done: local government produces local heritage.

At the other extreme, interpretation legitimating supranational identities is less easy to recognise in the iconography of modern Europe simply because of the weakness of any such scale identity. Indeed the most obvious examples in the built environment are relics of now defunct supranational entities that predate the nation-state, such as the dynastic regimes of Hapsburgs and Ottomans in Central and Eastern Europe, and the messages these convey have little remaining political relevance (Tunbridge 1994). However, a concept of global heritage does exist in two senses. There are governmental and non-governmental bodies that take a global view, through conferences, reports, and declarations to the world from the 'Charter of Athens' (1931) to the 'Charter of Venice' (1964). In particular Unesco and its agencies such as ICOMOS recognise that a location has a supranational significance by conferring the designation, 'world heritage site'. However, the official 'producers' of a world heritage are in practice only recognising, co-ordinating and encouraging national or local heritages which limits their authority, rather than shaping a competing alternative at a new spatial scale. Indeed, the long-standing concern of such global agencies with conventions on cultural property rights and national repatriation of perceived misplaced heritage (Unesco convention of 1970) actually reinforces the primacy of the national level as being 'correct' (Ashworth 1997).

Even more important than the international agencies is the global legitimation conferred by a world market for heritage. This is manifest in a worldwide popular anxiety expressed through a flow of concern, advice, and financial aid whenever the continued existence of a major monument, site or city is seen as being threatened. Global heritage tourism is a further clearly expressed manifestation that global heritage exists in the global village (Boniface and Fowler 1993). Each tourist visit expresses recognition that a site is part of the heritage of the tourist and not just of the inhabitants of the locality. This is not only an expression of an international title of ownership, or right of access, but has numerous practical implications for management, finance and interpretation.

It is not enough just to recognise that the conserved built environment conveys messages supporting identities at different spatial scales; the relationship between these messages is not always clear. The same places, buildings and historical narratives can be interpreted to convey spatially contrasting messages. These may be complementary and mutually reinforcing, co-existing independently or mutually incompatible and thus competing for the identification of those receiving them.

Meanings of European heritage

Interpreting a specifically European sense of place from a European heritage immediately confronts different meanings of the continental adjective. This is not just casuistry: for the definition in practice determines the choice, location and market for such heritage.

The heritage of Europeans

If all heritage is user determined then logically heritage 'belongs' to those for whom it is currently relevant or those who perceive themselves as having created it. It seems reasonable therefore to consider the heritage of Europeans as including heritage of whatever sort, and wherever now located, which was created by, or can be considered relevant to, Europeans. This has much to recommend it as European peoples have, at least over the past 500 years, demonstrated a remarkable capacity for global involvement of various sorts and thus a sense of Europeanness is only conceivable in a global context. The settlement of Europeans overseas and the globalisation of European trading and political systems has not only transplanted European languages, cultures and economies to very extensive portions of other continents, but also shaped links between heritage artefacts, such as architectural styles, urban designs and the like, that would make it illogical and artificial to include Novara but not Louisbourg, Bath but not Boston, Seville but not Santo Domingo. Equally as a result of this global interaction, so much of the remembered and memorialised symbolic past of Europeans occurred outside of Europe. There are a few exceptional cases, whose rarity does not deny their importance, where historical events occurring in Europe are commemorated elsewhere. Notably the 'holocaust' was a European crime located in Europe with Europeans fulfilling the roles of both victim and perpetrator. It is, however, memorialised most dramatically not in the places where it occurred but in the places where it is now most relevant to survivors, namely in Israel and the USA.

The definition of European heritage above, however, has three main difficulties. First, it presents an extremely wide selection of possibilities and does little to limit an already wide field. Second, if the purpose is to discover or create a distinctive place identity then European heritage cannot just be interpreted as a microcosm of a global phenomenon. Third, it raises the major problem of the treatment of the reverse case, namely the heritage that can be classified as non-European although physically located in European locations. Logically, for example, Islamic heritage in Europe, whether a relic of previous occupation, as in Spain or south-eastern Europe or of more recent immigration, as in many industrial cities, would have to be excluded from such an interpretation. This would remove one of the most important and interesting aspects of the use of heritage to support the shaping of new multicultural identities within a new sense of Europe.

The heritage in Europe
This, simply defined, is heritage occurring in what can be recognised as the continent of Europe. Of course the delimitation of that continent from the Eurasian landmass is highly tendentious and based upon few universally accepted criteria. A long discussion could ensue, and indeed has ensued in discussions of potential EU membership, on the marginal cases of Iceland, Greenland, Turkey, the islands of the Mediterranean (especially Cyprus and Malta), Israel/Palestine and perhaps even the Maghreb countries. The more intractable problem lies with Russia: exclusion seems illogical given

the historical and cultural involvement of that country with the other countries of Europe while inclusion extends the area of consideration to the Caucasus, Central Asian Republics, Amur River and Pacific Ocean.

Until very recently Europe was, in many important respects, both much smaller in extent and more easily delimited. The western continental fringe of countries, politically and militarily united in an Atlantic alliance since 1948 and increasingly economically interdependent from the early 1950s, formed a clearly defined entity that thought of itself as simply 'Europe'. Asia began on the east bank of the Elbe (echoing Metternich's eastern gate of Vienna) in contemporary economic and political reality if not in historical perspective. Now there is the acceptance, however unconsciously, of the idea of a core Europe of western European countries, almost coterminous with EU membership, and a fringe of possible, future and potential EU aspirants to the south and east. This is despite the non-membership of a number of western European countries (Norway and Switzerland in particular) and despite the subsidiary role it allocates to the countries that increasingly call themselves 'Central Europe'.

This may appear mere geographical quibbling but there are dangers involved in a too broad or indeed too narrow definition. The inclusive Europe from 'Vancouver to Vladivostock' may not be distinctive enough for the purposes of identity while the definition of European culture as that which can be viewed on a day trip from Brussels is likely to be too exclusive to be acceptable to many Europeans.

The heritage for Europe

A different approach to a definition would be from the side of demand. Central to the argument here is the idea that there is a European purpose to this search for a European heritage and thus logically the purpose can determine the scope. Europe, of course, has many purposes for its creation of heritage. The near ubiquitous economic commodification of the past as a central element within the important tourism industry ensures that heritage is a vital consumer product throughout Europe's increasingly free market dominated service economies. However, the concern here rests more narrowly with issues of place identification than with political entities and their legitimation. Thus European heritage would be that which contributes to this European purpose. The two main objections to this line of argument are not that it cannot be done but either that it should not, for various reasons, or that in practice it just is not done because there is nobody charged with doing it, and if there was, they would not know what to do.

The creators of a European heritage

Given the argument so far that a European heritage for a delimited entity is needed, then the question of who has the responsibility for creating and managing it is pertinent. The European scale institution with the longest involvement in the heritage of the built environment is the Council of Europe. This continent-wide intergovernmental forum has long regarded culture in general, and the urban built environment in particular, as a major focus of its responsibilities. It has for more than twenty years publicised best-practice examples of planning historic cities in various countries with the implied intent not so much of comparing European national practices, as using successful examples to stimulate the less active members. Equally promotional in its objective was the naming of years. 'European Conservation Year' (1970) was followed by arguably the most successful, 'European Architectural Heritage Year' (1975) and, subsequently, by 'European Campaign for an Urban Renaissance' (1981) and 'European Year of the Environment' (1989). These did provide national governments and agencies with an excuse and stimulant for increased heritage expenditure and raised the public profile of these topics. More recently the 'European City of Culture' designation has proved a similarly efficacious means of obtaining funds for cultural and tourism initiatives at the local city scale, although the meaning of the 'European' in the title remains undefined and usually unexpressed. In the latest initiative a very mixed bag of cities (Avignon, Bergen, Bologna, Brussels, Kraków, Helsinki, Prague, Reykjavik and Santiago de Compostella) have been designated 'European Capitals of Culture'. Again, the European dimension is largely unexpressed as the various cities attempt to capitalise upon their self-promotion as individual cultural products. Although its activities have been predominantly urban, the Council of Europe has also been involved in other heritage initiatives. In 1987, for example, it launched a cultural routes programme designed to celebrate the unity and diversity of European identity of which the first was the pilgrim route ('Camino') to Santiago de Compostella, selected as a 'deeply felt commitment to the European experience' (Council of Europe 1989); although it could equally be interpreted as part of a Spanish national, or even Christian, struggle against the Moors (Graham and Murray 1997).

By contrast, and somewhat surprisingly given the argument above about its stake in the topic, the EU has taken only sporadic interest in the heritage of the built environment and even the few initiatives that can be recognised make no particular use of a self-consciously European dimension. One difficulty is that the topic does not fit comfortably into the present structure of

EU administration or decision-making. At the executive level, responsibilities for heritage topics are divided between DGXVI (regional policy, including the allocation of subsidies for regional and urban programmes) and DGXI (environment, including the management of both the built and natural environment). Other directorates also cover various important uses of European heritage, such as DGXXIII (tourism), DGX (culture) and DGXXII (education). At the political level, responsibility is also divided among at least four of the twenty-one Commissioners' portfolios. This fragmented responsibility accounts in part, for example, for the failure of the arguments, put forward by DGXI, to have specific references to the historical role of European cities in nurturing a European civilisation included in the Maastricht Agreement (Williams 1996). In reality, European Commission concern with heritage amounts to no more than general exhortations that can be implemented only at the local scale through national conservation and physical planning systems. Thus, the vision of European spatial patterns and policies published as 'Europe 2000+' (European Commission 1994) includes among its eleven focus topics, 'heritage preservation and conservation of historic areas'; such platitudes hardly amount to a distinctive European heritage policy in either content or method.

This discussion of the relative ineffectiveness of official interventions into heritage at the European scale combines with two further important constraints on the development of a specifically European dimension to heritage. First, the dominant sphere of public sector intervention in the definition, preservation and presentation of heritage remains national governments and their agencies, operating in pursuit of notions of national heritage. Second, private commercial enterprises, which can be loosely bundled together as 'the heritage industry', play a major role in the presentation and use of the commodified past, including the heritage resources preserved and maintained by the public sector. Much of this heritage is part of a leisure industry that provides 'fun' experiences in response to a growing contemporary demand for the past as entertainment. The point is not that this constitutes a somehow less valid or 'authentic' use of the past, these terms being quite meaningless in this context, but simply that this is an alternative and competing economic use of the past to the political uses discussed here. Inescapably, therefore, any officially propagated public history would have to compete for public attention and the acceptance of its message with an existing, successful and highly effective commercial entertainment industry.

Content of European heritage

A completely different definition of the term European would seek meaning through content: it would attempt to identify heritage that is specifically European, as opposed to pertaining to some other spatial scale. Much of the rhetoric emanating from the European institutions seems to suggest that such a heritage exists apart from national or local heritages. This immediately raises the question of what heritage is, or could be conceived to be, distinctively European as opposed to the mere aggregate within Europe of national or local heritages. Three answers are suggested here.

The heritage of the European idea

The first defines European heritage narrowly as relating to the origins, evolution and achievements of what can be termed the European idea. This quite clearly offers an opposing alternative to the idea of national heritage described above. It thus provides a clearly comprehensible justification, goal and answer to the problems of selection and interpretation. Its purpose is the legitimisation through heritage of a European organisation, and ultimately state, in opposition to the nation-state legitimated through national heritage.

There could be a focus, presumably, on such topics as 'European capitals', in contrast to national capitals: cities with designated supranational, European functions, such as Brussels, Strasbourg and Luxembourg City within which there are sacralised spaces and buildings such as the Berlaymont/Place Schuman in Brussels or the European Parliament in Strasbourg. This could be supplemented by marking the various events, the summits and signings, and a new pantheon of European heroes (including, presumably, Monnet, Spaak, de Gasperi, Adenauer, Heath, if not Jenkins, Delors and Santer), together with the anthems, flags and other essential paraphernalia of a legitimate state.

There are two insurmountable difficulties with such an approach. First, there are just very few heritage resources to be found in the buildings, events and personalities from the European past that can be used in the creation of such a European heritage in competition with the national and imperial capitals, collections, monuments and heroes. The people, events, buildings created to house them and indeed the cities in which they are located are generally uninspiring at best and quite unable to compete successfully in popular imaginations with the personalities, events and structures which underlie national – or even regional – heritage narratives. Such a European heritage would simply lose a competitive struggle for the identification of Europeans. Second, the selection of artefacts and events to shape a specifically European Union heritage poses the question of how to treat the overwhelmingly dominant mass of existing heritage that does not support this scale of legitimacy. An Orwellian rewriting of the past, the fostering of a collective amnesia to counter collective memory and the physical destruction of its relics is beyond the current power of the European Commission. The choice therefore would be between policies of conscious ignorance and acceptance or an attempt to reinterpret national heritages as either primitive precursors to the European idea or as warnings of the consequences of destructive nationalisms. Neither of these policies would have much chance of success.

The heritage of European ideas

A less drastic but equally less focused approach would be to develop a specifically European heritage based upon those ideas, trends, aesthetic creations and activities that of their nature were continental rather than nation bound. Many general artistic, philosophical, political, economic and social themes suggest themselves as being intrinsically international, although not necessarily specifically European. Architectural themes from the Gothic to the postmodern, aesthetic fashions from Classicism to Romanticism, political movements from the Crusades to Marxism, economic and social trends from feudalism to liberal capitalist consumerism provide an almost inexhaustible quarry of possible resources for the selection of heritage that disregards national boundaries. The advantages of these heritage themes is that they are mostly safe (i.e. they create little dissonance), self-congratulatory (i.e. the recipient shares the achievement with the 'greats'), some are inclusive (i.e. they disinherit few excluded groups), and many may even surmount the barriers of cultural and linguistic communication. In this respect conserved built environments are in many ways ideal, being composed of internationally legible forms which are both an element in, and a stage for, wider cultural expressions, while acting as a primary resource for the international heritage tourism industry whose activities legitimate the heritage.

There are two difficulties. First, there is such an embarrassment of riches that there is no guidance in the selection from such a myriad of possibilities. Second, much of the interaction between Europeans that could form the basic themes is dissonant: that is, there is a discordance or lack of agreement and consistency between the messages emanating from the heritage and the identity needs of those receiving them (Tunbridge and Ashworth 1996. Two thousand years of intense interaction between Europeans has resulted not only in progress, whether artistic, social or political, but is also equally typified by pogrom, persecution and prejudice manifested in near-continuous internecine oppression, war and genocide. Europeans may not have invented these traits of the human condition and have had no monopoly of their practice, but they have developed them to a new apogee in global applications. Thus a European heritage based upon the acceptable complacency of cathedrals, eisteddfods and folk dances would find it difficult either to accommodate or to ignore ghettoes, concentration camps and battlefields. In short, how can such an interpretation manage the distasteful, the history that hurts?

A European identity in European conflict

Both of the above ideas for structuring a content of a European heritage founder on the dissonant nature of the European historical narrative. Simply much of the interaction between Europeans that could form the basis for such themes is dissonant in some way or other to some Europeans. The past is a contested resource and thus the recognition of any one claim upon it disinherits others, sometimes with serious results. This is manifested in several ways in Europe. The nation-state is generally perceived to be forged through a 'freedom struggle' for existence. Conversely a country with no 'war of independence', such as Canada (Ashworth 1993) or Australia (Anderson and Reeves 1994) has such severe problems of nation building that it needs to invent one. Further the region-states, or even less overt expressions of separatist identity within the nation-states, are equally defined by histories of subjugation and rebellion. Conflict is essential to these narratives and war, atrocity, repression and revolt are needed to produce the folk heroes and martyrs, as well as the folk villains and oppressors that differentiate the national character and virtues from the others.

The importance of these elements in existing national heritages may seem so self-evident as to be not worth arguing. The point here, however, is that it is so important that it can be neither ignored nor opposed. If that is so, then the only alternative is to accept its existence and to use conflict itself as the structuring theme for a European heritage. Only in this way can the content of European heritage embrace the distasteful – Katyn and Dachau as well as Chartres Cathedral and the Sistine Chapel. The Jewish Holocaust of 1933–45 remains pre-eminent, archetypally 'European' heritage and arguably the most serious challenge facing contemporary European society in managing its past. It is perhaps more comfortable to believe that a European heritage, which includes war and atrocity, commemorates only former divisions and should be ignored. However, the past, no matter how awful, can still be seen as constructive if one of the functions of European unity is to prevent its reoccurrence. Thus, Europe's camps, graves, battlefields and memorials are a past that cannot just be erased from human memory; the inheritance cannot be rejected, but must constitute part of its heritage alongside the more acceptable elements that support our ethnocentric notions of European cultural hegemony and civilisation.

Throughout Europe the 'landscapes of death' are memorialised as 'landscapes of memory', of contested pasts whether recent (such as Verdun, Ieper and the Somme to which can be added Srebrenica and Sarajevo) or more distant (Waterloo, Kosovo, Mohács). These can be transformed through time to convey rather than negate the notion of Europeanness. Although few places on earth have been fought over so continuously, one of the primary functions of European economic and political integration is to ensure that such events never occur again and that the short, and historically aberrant, window of peace that opened up in the second half of the 20th century be maintained. Thus the memorials, graves and battlefields across the continent, essential components of national heritage, might also be interpreted as a heritage of European reconciliation, testimony to the unacceptably atavistic. The 'museums of peace' (Kavanagh 1994), the war cemeteries and cenotaphs (Heffernan 1995), the concentration camps (Charlesworth 1994) and the battlefield interpretations can be read as landscapes sacred to the folly of warring nations and the wisdom of an idea of European unity rather than as a necessary sacrifice to the fatherland. In practice, however, this opportunity has so far been squandered. Most such interpretations tend to be military–technical, treating war as a strategic and tactical game, blatantly ethnicist or nationalist or, most commonly, where time has muted the ideological messages and realities of suffering, as entertainment.

At a more prosaic level a structuring of European heritage through the concept of dissonance recognises that the past is a resource in conflict, but is itself seriously dissonant with the currently dominant interpretations of most of what could be termed the heritage industry, which is strongly wedded to a 'history is fun' approach to the past. Much of the contemporary market for heritage is quite simply seeking entertainment and much heritage is maintained in existence principally to supply fun experiences for this leisure market. If this implies, as it increasingly does, 'Schindler tourism' in the heritage of the Jewish Holocaust in Kraków-Kazimierz with optional coach excursions to Auschwitz (Ashworth 1996), then how do we react?

Heritage is Europe: Europe is heritage

Now a different argument will be presented, namely that the delimitation of area and the choice of content for a European heritage has already been made and not by statesmen operating on a European scale in European institutions but by local planners implementing essentially local schemes and policies. As a consequence heritage has become a fundamentally European idea, manifested in a European movement that has resulted in the shaping of a distinctive European built environment, recognised as such by both Europeans and others.

Heritage is European in two senses. First, a conscious concern for the relics of the past, their conservation and heritage interpretation developed across the nation-states of Europe in much the same way and at much the same time, resulting in broadly similar organisational structures, legislation, practice and thus conserved historic cities (Ashworth 1992). The countries around the North Sea were often the legislative leaders, those around the Mediterranean followed, but the gap was always short and the similarities obvious. We can thus argue that if the European city exists as an idea then it is composed of conserved urban forms and the idealised urban life style these express. Such an archetype was created, not as might be thought by a thousand years of an essentially unique urban historic experience but by less than a hundred years of a standardised continent-wide conservation planning. Second, this planning process was European in another sense, in that although other continents have distinguished urban histories and architectural creativity, some of which have been valued and protected, urban conservation as discussed here was in essence a European idea prop-agated by European schools of planning, diffusing later elsewhere, most usually first to cities of European settlement overseas (see the detailed cases of Boston, Sydney or Pietermaritzburg in Ashworth and Tunbridge 1990). This has numerous implications from the commercial, with the European cities being the product leaders in the cultural and heritage tourism industries, to the political, with 'global heritage' and its interna-tional institutions being little more than European conservation writ on a world stage (Ashworth 1997).

There is a major objection to this assertion, which returns to the argument of the initial assumption about the link between heritage and place iden-tity. The question is whether heritage as a planning process encourages heterogeneity or homogeneity. The conservation of structures and forms from the past has been and is still strongly linked to the idea of diversification through the uniqueness of the historical experience of places and is explicitly undertaken as a projection of, and stimulus to, such a unique identity of a specific place. This largely unchallenged conventional wisdom is contradicted by the practice of conservation itself, which contains powerful intrinsic trends in exactly the reverse direction, that is towards the standardisation of forms and thus homogenisation of places. This may be occurring at two levels of generalisation.

First, it is possible to recognise national styles of urban 'heritagisation' emanating from distinctive national schools. There is, for instance, a 'French School of Conservation' (Kain 1981) characterised by relatively lavish public expenditure on set-piece national projects, each cloning such a Parisian archetype as the Place de Vosges in many a provincial town centre. Similarly a 'Polish School' (Milobedzki 1995) painstakingly and self-consciously reconstructs an idealised Polish 'Jagellonian' urbanism. The 'German School' reproduces a rediscovered German 'vernacular' style in numerous urban conservation projects as both an artistic reaction to bland 'modernism' and as an assertion of a new national confidence after a generation's submission to international political dominance (Soane 1994). There is even a 'Dutch School' which replicates throughout the country the obsessive regard for domestic detail and small-scale structures and spaces of Vermeer's image of Delft. If these and many other such possible national 'schools' actually exist and are nationally dominant then they would clearly produce a national heritage identity at the expense of locally distinctive identities at the scale of the city and region.

Second, the argument can be extended to the continental and even global scales. At the level of detail it is easy to recognise a 'catalogue heritagisation' of stereotypically historical street furniture, paving materials and signage while new and existing buildings are treated to a standardised 'neo-vernacular historicist' embellishment. The cities of Europe, or at least the expanding group that regard themselves as 'historic', have created by planning action historic districts that are largely indistinguishable from each other, which in turn reinforce the image among Europeans of how a 'real' European city should appear.

When Stokstraat (Maastricht), Stonegate (York), Elm Hill (Norwich), Bottcherstrasse (Bremen) and even Louisbourg Square (Boston) or with only minimal fantasy 'Gastown' (Vancouver) are all standardised 'historic', then there is a paradox that 'involves at once the devaluation and the valorisation of tradition and heritage' (Robins 1991: 40).

Conservation architects, heritage planners and urban political managers are fashion conscious; professional training and subsequent networking establishes and transmits an acceptable consensual style of practice; and peripatetic commercial developers with access to international capital investment favour provenly successful formulas. Thus similar building restoration work, townscape schemes and urban revitalisation projects are replicated regardless of the distinctive local historical experience, geographical environment, or locally symbolic meanings. Similarly there is an international propagation of 'best practice' through global governmental organisations such as Unesco or ICOMOS and at the continental scale through, especially, the Council of Europe. There is also a proliferation of various European associations of cities (whether under semi-official European patronage such as 'The League of Car-Free Cities' and 'Quartiers en Crise', or 'unofficial' such as 'The Walled Towns Friendship Circle' or 'The European League of Historic Towns') which encourages the transfer of technical and artistic practice and thus reduces rather than increases the local distinctiveness of the conserved urban form.

Thus we arrive at the conclusion that although urban conservation was and is motivated by a wish to enhance local place identities, the more it is practised the less distinctive that identity is likely to become. If pressed to define the content of what is typically European as opposed to appertaining to some other continent, then many Europeans would articulate this through the 'Europe of the cities', the environment in which most Europeans live, work and recreate, and specifically through the 'Europe of the historic cities'. One of the most prevalent visions of Europe is Florence, Bath and Heidelburg (now extended to Telc, Eger and Kraków), evoked even among the many who do not live in these particular environments, cities or even countries. In these senses a European heritage already exists in the European imagination and is deliberately sought out and experienced by millions of tourists from this and other continents as well as willingly financed and defended from threat in well-supported campaigns to 'save our European heritage'.

Europa Nostra?

There is globally evident, but most obviously in Europe, an increasingly complex articulation of territoriality, sovereignty and identity. Centripetal forces, whether the creation of continental economic, political and increasingly also social and cultural structures, or convergence in life patterns, styles and tastes, are being superimposed upon the patterning of nations and their nation-state creations of the later 19th and early 20th centuries. Simultaneously, however, regionalised and localised decentralisation is apparent in new forms of territorial sovereignty, jurisdiction and the identification of citizens. The interpretation of the heritage of the built environment plays various, and often ambiguous, roles in each of these trends.

It is apparent that unavoidable tension, dissonance and conflict exist among the various but simultaneously present scales, meanings and interpretations of heritage throughout Europe and, that within this heterogeneity of meaning and motivation, the idea of a distinctly European heritage is as yet poorly developed in comparison with other spatial scales.

However, if the function of a European heritage is to create a European dimension that can be added to already complex formulations and layerings of identity, this is not only possible but to an extent already exists. Given the fragmentation of territoriality and sovereignty that is characteristic of the New Europe, it is important not to equate the creation of a European heritage with an all-encompassing, pervasive European identity. Above all, therefore, a European heritage must be manipulated as a mosaic of similarity but also difference that reflects the political and cultural realities of overlapping layers of identity and empowerment. If there is no one landscape or iconography that can encompass Europe's identity, then a European heritage has to portray diversity as a positive quality, symbolic of reality. Nor can it comprise those elements that are common to all as this would result merely in an anaemic heritage in which the hard questions posed by the past are obscured by superficial and complaisant narratives of progression and European cultural hegemony, which contain their own dangers given the shallowness of the grave into which the European past of conflict has been very recently buried.

If territoriality, sovereignty, nationalism and the state need no longer all be bundled together (Anderson 1996) then there are many possibilities for more inclusive, pluralist and overlapping structures, identities and senses of place, all of which could be validated through heritage interpretation. The meaning and consequences of Europeanness are a challenge that the New Europe is beginning to face. The central importance of heritage interpretation, as well as its content and meanings, will be inescapable.

References

Abercrombie, N., Hill, S. and Turner, B. S. (1980) *The Dominant Ideology Thesis*, London: Allen and Unwin.

Anderson, B. (1991) *Imagined Communities: Reflections on the Origins and Spread of Nationalism*, London: Verso Books.

Anderson, J. (1996), 'The shifting stage of politics: new medieval and postmodern Territorialities?', *Environment and Planning A: Society and Space*, 14: 133–53.

Anderson, M. and Reeves, A. (1994) 'Contested identities, museums and the nation in Australia' in F. Kaplan (ed.) *Museums and the Making of Ourselves: the Role of Objects in National Identity*, London: Pinter.

Ashworth, G. J. (1992) *Heritage Planning*, Groningen: Geopers.

Ashworth, G. J. (1993) *On Tragedy and Renaissance: the Role of Loyalist and Arcadian Heritage Interpretation in Canadian Place Identities*, Groningen: Geopers.

Ashworth, G. J. (1996) 'Jewish culture and holocaust tourism; the case of Krakow-Kazimierz', in M. Robinson (ed.) *Tourism and Cultural Change*, Newcastle: University of Northumbria, pp. 1–12.

Ashworth, G. J. (1997) 'Is there a world heritage?', *Urban Age* 4(4): 12.

Ashworth, G. J. (1998) 'The conserved city as cultural symbol: the meaning of the text', in B. J. Graham (ed.) *Modern Europe: Place, Identity and Power*, London: Methuen.

Ashworth, G. J. and Graham, B. J. (1997) 'Heritage Identity and Europe', *Tijdschrift voor Economisch en Sociale Geografie*, 88(1): 381–88.

Ashworth, G. J. and Larkham, P. J. (1994) *Building a New Heritage: Tourism, Culture and Identity in the New Europe*, London: Routledge.

Ashworth, G. J. and Tunbridge, J.E. (1990) *The Tourist-Historic City*, London: Belhaven.

Ashworth, G. J. and Voogd, H. (1990) *Selling the City: Marketing Approaches in Public Sector Urban Planning*, London: Belhaven.

Boniface, P. and Fowler, P. J. (1993) *Heritage and Tourism in the Global Village*, London: Routledge.

Bourdieu, P. (1977) *Outline of a Theory of Practice*, Cambridge: Cambridge University Press.

Charlesworth, A. (1994) 'Contesting places of memory: the case of Auschwitz', *Environment and Planning A: Society and Space*, 12: 579–93.

Council of Europe (1989) 'The Santiago de Compostella Pilgrimage Routes', *Architectural Reports and Studies*, 16. Strasbourg: Council of Europe.

European Commission (1994) *Europe 2000+*, Brussels: European Commission.

Featherstone, M. (1990) *Global Culture: Nationalism, Globalisation, Identity*, London: Sage.

Gold, J. R. and Ward, S. (1994) *Place Promotion: the Use of Publicity and Marketing to Sell Towns and Regions*, Chichester: Wiley.

Graham, B. (1997) *In Search of Ireland: a Cultural Geography*, London: Routledge.

Graham, B. J. (ed.) (1998) *Modern Europe: Place, Identity and Power*, London: Methuen.

Graham, B. J. and Murray, M. (1997) 'The spiritual and the profane: the pilgrimage to Santiago de Compostella', *Ecumene*, 4(4): 389–409.

Habermas, J. (1973) *Legitimationsprobleme im Spätkapitalismus*, Frankfurt am Main: Suhrkamp.

Heffernan, M. (1995) 'For ever England: the western front and the politics of remembrance in Britain', *Ecumene*, 2: 293–324.

Horne, D. (1984) *The Great Museum: the Re-presentation of History*, London: Pluto.

Kain, R. (1981) *Planning for Conservation: an International Perspective*, London: Mansell.

Kavanagh, G. (1994) *Museums and the First World War: a Social History*, London: Pinter.

Masser, I, Sviden, O. and Wagener, M. (1992) *The Geography of Europe's Futures*, London: Belhaven.

Milobedzki, A (1995) *The Polish School of Conservation*, Kraków: International Cultural Centre.

Relph, E. (1976) *Place and Placelessness*, London: Pion.

Robins, K. (1991) 'Tradition and translation: national culture in its global context', in J. Corner and S. Harvey (eds) *Enterprise and Heritage: the Cross Currents of National Culture*, London: Routledge.

Schimany, P. (1997) 'Soziokulturelle Auswirkungen des Tourismus', *Passauer Papiere zur Sozialwissenschaft*, Passau: Heft 16.

Soane, J. (1994) 'The renaissance of cultural vernacularism in Germany', in G.J. Ashworth and P. J. Larkham, (eds) *Building a New Heritage: Tourism, Culture and Identity in the New Europe*, London: Routledge, pp. 159–78.

Tunbridge, J. E. (1994), 'Whose heritage? Global problem, European nightmare', in G. J. Ashworth and P. J. Larkham (eds) *Building a New Heritage: Tourism, Culture and Identity in the New Europe*, London: Routledge, pp. 123–34.

Tunbridge, J. E. and Ashworth, G. J. (1996) *Dissonant Heritage: the Management of the Past as a Resource in Conflict*, London: Wiley.

Williams, R. H. (1996) *European Union Spatial Policy and Planning*, London: PCP.

9 Mediating the shock of the new: interpreting the evolving city

BRIAN GOODEY

Although still popularly regarded as a whispered word at the shoulder of an international leader, 'interpretation' in its minority meaning, should need little initial definition to the reader who has been drawn to this title. Whether interpretation is essentially a set of communication processes designed to enhance and conserve the qualities of a site, setting or feature, or whether it is (in my view) a process of adding value to the experience of place, its short history and major principles are shared by modest professional interest groups in several countries.

Thus far, however, the process of interpretation has been largely confined to drawing the visitor or viewer into conservation of the past, with the term 'heritage interpretation' favoured by many. Its earlier source, 'countryside interpretation', has been less restricted to revealing past processes and landscapes, often involving discussion as to the present results of human impact, and extending to a justification of present and visible management interventions.

Seldom, if ever, has the interpretive process been drawn to future, or emerging environments. It is the discussion and opportunities which surround the interpretation of future environments which concern this chapter. Three matters are explored:

- experienced examples of the postmodern complexity of design, explanation and meaning in the interpretation of the built environment;

- key issues concerning the recent role and performance of interpretation;

- settings and opportunities for interpretation in the evolving built environment, and the linkages and skills required to achieve modest gains.

Experienced examples of the postmodern complexity of design, explanation and meaning in the interpretation of the built environment

The basis of all interpretation is observation to be backed up by research, and by the structuring of themes and stories which will engage the user or visitor. The interpreter is thus in descent from the 18th-and 19th-century topographers and, in the built environment, from street and building enthusiasts who endorsed the varied qualities of public places. Among them, Sir John Betjeman and Ian Nairn stand out as major influences on a way of looking enjoyed by post-war generations with Jonathan Meades currently reinterpreting the latter's approach.

In London I still seek out the places marked by Nairn (1966, rev. Gasson 1988), and others which he missed. Nairn showed the true value of a quiet pub table. Betjeman will always be associated with railways; he made a number of signal 'rail-trail' films, notably *Metroland*, and revelled in Paddington as his London terminus (Betjeman 1981). Come, walk around some urban places with me and 'listen' to the messages they convey.

The Blind Beggar, Whitechapel

The building shell is of London stock bricks from the 18th century, part of a larger, revised brewery; the interior is eclectic, modern brick fireplace, recent imitation Victorian joinery, applied leaded windows. It's all new, but looks old. Gold-framed picture of a stagecoach, etched glass mirrors (but with US and French images). A 360-degree survey against the backdrop of the Spice Girls, and an earnest discussion of *Richard III* in the Great Hall, shows that every element here hints at history, but is modern. '*Blind Beggar* T-shirts for Sale, Good Quality', but why? Why is this run-of-the-mill pub of any interest? It is 'dumbed down', hiding any sign of its particular history or relationship with place behind a shop-fitted display. Possibly the intention, and certainly the result, is a comforting, unchallenging, encounter with a WASP world, determinedly different from the Asian street market outside in Whitechapel. It is a 'heritage' world which only hints at the past of its surrounding former brewery, much of which is now a thoroughly modern Sainsbury's.

A mention of my lunch stop to the cabby who drove me to Paddington immediately raised his memory of ferrying the infamous Kray Twins from their drinking club in Stoke Newington to *The Blind Beggar*, though not on the night when a gang murder ensured its place in local history.

J.J. Moon's Bar, *Departures, Terminal 4, Heathrow (1996)*

Encrusted bay of etched glass and pine panels, rose trellis carpet – pause for bacon and tomato triple-decker – seating is tight (and will be tighter). Lighting low and gas styled; conspiratorial, antique image is broken tastefully by the bright lights of the slot machine and departure screens. Certainly sufficient here to allow the interior designer to provide publicity photographs of the 'traditional' pub in a glazed terminal setting. The character is most immediately and carefully caught in an individually lit, framed portrait above some booths: 'Col. F. S. Cody', a throwback hippie if ever there was one, posing in sepia before me.

Look in detail at the panels (of which there are many) and two entwined themes are present: the early history of flight, its heroes, hardware and daring – Lindbergh, Amy Johnson and Cody; in more bookish style, with historic prints, plans, axonometrics, sepia portraits, houses and the rest, are those panels which most visitors avoid. This is easy to do as most are above tables and the text is very pale. Make the effort and the story of what was here or hereabouts tumbles out: Hounslow Heath, the early days of the Ordnance Survey, gunpowder works, highwaymen. It is certainly a form of interpretation just where it might be useful, but the visitors don't relate; perhaps it is difficult to think beyond the Harrod's Duty Free opposite. Interpretation, perhaps, but with no sequencing, no typeface hierarchy or story line – but could it be read if there were one?

Gatwick Village

The unfettered is alternative described by Kenneth Roy:

> If you wish to see the place which is, for so many pilgrims, the last sight of England. And quite a sight it is, too. Yes, there is somewhere in West Sussex a place called Gatwick Village, though it is not the picture postcard image of an English village. Tourists will look in vain for the cricket pitch, the Norman church, the froth of real ale in an oak-beamed pub, the grungy kids outside the Spar shop, the Sunday afternoon bikers, and the other much-loved features of rural life. At Gatwick Airport they have refined the ideal by creating an indoor village, with round-the-clock security and regular flights for the relief of terminal boredom. Here, indeed, is the quintessential village for our times. It has proper streets with banks, shops, restaurants of a sort, and what they call an amusement arcade, not that anything could be less amusing than an amusement arcade.

Roy 1995

A cab arrives at Paddington

Speedier than usual – we discuss the latest approach for taxis to Paddington Station. 'It changed again on Friday, we'll have to approach from the front,' notes the driver. My mind rapidly circumnavigates the complex site to work out where the front, designed as such, is located. Memories of a war memorial under an arch finally settle it as adjacent to Platform 1. Logical, except that until very recently the major foot entrance was down the approach ramp near Platform 9. Is it now Platform 9? Into Brunel's intended gateway to New York (via a ship, his ship, from Bristol) and soon (another cab rumour is that it is on Monday) to become the new gateway to Heathrow, at last achieving Brunel's aim. In a sea of builders' hoardings and stranded seating I glimpse an unscheduled, sleek, dark new train which is probably the Heathrow Express in waiting. A detailed trawl of all available boards (usually well out of public view) reveals nothing of Railtrack's intentions and the significant new piece of railway history about to be opened; but of leaflets, exhibition panels, a video, plan or expectation there is no sign. Here is a vacant audience of some four hundred people waiting for several trains, eager to pursue any hint of information, and nothing. Brunel's statue and the glass-tombed Paddington Bear are both marginalised. Begrudgingly the information assistant hands me a leaflet for the 'London–Heathrow Fast Train' with no starting date, although the 'Heathrow Express' begins in June 1998.

I retire to *Coopers* (since demolished), the station bar, where the environment of instant history offers framed evocations of beer barrel cooperage of the past, something which the pint as pulled is unable to achieve.

Key issues in interpretation

Of the environments recently experienced above, *The Blind Beggar* and Paddington Station both fail to engage their users with any direct reference to their past or contemporary states. The Gatwick example endorses what we might now expect, past heritage reduced to a simple social image, while the Terminal 4 bar at Heathrow stands out as a considerable surprise. Yet, as Susan Hill illustrates, fiction, film and drama are full of richly framed images of the city past:

> If I close my eyes, I am sitting in the cab, crawling through the fog on my way to King's Cross Station, I can smell the cold, damp leather of the upholstery and the indescribable stench of the fog seeping in around the window, I can feel the sensation in my ears, as though they had been stuffed with cotton. Pools of sulphurous yel-

low light, as from random corners of some circle of the Inferno, flared from shops and the upper windows of houses, and from the basements they rose like flares from the pit below, and there were red-hot pools of light, from the chestnut-sellers on street corners; here, a great, boiling cauldron of tar for the road-menders spurted and smoked an evil red smoke, there, a lantern held high by the lamplighter bobbed and flickered.

Hill 1983: 26–7

For some time it has seemed as though interpretation has lost its way. While individual schemes may have been successful in engaging and enhancing the experience of visitors, the profession itself has failed to advance into new areas. It has relied instead on the ever-willing support of designers and media salespersons for a sense of subject development and contrived 'experiences', only a few of which enhance the visitor's understanding of place (Goodey 1994). Such have been the inroads made by managers and designers into the ill-formed and poorly advocated purposes of interpretation that any development of the subject now requires a fundamental reappraisal in the light of major cultural changes which seem largely to have passed the interpretive world by.

As exemplified in the *The Blind Beggar* pub refurbishment and the casual introduction of a new rail service, the use of some form of interpretation to add value to new places and products is not regarded as essential. Researched historical antecedents or contexts are seldom seen as a useful device when presenting commercial places, indeed the very reference to history may introduce unwelcome 'noise' in the favoured promotional message. Clearly a recast family pub like *The Blind Beggar* should not advertise its criminal associations – although the T-shirt promotion hints at concealed pleasure at notoriety. Any bookshop has the story on its shelves, and London's most popular walking trails head straight for the East End criminal nexus (see Foley and Lennon 1996 for an elaboration of the issue). Railtrack favours Paddington Station in its images of corporate investment in the public good, but again one senses that past images of steam and engineering heroes are somewhat distant from the intended modern service.

There appear to be five major factors which, in the past ten years, have shaped public, and therefore business, attitudes towards interpreting environments in the manner traditionally advocated by the founding fathers, although it is as well to admit that those founders seldom reflected on urban or industrial places. These factors are charging, promotion, seeing globally, virtual places and layering.

Charging

In the past ten years, society has moved from the unwritten understanding that most environmental experiences, whether rural or urban, were free enjoyment, with the only rationing being in terms of time, to the expectation that every encounter has its price. This is not only a reference to the required erection of pay boundaries around former public facilities, but also to the belief that nothing is provided without strings attached. Admission charges raise expectations as to quality, novelty and a managerial structuring of routes and information, with the proximity experience of throughput and flows ruling over revelation.

Today the mere presence of information associated with a site increasingly implies a promotional overture or funnel towards further expenditure. The possibility that information or facilities are provided to add to the immediate quality of place and to the broader quality of life is fast departing. If hospitals can charge for their car parks and cathedrals for admission then pay boundaries are the norm.

Promotion

Any role enjoyed by the interpreter in the past has now been largely usurped by the promoter who, under various corporate guises, is responsible for relationships between the owner and operator on the one hand and the customer or user on the other. Much of their effort seems devoted to protecting their employers from the public and directing public enquiries or interest into safe areas. Indeed, the issues of liability and the danger of legal proceedings seldom seem far from view, obscuring any opportunity for greater understanding (as in Trafalgar Square, Goodey 1993).

From a facility providing interpretation sufficient for the user to launch a series of probing encounters with a site or building, the management potential of interpretation seems to have all but extinguished the communication opportunity. At Paddington Station it seems quite clear that Railtrack does not want members of the public, or worse still enthusiasts, probing into new rolling stock or services before the announced date of operation (whenever that it is). Patterns of training for public relations or advertising are not known for their concern for exploration or historical reference; the SWOT analysis is regarded as an awesome research tool. From government to pop groups we are aware of the hold which promotion techniques now have on the communication between power and the public. Although we may be cynical, we are also losing the ability to seek more information.

Seeing globally, disappointed locally

The increase in domestic information sources, especially those on screen, has enlarged the geographies of most viewers. But the new geography is not one of experienced place, but rather of isolated, uncontextualised events or images. Disasters, political change, conflict, natural environments, human achievements and new structures become fleeting images on a map which may be ordered as much by the chronology of, or associations with, the information received as by their spatial arrangement.

News and documentary originators strive for the best and most effective images and, in a rapidly moving market, succeed for an instant. We are exposed to the biggest, the best, the most gruesome, the most realistic. If we want more, three alternatives are open. We can re-run the media experience, we can decide to go and see 'excessive environments' for ourselves (Goodey 1998), or we can seek a more local reference. Choosing the last, we will inevitably be disappointed by the quality, context and lack of immediacy. Britain's wildlife is invariably small, brown and hidden compared with TV nature photography and safari park performances on the screen. The majority, therefore, seek sensation, an aggravated experience, rather than the opportunity to explore and engage when visiting traditionally interpreted sites. Although the colourful leaflets and panels introducing nature sites were nearly always excessive in their claims, much of the public now knows that they are.

Virtual places

For younger generations, the interpreter's future clients, the preceding factors have been resolved through resort to artificial, largely screen worlds. The process was evident with the growth of concentrated and contained 'experiences' which initially drew heavily on interpreters' skills before moving quietly into the land of set design. But the rapid extension of virtual worlds to education and entertainment now suggests that future generations will maintain their commitment to increasingly enhanced screen and artificial experiences rather than to what is somewhat lovingly called the 'real' world. Although interpretation does have a significant role in presenting screen experiences, the essential foundation in environment and place is under threat. The justification of conservation education for interpretation has been largely lost in this transition.

Layering

A further challenge to interpretation is stimulated by the ability of the computer to respond to non-linear and uncontextualised enquiry. The tradition of interpretation has been to tell stories, nested within themes, adding up to a contained and somewhat imposed image of place. While we are frequently reminded of the diversity of markets available to each site and the need to cater for age, sex, ethnic origins and abilities, these variations are usually around a core theme. Thus, a heathland is revealed in terms of its ecology and human responses, a city in its built chronology from medieval times.

Increasingly, however, knowledge and experiences are sought in fragments which, while relating to place or object, do not require an established story-line for their reception or digestion. Given the density of human use, a popular place is likely to reflect a layering of users and opportunities for experience, with participants overlapping in both space and time. Certainly the future of the English countryside is of a landscape layered with often conflicting searchers for an increasing variety of experiences (Goodey 1994c). The lives of most of such users will have the potential for enhancement, with varying degrees of commitment to conservation, but new patterns or methods of interpretation need to be developed in recognition of the multivalent environment.

These factors begin to define the new and unsettling professional remit for interpretation. It may all be too much; perhaps the generation of interpreters with their feet on the soil will pass and their purpose will pass with them? As one with investment in that tradition I should hate to think that this is so, especially as in the urban and built context, never adequately addressed by professionals in the past, the mission seems more relevant than ever if we accept that city centres represent the focus of our evolving cultural life, with buildings the most evident markers of cultural change (Plate 9.1).

Central cities are under threat as never before, especially since in many countries the exchange function has flown to the periphery. Aside from the property investment which is their biggest guarantee of survival, central cities maintain the record of past commercial, public and design achievement, as well as representing a spatial geography which is maintained in the popular mind. Just those issues of conservation education and communication which engaged earlier interpreters of the natural environment are now urgently required for the built. While there is extensive public agreement as to the need to conserve habitats and species in nature, there is a severely restricted awareness of the importance of local urban morphological traditions, or of the significance of many listed and conserved structures. There is almost no public knowledge of how the service systems of a city function.

Settings and opportunities for interpreting the built environment future

If urban conservation were a matter that readily engaged the public mind, we would be flush with urban studies centres (now largely closed since their heyday in the 1970s) and every city would have a museum devoted to its growth, with effective interpretation linking exhibits to the space beyond. But such facilities, though common in the countryside context, are all but absent in the urban. The absence of any effective infrastructure for urban interpretation – save for the perpetuation of urban trails – is a fundamental problem which must be resolved before the more important issue of the urban future is approached.

Plate 9.1
Opportunity lost: the Peabody Trust, whose origins are worth remembering, forgets itself when converting a new hostel in central London. Given the size of the hoardings, more could have been said
Source: Brian Goodey

There are so many pointers in favour of urban interpretation that its absence is initially a conundrum. Urban areas are dense, allowing easy access by many paths – a public space network which is the envy of any countryside manager. Most features are more evident and approachable than in the countryside context and, as nearly every user and visitor lives in a home, so the building blocks of city making have been directly experienced. Changes to the urban fabric are advertised by planning authorities and cannot escape the notice of passers-by. Plans and impressions often feature in the local press, or are on public display. The media and popular discourse on the city readily embraces both conservation issues and new developments. A transect of at least part of the city is a daily experience for many.

For generations, however, familiarity has bred contempt: contempt for the pressures of a working rather than leisure environment; contempt for those who manage so badly; contempt for the wealth and arrogance of those who prosper; contempt for the influential who seem to gather around the city's very name. The central city is visible evidence of the locus of power in society, as was (and often remains) the countryside wall or fence which rings the private estate. The past decade of elevation and polite conflict between leagues of world cities has only widened the gap between the city as promoted and the city as experienced. If cities are to maintain their multifunctional qualities then these two cities – promoted and experienced – must be reconciled.

Here, then, is a major and urgent role for interpretation, a distinctively original function to add value to the experience of the city and its buildings past, present and future. Although the skill base of interpretation may be oriented towards the past, albeit a past which now embraces through conservation structures and schemes of the 1960s and a few more modern buildings, it is interpretation of the future which offers the greatest potential.

I share with many of my generation memories of London in the immediate post-war period. Casual conversations still raise the image of well-known bombed sites, even though the commemorative sculptures are now neglected by most visitors. (I have the Fire Brigade memorial at St Paul's Cathedral in mind as I write.) When developers entered the bombed sites of the 1940s, they erected viewing platforms (one, at least, with a phone connecting the viewer to the site office) so that lunchtime workers could share in the rebuilding of the city. Detailed plans were displayed to draw the viewer into the future and its prospects. In Switzerland I have seen a site where the outline of the intended new structure is superimposed on an image of that about to be demolished. This was similar in form and impact to a detailed panel in one of the Paris parks where the timbered areas to be felled were backed by the intended new landscape after twenty years of growth.

Such has been our preoccupation with the past that we have fought shy of stimulating experience of the future. As I write, London's Millennium Dome is an apposite example. In the media we are fed one distant architectural image of the feature, while its attractions and constituent parts are fought over in media sound bites. There is little to raise expectation regarding the future design or opportunities of the building. In discussion with developers on this matter I have been told that any detailed information, rather than promotional hoardings, is likely to lead to further enquiries and requests for additional information which are not seen as essential to the promotional budget. The building, its fittings, contents and image should be sufficient.

Sufficient they may be for the developer, but are they sufficient for the surrounding public who will have to live with the building and its functions? Statutory public participation in the planning process, surely an opportunity to open up experience of the future, has become institutionalised and stunted through lack of local authority imagination and a fear of public debate, which is seen by most parties as time-wasting. Without a growing knowledge and sense of expectation of what a new building or scheme will be, there is little chance that public affection for the evolving city will develop. City promotion and High Street management (another interesting professional impact on interpretation) will advance a fragmentary and unquestioning set of initiatives focused on new retail opportunities, thus isolating the new structure from its context.

In order to advance the purpose, and therefore the role, of the interpreter in the future city we need to look at the skills and linkages which will be required. I have no doubt that the fundamental purpose remains close to that of interpreting the natural environment of the 1950s. Given continual investment in the city, and the increasing public space remit advanced by most urban authorities and experts, how can the public be offered its full range of experiences and encouraged to conserve its unique qualities?

Initiatives, skills, media and linkages

With the aim of bringing the contemporary central city alive in more than its retail and heritage dimension, and in drawing its resident and visitor publics into dialogue with the future, what initiatives, skills, media and linkages are appropriate?

Initiatives

Increasingly, and for many of the reasons noted above, interpretation finds itself fighting a rearguard action for dated environmental and communication concepts. In moving to the city of the future, it is essential to take initiatives which build on and enhance future-directed trends. While this does not mean 'going with the flow' and the abandonment of principles, it does imply a considered perspective on likely developments.

A key feature of the future and present city is the evolution of urban places as a mosaic of identifiable character zones. We are well aware of the often imposed heritage areas. 'Treated in this way, a historic city becomes a set of stimulations and simulations in a highly controlled, pedestrianised environment – or, in short, a shopping mall' (Moore 1993, on York). The urban core (Goodey 1994a; Glasson *et al.* 1995) is being joined by ethnic districts, inner suburban villages and peripheral districts surrounding the city. In what may often appear to be an increasingly characterless city when viewed from the road, commercial and community interests, assisted by successive governments, have built on local character and populations (Goodey 1995). Local published histories abound and schools have developed their own interpretive curriculum materials to meet structured fieldwork requirements. But aside from the central heritage zone, little consideration has been provided by interpreters. Communication about place is severely institutionalised and fragmented, making the evolutionary approach of Bath's building museum a rare example for learning (Goodey 1993a). In future we should expect to visit a city, roam on public transport networks and plug into interpretation of local character.

Roaming implies accessibility, both through the urban space net and into buildings and places which are or could be available to the community and to visitors. While the next decade promises increased pressure for rural access (and offers another immediate and thus far neglected opportunity for interpretation), access within the city has decreased over past decades. The combination of public sloth, the unwillingness to walk any distance in the city and security restrictions have reduced both the demand for and the provision of access. With increased public transport and fewer urban places dedicated to single-use manufacturing or commerce, there is immediate opportunity for interpretive initiatives which both enhance journeys and signal possible destinations (Plate 9.2).

In terms of traditional interpretive devices such as signs, panels and leaflets, the future could provide opportunities for the effective co-ordination of casual interpretation. On street and on site hints which encourage exploration or jog the memory are essential in the city, where mobility has largely destroyed vernacular knowledge. Such hints should appear casually, and certainly not as part of an overall plan. However, if they are the result of local initiative then the spread and quality will be uneven so some overall planning is essential. The immediate challenge is for an urban interpretive plan which achieves some authority in place-making circles. With the growth of value evident in place-making schemes (as, for example, Calthorpe 1993; Cruickshank 1989; Duany and Plater-Zyberk 1991; Essex County Council 1998), the incorporation of an interpretive plan which links conservation with potential community life is not impossible to achieve.

Perhaps the greatest challenge to the complexity of professionals, funders and designers who shape the future city is to effectively involve present and future citizens and users. Without their support through residence and

Plate 9.2
Every opportunity organised: overloaded Liverpool heritage sign which manages to merge modern functions (e.g. car parks), recent history (The Beatles) and heritage (Maritime Museum) in one sign
Source: Brian Goodey

spending, the most glamorous architectural schemes will fail. Involvement in the process of urban evolution is the single, most important challenge to urban authorities and is being met by a variety of initiatives, many of which currently employ focus group or 'visioning' techniques (see, for examples Gallagher 1991; Rattenbury 1994). Reviewing the initiatives taken by those responsible for Agenda 21 sustainability issues, it is clear that interpretation of the future city is being pursued and formalised, often in parallel (but entirely unrelated) with model-based exercises to engage the public in a city's future form. Both patterns of futurological discussion seem to emphasise physical structures, morphological patterns and management policies, while neglecting the personal experience of the coming urban place (discussed in the Brazilian context by Goodey and Murta 1995). It is here, particularly, that interpretation should have a major role to play, not the least in demystifying understanding of the present built environment.

Skills

The key skill evident in the best interpretation is the ability to bring alive and into focus hidden, yet commonplace, layers of the world about us. What, on first sight, seems to be a crumbling ruin is repopulated in our imagination; the bleak countryside site is encouraged to yield a disguised world of ecological exchanges and dramas. It is exactly these skills which are now required for our contemporary urban places. How heavily we rely on historical fictional reconstruction (as in Hill 1983, above) or on the thrill of deviant pockets beyond our daily lives (as in the success of the film *Trainspotting*). Why, however, is the richness of the city neglected? *The Power of Place* by (Hayden 1996) provides an extended text which addresses this issue. It offers urban landscapes as public history, emphasises the importance of character zones and of local populations experiencing the landscape. It follows in the tradition of several urban analysts, such as Lynch and Cullen, who have been almost entirely neglected by interpreters.

So obvious should be the translation of good interpretive practice and skills from country to town that we need to ask why it has not occurred. Why have we not recognised the potential for individual sensory experiences in urban places (for practical examples, see Peterson1990) and provided appropriate settings? We can reveal in graphic detail the processes which have shaped our landscape, but we have seldom turned our attention to, for example, the complexity of underground services which keep the city running.

Two major reasons are suggested. The first is that the countryside has been seen as a positive leisure retreat from the working and largely negative city. This pattern of perception is slowly changing as the countryside becomes a battleground for overlain demands on space and quiet, while the post-industrial city is proposed as a secure yet stimulating, environment for life and leisure. Following from this, the professional client configurations and policy approaches to town and country have, in the past, stood in stark contrast. The process of countryside management welcomed interpretation as a means of endorsing leisure and conservation policies, while urban management often saw such processes as inhibiting the rapid change and growth which maintained urban power. Again, patterns of thought are beginning to shift with issues of environment, conservation and cultural innovation fuelling a concern for the quality of urban life where interpretive communication should find a role.

Media

Difficult as it is to believe, the fundamental issues in interpretation do not concern media selection, but rather the purpose and form of the messages to be communicated. In the urban context, this is where thought and debate are urgently required. Once a new set of principles for a specific

Plate 9.3
Humanising humour: public seating in 'Cow Town', Calgary, against a thoroughly modern backdrop
Source: Brian Goodey

context have been developed with the community, the opportunities for presentation will be found to be far richer than in rural or most conservation settings. By definition, global cities are the focus for communication, and media opportunities are rapidly filtering to all parts of the urban system. Local computer networks, desktop retailing and banking, and touch screen information systems all bring the individual into immediate contact with the city system.

Two distinct, but potentially closely related, contexts for interpretive innovation in the city are waiting for our attention. The first, and more traditional, is the enhancement and extrapolation of physical form where art in the environment currently fills the interpreter's role but pursues a very different agenda. The experienced environment needs graphic, written or designed hints as to experiential opportunities which go far beyond the street map or name plate. In supporting such place-based initiatives we must also resolve the perpetual inadequacy of printed support, as well as the more difficult challenge of accepting that the population is likely to increase its spontaneous demand for meaning in place, as with the death of Princess Diana (but see also Azaryahu 1996). This has to be done before we can sensibly become involved in the challenge of electronic support, the area where interpretation of the future city must surely grow.

The skills and technology are available to link citizens and visitors with the evolving physical and management plans for a city. The future experiences of a city can be partly moulded by those who will enjoy them with at least fragmentary experience of simulation, onscreen participation and vision building etc. already available, though widely distributed between unlikely partners and experimenters. Linkage is the key.

Linkages

The future success of our cities and built form is likely to be measured in the quality of human experience which they offer and sustain; people are likely to be looking forward to what is coming next. This is an essentially new remit for the management of urban place and few existing professional or managerial structures are up to the mark. But new groupings are rapidly emerging – a number of British environmental professions have formed the Urban Design Alliance (1997) and the Prince of Wales, an early advocate of urban quality, is fundamentally revising his approach to urban regeneration.

Four key processes in city management – development, planning, community and promotion – will be subject to redefinition in the UK by the year 2000. As in the countryside, the tension between globalisation of issues and the popular demand for experienced place will be the running subscript in this redefinition. If, as currently suggested, the burden of providing some five million new homes in Britain over the next twenty years is to fall on cities, then urban place will be fundamentally redefined. Interpretation has been too modest to claim any part in these exciting developments, but its purpose deserves to be considered and, if not inserted into the process, is likely to be reinvented by those who recognise the importance of human experience in the future success of cities.

Plate 9.4
A success story: Croydon's Lifetimes Exhibition – at last a reason for living in Croydon and being part of something great
Source: Brian Goodey

The immediate avenue for discussion would seem to be through the cultural infrastructure which is closely associated with interpretation in the city – museums, galleries, education centres and public art initiatives. All have achieved a more evident urban voice than interpretation but offer, perhaps unwillingly, the context for involvement (Taylor 1981). A further stimulus to such engagement could be a current review of Peter Hall's (1967) neglected call for interpretation, 'The great British history parkway drive-in', or a detailed examination of various initiatives in that unlikely city-in-waiting, Croydon (Goodey 1993b; MacDonald 1996). (See Plate 9.4.)

Conclusion

Of the limited but variously urban spaces discussed, Paddington Station stands out as a public context where enhancement of the (waiting) experience is overdue. Future architectural impressions suggest another Liverpool Street Station, possibly deserving of design awards, but like Liverpool Street totally lacking in any messages which suggest both the heritage and current complexity of the structure and its services. It may well be that Railtrack is encouraged to add to the Brunel statue (and underground tile work) with art in the environment references to past or present function.

How about a percentage for interpretation in all urban schemes? This could and should embrace the percentage for art concept. The success of art initiatives in urban spaces has been achieved through a long succession of individual and group initiatives which showed the cultural and employment advantages of increased public art, but which also suggested the human profit to be achieved (Goodey 1994b; Roberts and Erickson 1996; Miles 1996). Advocates pointed continually to an enhancement of human experience and the quality of life. If we believe in the purpose of interpretation, we could surely do the same; in which case Gatwick Village may be a major opportunity in an edge city with potential for airport interpretation, rather than a sad journalistic joke.

The future for interpretation within the urban future is located in engagement with developers, urban designers and artists. Interpretation has a very specific approach to offer, one which complements the work of urban artists and can engage the broader public. Current experiments, such as the Architectural Foundation's 'Beacon' video soapbox (Building Design 1998), restate the potential of interactive electronic media for learning about and participating in the form of a city.

References

Azaryahu, M. (1996) 'The spontaneous formation of memorial space. The case of *Kikar Rabin*, Tel Aviv', *Area*, 28(4): 501–13.

Betjeman, J. (1981) *London's Historic Railway Stations*, London: John Murray.

Building Design (1998) 'It's good to rant', *Building Design*, 9(IV): 10.

Calthorpe, P. (1993) *The Next American Metropolis*, New York: Princeton Architecture Press.

Cruickshank, D. (1989) 'Model Vision: Leon Krier's designs for expanding Dorchester', *Architect's Journal*, 28(VI): 24–9.

Duany, A. and Plater-Zyberk, E. with Kreiger, A. (eds) (1991) *Town and Town-Making Principles*, New York: Rizzoli.

Essex County Council (1998) *Design Guide for Residential Areas*, Essex County Council: Chelmsford.

Foley, M. and Lennon, J. J. (1996) 'Editorial: heart of darkness', *International Journal of Heritage Studies*, 2(4): 198–211.

Gallagher, M. L. (1991) 'Des Moines and the vision thing', *Planning*, December: 12–15.

Gasson, P. (ed.) (1988) *Nairn's London*, Harmondsworth: Penguin.

Glasson, J. G., Godfrey, K. and Goodey, B. (1995) *Towards Visitor Impact Management: Visitor Impacts, Carrying Capacity and Management Responses in Europe's Historic Towns and Cities*, Aldershot: Avebury.

Goodey, B. (1993). 'The heart of the matter, Westminster, New Year's Eve', *Town & Country Planning*, Jan.–Feb: 24–5.

Goodey, B. (1993a) 'Beauty of Bath', *Town & Country Planning*, April: 93.

Goodey, B.(1993b) 'I've seen the future …', *Town & Country Planning*, 62 (10): 250–2.

Goodey, B. (1994) 'Warwick's kingmaker', *Interpretation Journal*, 56: 8–9.

Goodey, B. (1994a) 'Spreading the benefits of heritage visitor quarters', *International Journal of Heritage Studies*, 1(1) : 18–29.

Goodey, B. (1994b) 'Art-full places: Public art to sell public places', in J. R. Gold and S. K. Ward (eds) *Place Promotion: the Use of Publicity and Public Relations to Sell Towns and Regions*, London: Belhaven, pp.153–79.

Goodey, B. (1994c) 'Leisure landscapes', *Landscape Research Extra*, 15: 7–8.

Goodey, B. (1995) 'Building a context for neighbourhood cultural regeneration', *Culture and Neighbourhoods: Vol.1 Concepts and References*, Council for Cultural Co-operation, Council of Europe Publishing, pp. 63–70.

Goodey, B. (1998) 'Change as an attraction: the qualities of the contemporary urban tourist resource', in R. French (ed.) *Challenged Tourism*, Proceedings of the 2nd GAU International Tourism Conference.

Goodey, B. and Murta, S. M. (1995) *Interpretacaio do Patrimonio para o Turismo Sustentado um Guia*, Belo Horizont : Edicao Sebrae.

Hall, P. (1967) 'The great British history parkway drive-in', *New Society*, 3(VIII): 151–15.

Hayden, D. (1996) *The Power of Place: Urban Landscapes as Public History*, Cambridge MA: MIT Press.

Hill, S. (1983) *The Woman in Black*, London: Mandarin.

MacDonald, S. (1996) 'Lifetimes: a multimedia history', *Interpretation*, 2(1): 21–3.

Miles, M. (1996) 'Imaginative interventions: art and craft in city design', *Urban Design International*, 1(1): 81–8.

Moore, R. (1993) 'A new York, but not a better one', *Independent*, 7 July.

Nairn, I. (1966) *Nairn's London*, Harmondsworth: Penguin.

Peterson, R. A. (1990) 'Designing cities without designing buildings?', *Urban Design Quarterly*, April: 6–11.

Rattenbury, K. (1994) 'Visions for Woolwich', *Building Design*, 25 February: 15–18.

Roberts, M. and Erickson, B. (1996) 'Artful change: public art and city regeneration', *Urban Design International*, 1(2): 163–71.

Roy, K. (1995) 'Joke village getting by on a wing and a prayer', *Observer*, 1(X): 10.

Taylor, L. (ed.) (1981) *Urban Open Spaces*, New York: Rizzoli.

Heritage that hurts:
interpretation in a postmodern world

DAVID UZZELL AND ROY BALLANTYNE

Concept of hot interpretation

The term 'hot interpretation' was introduced to the field of heritage interpretation in 1988 (Uzzell 1989). The concept arose as a response to the failure of many interpretive designers and providers to acknowledge that visitors to heritage sites do not experience heritage simply as a cognitive experience. The principle behind hot interpretation is that although a detached, cool and objective approach to the presentation and assessment of information and subsequent decision-making is seen as highly desirable in our society, there are many decisions that we make in both our private and public lives where a purely rational Vulcan-like approach to the world is difficult, impossible or even undesirable. Whenever we are presented with choices, we rarely stand by as disinterested observers. Of course, we hope our judgements will be thought through carefully, having drawn on as much information as possible and weighing up all the pros and cons of alternative options. However, our feelings, emotional instincts and reactions play an important role in our decision-making.

Emotions colour our memories and experiences and thus our selective attention to information. Our minds are not virgin territories and our past experiences and decisions influence our future actions. This applies to all areas of our lives whether concerning career, marriage, consumerism or health. To deny the emotional side of our understanding and appreciation of the world and our relationships is to deny the very humanity that makes us part of the human race. This should not be interpreted as if there were two types of thinking which exist independently of one another – cool and dispassionate, and hot and emotional. Neither are we arguing that the latter has priority over the former. What is suggested, however, is that issues which involve personal values, beliefs, interests and memories will excite a degree of emotional arousal which needs to be recognised and addressed in interpretation.

These ideas are not new to interpretation. 'Good' interpretation has always reflected this. Tilden (1957:8) defined interpretation as 'an educational activity which aims to reveal meanings and relationships through the use of original objects, by firsthand experience, and by illustrative media, rather than simply to communicate factual information'. Meanings and relationships necessarily have an emotional dimension yet these have often been excluded from interpretation. This may have something to do with the scientific and academic background to most interpretation where emotion is seen as contrary to objectivity. Two of the six principles of interpretation put forward by Freeman Tilden over forty years ago surely presumed an affective component. Tilden (1957: 9) argued that 'the chief aim of interpretation is not instruction but provocation'. How better to provoke than through addressing the affective side of the visitor's personality? He also advocated that interpretation must 'address itself to the whole man rather than any phase' (Tilden 1957: 9). This must include people's feelings and emotions. A reading of Tilden's book forcefully reminds one that interpretation is about kindling a spiritual awakening in visitors to the wonder of the world around them. For Tilden then, interpretation which does not lead to an emotional experience of the world is deficient in some important respect.

Plate 10.1
Interpretation in the Campo del Ghetto, Venice. In 1938 approximately 200 Jews, one-quarter of Venice's Jewish population, were rounded up and deported to German concentration camps
Source: David Uzzell

There are some areas in heritage interpretation which have a strong affective and emotional impact on people. This might be because the interpretation touches on personal memories: for instance, at battlefield sites where loved ones were killed. Interpretation could equally have resonance at a collective level such as at a site where a nation achieved its independence from a colonial power or where a pressure group won a famous battle to protect a threatened landscape. Likewise, emotional responses could be fired through interpretation related to issues which evoke strong ideological beliefs and convictions such as the protection of a rare bird or plant species or opposition to non-renewable energy sources such as nuclear power.

Interpretation that appreciates the need for and injects an affective component into its subject matter, where appropriate, is 'hot interpretation'. Hot interpretation accepts that we are subject to a full repertoire of emotional responses – the palette is very varied, more varied than is typically acknowledged, anticipated or encouraged through interpretation. Furthermore, there are strong theoretical grounds for believing that we will not be as effective as we could be as communicators and people in the business of changing attitudes and behaviours in respect of serious environmental issues if we exclude an affective dimension in interpretation. If the affective element required for effective attitude change is absent then interpretation is unlikely to achieve its objectives (McGuire 1985).

It would be strange if heritage did not have an effect upon us. This surely is the point about heritage – it is value laden. Of course, we can value things which are old simply because they are old, but when our perceptions are coloured by thoughts about their origins, their construction, their context and who used them, it would be an insensitive and insensible person who claims that heritage does not provide the spark of an emotional charge. Heritage resonates for us because it not only relates to our past but is an important part of our present and future. This is not meant in the sense of 'having' but rather in the sense of 'being'.

Emotional engagement with the heritage

The resonance of heritage applies equally to the natural and cultural landscapes and artefacts. It can emerge out of the heritage itself or can be mediated by interpretation. The function of interpretation in this case is to make links, to remind us, to make us aware. The degree to which interpretation 'works on us' and the strength of the affect will be conditioned by a number of factors. Five such factors have been identified here which serve to influence our emotional engagement with either the heritage itself or its interpretation: time, distance, experiencing places, the degree of abstraction and management.

Time

The issue of time and meaning in the context of interpretation is addressed elsewhere in this book (Chapter 2). However, there are some issues related to time that have a particular bearing on hot interpretation. Uzzell (1989) has demonstrated how the meaning and resonance of events from the past changes as time separates us from those events. Three examples of the interpretation of war and conflict were described, ranging from events which happened fifty, eighty and seven hundred years ago.

The first case study related to the massacre by the Nazis of virtually all the men, women and children from the village of Oradour-Sur-Glane near Limoges in France in May 1944. Suspected of harbouring resistance fighters who had a few days earlier ambushed a German patrol, all the men of the village were taken to various houses, garages and public spaces and summarily executed. Following this, all the women and children were rounded up and taken to the Church. They were barricaded in and grenades were

Plate 10.2
Entrance to Oradour-Sur-Glane, France
Source: David Uzzell

thrown into the building which was then torched. Over 640 villagers were killed and the village destroyed. It was decided after the war that the village should not be rebuilt, but a new one should be constructed on the outskirts. The old village was turned into a national memorial by the French Government as a permanent reminder of what had happened (see Plate 10.2).

Today it is possible to visit the village and walk down the destroyed streets and into the shell of the Church. In the mid 1980s a guide, related to one of the villagers who had been killed, took visitors around the town and explained in detail the chronology of events. It is also possible to buy various guidebooks and leaflets which graphically depict with contemporary photographs what happened. There is additional interpretation in the form of a small museum which contains the personal effects of those who were immolated. Returning to the village several years later it seemed that there is a subtly different atmosphere. Maybe it is the tourist detritus that could be found on the ground, or maybe it is the presence of more young families. Whatever the cause, the place itself seemed to have changed from being a memorial and a place of remembrance to a tourist attraction. As Oradour-Sur-Glane moves from being a memorial to a day-trip destination, it may also move from being an affective to a cognitive experience. For many French people (and non-French too) who had experienced the war, the name Oradour-Sur-Glane would have a powerful resonance and retain its place in the French collective memory. Clearly this is not the case for all visitors. Although the French authorities originally decided that visitors should not be spared the horror of what happened, one suspects that the anger and anguish will slowly be muted. The numbers for whom Oradour-Sur-Glane provides a cathartic experience are declining.

The second example of the way in which time affects the emphasis which is placed by interpreters on events and consequently what those events are made to mean to us is illustrated by reference to a major conflict just over eighty years ago. The presentation and interpretation of World War I displays at the Imperial War Museum recently came in for criticism because it seemed that war was reduced simply to being a story about the application of technological and industrial developments to the slaughtering of millions, as if the most significant aspect was the military technology. This museum was not alone in this kind of presentation – quite the contrary, it was the norm. However, the displays have now been transformed in a successful attempt to interpret the 'meaning and significance' of the war in its many dimensions. But there are still many museums around the world where the sartorial elegance of the soldiery and the impressiveness of the instruments of war assumes as much if not more significance than their purpose and effect. As we go back in time we seem to be more willing to ignore suffering and treat events in a more disinterested way as if they are from a 'foreign country' (Hartley 1953).

The third example illustrates that as we progress in time not only are the emphases of history changed but history can become rewritten or forgotten altogether. At the time when the first study was written, the interpretation of Clifford's Tower in York did not just minimise the history but failed even to tell the story of the 'ethnic cleansing' of the Jewish population of that city in a wave of anti-Semitic riots which occurred in various parts of the country after the Crusades, some 700 years ago. The interpretation of the Tower's history focused on who had lived there, its changing role over the centuries and its building materials, but no mention was made of the fact that the Jews of York were corralled into the Tower and, when faced with annihilation, committed suicide. Those who did not die at their own hands were tricked into opening the Tower's gates on the promise of clemency, but were then slaughtered. In the case of Clifford's Tower, it was not a case so much of history being rewritten, but rather history being forgotten. The displays at Clifford's Tower have since been changed by English Heritage. However, how many other heritage sites exist where shameful events of our past are forgotten altogether because they are seen to be so temporally distant that it is expedient to forget their occurrence. (See Plate 10.1.)

Experiencing Places

When we talk about experiencing place and events, especially in terms of our emotional reactions, it is difficult to know to what degree other people share similar feelings. Even more problematic, of course, is specifying what we mean when we talk about a place or an event having a particular atmosphere. Where is this atmosphere? It is hardly 'out there' like a magic ingredient which has been added to the oxygen, nitrogen, argon, carbon dioxide and water vapour (not counting, of course, the carbon monoxide, sulphur dioxide and lead). If it is not out there, then clearly it is some form of projection from ourselves; we impose our feelings and emotions onto the scene. This can be illustrated by a consideration of the atmosphere in London in the week following the death of Diana, Princess of Wales.

Many thousands of people travelled to London to pay their last respects by signing the books of condolences at St James's Palace and leaving flowers outside both St James's and Buckingham Palace. This was reported daily on TV, radio and in the press. TV reporters stood in front of the carpet of flowers or alongside the quarter-mile-long queue of mourners and tried to share the experience with the nation by commenting that 'there is a muted and melancholic atmosphere here in The Mall'. A picture was painted of clothes-rending mourners queuing under a pall of gloom and sadness. Yes, the occasion was sad like any untimely death, perhaps especially so in the case of someone who meant so much for all sorts of reasons to so many people. But when one of us walked down The Mall on the Wednesday following Diana's death, I cannot say that there was a tangible atmosphere – not for me anyway. This should not be taken to mean that I did not feel something about the tragedy that had happened in the early hours of the previous Sunday morning, neither does it imply that such 'atmospheres' do not exist. They clearly do, but they are not a ubiquitous experience for all people, all of the time, in every situation.

Space is endowed with 'atmosphere' according to activities and memories of what has occurred there. For instance, a person walking up The Mall a few days previously would have relied on other past events and memories to create 'an atmosphere'. Similarly, for some visitors with memories of World War II, Oradour-Sur-Glane is undoubtedly a highly provocative environment generating an emotive 'atmosphere', while for others perhaps this is not the case. What are the implications for interpretation? Should hot interpreters be trying to create an 'atmosphere'? Who is the target audience – those with firsthand experience of the situation or general visitors? The answers to such questions are important in designing hot interpretation. As seen later in this chapter, the nature of hot interpretation of Aboriginal cultural heritage is greatly influenced by responses to questions relating to target audience (tourists or Aboriginal communities) which impact upon the purpose of the interpretation.

As time separates us from past events our emotional engagement is reduced. Does the time period separating events affect our decisions regarding the presentation of information, emotional reaction and issues of taste? A few examples of recent events are discussed below, promoting reflection on the impact that distance, in terms of time from 'hot' events, has upon interpretation decision-making. These examples raise questions about what should be interpreted, how it should be interpreted and when. They also illustrate the relative nature of visitor emotional engagement, a consideration of which impacts upon decisions regarding the choice of interpretive techniques needed to make historic hot events and places 'live' for those who have little empathy or connection with such events and places.

Late in the evening of the 22 December 1988, the BBC was due to show the film *Fear is the Key*, but the continuity announcer came on and said that due to the crash of Pan Am Flight 103 over Lockerbie, it had been decided that it would be inappropriate and distressing for some viewers and therefore the film would be shown at a later date. Of course, one can understand this decision and arguably it was the appropriate and most sensitive thing to do. But why should it be more acceptable to show the film at a later date – would not the elements which potentially made the film distressing still be present? What will have changed over the intervening period? In the case of news we seem to be prepared to forget quite quickly, while this is not so with recent history. This may present interpreters with particular problems.

The recency of hot events can make interpretation difficult as they cannot easily be placed in a larger historical continuity and context. But it is also problematic for a reason associated with the issue of hot interpretation. We have seen that war loses its emotional sting with the passing of years. Both we as providers of interpretive events and visitors as their consumers, appear to feel no twinge of conscience or unease at sitting down to watch two warring factions pretend to slaughter each other in an historical re-enactment of a Civil War skirmish. But why should the passing of time make this almost voyeuristic behaviour an acceptable form of entertainment when applied to an event 100 or 200 years ago, but not acceptable in the context of re-enactment of a battle fought ten years ago? Would we consider it appropriate and 'tasteful' to see a re-enactment between interpreters dressed as Serbs and Bosnians engaging in 'ethnic cleansing' or street fighting from Sarajevo?

The difficulties of interpreting recent hot issues are clearly illustrated by events occurring at the Port Arthur Historic Site in Tasmania, Australia (Plate 10.3). Port Arthur served as a prison to over 12,000 convicts transported to Australia from Britain between 1831 and the 1870s. Tragically, in 1996 it became the site of Australia's worst massacre as Martin Bryant, armed with an automatic rifle, first entered the Blue Arrow Café and opened fire on visitors before roaming around the 40- hectare site of historic buildings indiscriminately shooting people. Prior to the massacre, the site was very popular with visitors who 'enjoyed' the interpretation and stories of the hard life and characters who inhabited the Model Prison, worked and died at the site and were buried on the Isle of the Dead. The Ghost Tour, which recounted all the strange and horrible events that occurred there, was very popular with visitors. After the massacre, interpreters were left reflecting upon the nature of their interpretation of the site and whether distance in terms of time had led to the 'gentrification' of both the buildings and the stories of what was a feared and terrible place for so many. Did the interpretation exploit the horror and misery of being a convict at Port Arthur? What attracts people to come and pay to be entertained at such a site? Should such a site be interpreted – what would the convicts imprisoned there have thought?

It is interesting to contemplate that the site was ordered to be destroyed once transportation was stopped, but the order was never carried out. Why would people at the time want it destroyed? Were they too close to the experience of what life was like there – would interpretation have been viewed as tasteless?

Interestingly, a similar situation has now developed; the Blue Arrow Café, where most of the victims lost their lives, may be demolished. Is the Blue Arrow Café any more a reminder of horrific events and sorrow than the Model Prison building or others on the site? This was after all a place where convicts were so traumatised that they would draw straws to determine who would murder whom (as suicide was considered an unforgivable sin) so that both the murderer (who would be hanged) and the murdered would escape forever. Should not the Blue Arrow Café be considered as a future

Plate 10.3
Port Arthur historic site in Tasmania, Australia
Source: Roy Ballantyne

exhibit on the Ghost Tour? Our attitudes towards the recent past and the way in which it engages our emotions are interesting issues that need to be addressed by those responsible for interpretation.

Abstraction

Another factor which impinges on our emotional reaction to interpretive experiences concerns the degree of abstraction of the heritage being interpreted. Again this interacts with time, suggesting that the relationship between time and emotional involvement is not necessarily linear or negatively correlated. The interpretation of the Cold War presents an interesting example as it is both a recent event and, as the name suggests in the context of this chapter, not perhaps particularly promising in terms of hot interpretation.

The Cold War was unlike any previous war; it was a placeless war. There were, of course, sites which were strategically critical and place bound such as Fylingdales and as much in the 'front line' as any trench on the Somme. But the Cold War was also everywhere, as well as nowhere. While for many people it was real and costly, it was also an attitude of mind as two ideologies clashed in propaganda battles. It was not so overtly situated as previous wars. It extended across continents, although it did find visible expression where the two ideologies met at the borders of the countries separated by the Iron Curtain. The Cold War was as much about threat and potential harm, albeit on a cataclysmic scale, as about conventional death and destruction. Finally, the Cold War was also both a highly public and a highly secret war. All these factors make its interpretation problematic for those more used to dealing with plaques and audio-visual guides than to battle-field sites.

Cold War sites are different from other war sites inasmuch as they are often not the scenes of actual conflict and death. Their importance and value lie in what they represent and what they could have been. War sites visited by the public are invariably either where battles took place or exceptionally from where war was managed, like the Cabinet War Rooms in London. In the case of Cold War sites, while everything about them certainly meant business, they were at the same time about not being used. They are silent and cerebral in contrast to what most visitors assume and look for on a battlefield site – the noise, the clamour and the tangible. It is ironic that Janis and Mann (1979) chose to emphasise the argument that even if dispassionate objectivity were possible in our decision-making with regard to personal or societal issues, it is questionable whether it is desirable – by reference to one of the most memorable satirical films of the Cold War era: 'A world dominated by Dr. Strangelove and like-minded cost accountants might soon become devoid of acts of affection, conscience and humanity, as well as passion' (Janis and Mann 1979: 45).

Distance

The third factor that relates to our emotional engagement and response to heritage, and interacts with both time and abstraction, is distance. Both physical and psychological distance from people, places, events and artefacts can accentuate or moderate one's emotional involvement as well as one's knowledge, concern and, of course, action. This is well illustrated by some research we have undertaken over a number of years to examine the awareness and attitudes of the public to global environmental problems (Uzzell, in preparation).

A large sample of environmental science, environmental education and geography students studying in the UK, Slovakia and Australia were asked to rate the seriousness of seven environmental problems (water pollution, atmospheric pollution, noise pollution, acid rain, deforestation, global warming, ozone holes). The problems were rated on a five-point scale varying from 1 (extremely serious) to 5 (not serious at all) as they were perceived to affect individuals, their town, country, continent and finally the world. It was decided to use a sample of environmental studies students as it was felt that they would probably be well informed about environmental problems and therefore a yardstick against which one could measure other populations.

Overall, it was found that there was a statistically significant difference in the way that students perceived environmental problems at the five areal levels. Environmental problems were considered to be more serious as geographical distance from the perceiver increased. The effects of environmental problems on the world were perceived as more serious than their effects at the continental, country, town or individual level. Similarly, problems at the continental level were viewed as more serious than at the country, town or individual level, and so on. This trend held true for all three national groups, with a minor exception in the case of the Australian sample who, for understandable reasons, made no distinction between the severity of environmental problems at 'country' and 'continent' areal levels, presumably as a consequence of the sheer size of Australia. One interesting paradox revealed by this research is that students from the UK thought that the most serious evidence of global environmental problems would be found at the other end of the world (i.e. Australia), while Australian students believed that the most serious evidence of global environmental problems would be found at an antipodean distance (i.e. the UK).

The research went on to ask students in each country who they perceived as being responsible for addressing and solving environmental problems. It was generally found that students saw themselves as being responsible for local problems but felt that governments and agencies should be responsible for problems at the national and international scales. This finding is intersting, however, as students do not perceive local environmental problems to be particularly significant compared with global problems. This allows them to abrogate their need to deal with environmental issues by passing the responsibility on to governments and international agencies.

The relevance of this for hot interpretation is twofold. It is suggested that the amount of mass media attention given to global environmental issues may actually mean that they are more salient for people at a global rather than local level. The amount of television and newspaper coverage given to global warming and consequential sea level rises, destruction of the ozone layer through the emission of CFC's, cutting down of rain forests and species depletion has placed global environmental problems near the top of the public's environmental agenda. The maxim 'Think globally – act locally' was coined many years ago in an attempt to overcome the phenomenon whereby the public becomes highly aware, largely through mass media images, of the destruction of ecosystems and wildlife, but fails to appreciate that the same destructive processes operate on their own doorsteps. Events such as Rio only serve to emphasise the seriousness of global as opposed to local or even national environmental problems, despite follow-up initiatives such as Local Agenda 21.

Second, processes of global environmental change operate across considerable spatial and temporal social distances (Pawlik 1991). It is often the case with environmental problems that they are 'exported' from one region to another. Thus, an individual who receives the benefits of an environmentally damaging action is not likely to suffer its consequences. As social learning is facilitated by the interpersonal proximity of the individuals involved (Bandura 1977), learning through feelings of responsibility and/or empathy with the 'victim' will thus be inhibited (Pawlik 1991). Because of these processes we are less likely to have an emotional engagement with the 'victims' of the environmental damage we cause.

How should interpreters respond when faced with the knowledge that personal responsibility decreases with distance and that environmental winners and losers are generally separated by large distances? Surely, they need to ensure that the interpretation of environmental issues helps to make people aware of local actions on national and global 'others'. Attention should be paid to interpreting links between environmental winners and losers. A hot interpretive approach would be valuable in this regard, engaging visitors emotionally and helping them to identify with and acknowledge responsibility for environmental problems. In this way interpretation could enhance mutual understanding and appreciation and promote personal action facilitating environmentally sustainable practice at different spatial scales.

Management

The final factor which is important in influencing the affective impact of interpretation concerns the interpretive media itself. As a factor it is very much related to the promotion, marketing and management of an interpretive site, as discussed in the previous section. The pen may be mightier than the sword, but all the evidence suggests that when it comes to interpretive media the public prefer historical re-enactments, first person interpretation and demonstrations. Of course, the word can be powerful and effective such as the letter home from the front or the interpreted list of species lost this century through the destruction of the environment, but visitors can relate to people-based interpretation precisely because it invariably contains the full human response – the affective as well as the cognitive. Interpreters have long known this. But perhaps what they have not considered is the question: does people-based interpretation lead to a particular or a restricted set of emotions and feelings being portrayed? The French film director, François Truffaut, once said that it is not possible to make an anti-war movie because all war movies, with their energy and sense of adventure, end up making combat look fun. This is an oversimplification and contradicted by evidence (for example *Platoon* and *Saving Private Ryan*), but the point being made is that it may well be that certain types of presentation lead to certain types of interpretation.

Those responsible for interpreting and managing battlefield sites face a particular dilemma. On the one hand there is a desire to tell the story, to convey not only an accurate technical, logistic and strategic account of the conflict, but also to capture what the conflict meant at a human level for those involved so that the story told is as complete and 'truthful' as possible. But the truth can be nasty. In wars people get injured, maimed and killed in the most appalling ways. Children are orphaned and spouses are widowed. This is part of the truth. On the other hand, the owners and managers of battlefield sites are also required to attract as many visitors as possible and provide them with an 'entertaining day out for all the family'. These two objectives may not be compatible. It is a dilemma which is not easily resolved. Many managers take the line of least resistance and present a sanitised form of truth which will not upset, offend or challenge. If there is an attempt to engage the visitors' emotions, it may be restricted to superficial feelings which do not last beyond the visit. More often than not no emotional response is called for or encouraged.

What is the use of hot interpretation?

Hot interpretation as a concept has been discussed here largely in relation to the interpretation of war. This is because war tends to be a rather emotional subject which excites a strong affective response. But it has equal application to the many different subjects for which interpreters are responsible such as environmental destruction and pollution; species depletion; religious, sexual and racial intolerance and discrimination; class and caste issues; social reforms and differential access to health, welfare and education. It is not a coincidence that hot interpretation should have particular relevance and application to the interpretation of war and conflict. The reason for this is that conflicts between people are invariably emotional affairs. Therefore, wherever we find conflict between people there ought to be a role for hot interpretation and, arguably, the interpretation will be incomplete without this element.

We believe that the function of hot interpretation is twofold. First, interpretation that has an affective dimension will more adequately convey the meaning and significance of the heritage of the people, places, events and artefacts. In a sense, this is the touristic function of hot interpretation. Hot interpretation can, however, be used pro-actively and politically. This is the community development function of hot interpretation.

One example of this community development function is described in Ballantyne and Uzzell's (1993) paper concerning the role of hot interpretation in facilitating community healing in post-apartheid South Africa. As South Africa emerges from the trauma of its racial past, interpretation of the apartheid system and its city structures can help promote the process of reconciliation and nation building. In this regard, a hot interpretation approach is an ideal vehicle to promote community reconciliation in relation to forced removals. The effect of the Group Areas Act 1950, which led to the legal separation and forced uprooting of large numbers of the population, has left a legacy of deep bitterness. Removals were, and still are, a very 'hot' issue which the community needs to address. Of all the many forced removal areas in South Africa, District Six in Cape Town is perhaps the most infamous (Plate 10.4). Any visitor to Cape Town cannot escape noticing the 'scar' on the side of Table Mountain and inhabitants of the city well know the emotional impact of that space:

> Today the bare, scarred earth, and the hate and anger which its destruction generated have created a special kind of monument. On the one hand it bears witness to the crude, inhuman and ruthless vandalistic spirit of the South African ruling class and its equally crude and hateful race mythologies and policies, as well as its arrogance and violence with which it pursues its policies
>
> *Dudley 1990: 197*

Plate 10.4
District Six,
Cape Town,
South Africa
Source: David Uzzell

Such a 'hot' monument to apartheid cannot be interpreted without acknowledging and dealing with the emotional aspects which surround it – to ignore the 'heat' in its interpretation would be to fail the community. This does not mean that a hot interpretation of District Six should be used

to whip up further hate against those who were responsible for and profited from the removals. Rather, it is argued, that a hot interpretation of the history of District Six and its peoples should be designed to promote a healing of the anger and facilitate reconciliation in the community. A hot interpretation approach could help bring about Jeppie and Soudien's (1990:16) vision for District Six to become 'a healing symbol for a new and reconciled South Africa'.

The establishment of the District Six Museum in Buitenkant Street, Cape Town, in 1992 (Plate 10.5) has gone part of the way towards achieving some of the aims of a hot interpretive approach. It is truly a 'people's' museum and has been established through the goodwill of the community. Housed in the old Central Methodist Church, which in the days of apartheid was the venue for protest meetings, prayer vigils and a sanctuary for those physically and psychologically injured by police during protest actions, the museum has been very successful in attracting Cape Town community members and tourists through its doors. Exhibitions have focused upon community 'memories' of living in the area. Methods of interpretation have generally been hot in nature as exhibits encourage people to remem-

Plate 10.5
District Six Museum,
Buitenkant Street,
Cape Town,
South Africa
Source: Roy Ballantyne

ber or imagine the impact of removals upon people of the area. Past members of District Six are normally around to personalise the visitor experience. The impact of visitor interaction with those who lived the experience can be quite dramatic as personal experience and stories are related. People who 'watched' the removals and those who were moved often become engaged in conversation and leave with a greater understanding of what happened there.

The District Six Museum does not have flashy exhibits and the presentation of material is easily criticised. However, like the Checkpoint Charlie Museum in Berlin, the visitor is emotionally engaged by the significance and reality of the stories of the area and its people (Uzzell 1989). Although research needs to be undertaken to assess the impact of the museum and its interpretation, observation suggests that, like visiting a holocaust museum, people are profoundly affected.

Another example of the way in which hot interpretation could be used to bring about community development is described in a paper by Ballantyne (1995) which investigated conceptions of Aboriginal heritage and their implications for interpretive practice. In this study, interviews with interpreters of Australian Aboriginal heritage identified two ways of conceiving it with implications for the aims, content and strategies of interpretive programmes. Simply put, Aboriginal heritage can be understood to be either 'a thing of the past' or as 'evolving and contemporary'. It is suggested that a hot interpretive approach is suitable for addressing a number of issues involving contemporary, post-contact, Aboriginal heritage: for example, the positive role played by Aboriginals in Australian society, the nature of cultural beliefs and practices today, landrights, massacre sites, life on mission stations and the 'stolen generation'. Due to the cultural context within which such interpretation is to be presented, it is important that the interpreter adopts a sensitive, consultative approach and undertakes interpretation 'for' the community.

Those undertaking a hot interpretation of Aboriginal heritage should aim to interpret with, rather than about, Aboriginal people. Undertaking Aboriginal interpretation is at the best of times fraught with difficulties. Many well-meaning interpreters have found to their cost that what and how they have interpreted has not found favour with the Aboriginal community. An example of this would be the interpretation of Aboriginal heritage at the Ayers Rock Resort Visitor Centre in central Australia. In Aboriginal communities there are a number of 'mens', 'womens' and community stories and secrets which mean that what and how heritage is interpreted must be negotiated and at the discretion of the community.

A hot interpretation of post-contact heritage issues could play an important role in helping Aboriginal communities to tell their stories, as well as foster an understanding on the part of their fellow Australians about the history of the impact of European settlement upon Aboriginal peoples and their culture. As one Aboriginal interpreter suggested, it could play a role in helping people:

> to mature and come to terms with facts instead of covering up lies. Look at the Jews in Germany – they got wiped out, the same thing happened here and yet they tell us to forget about it, it's in the past. How can we forget about it? We know that our grandfather's father was beheaded over there ... to teach us a lesson. We can't forget about it.
>
> *Ballantyne 1995: 16*

Conclusion

Why are interpreters wary of employing hot interpretive techniques? Some are concerned that hot interpretation will be used simply for cheap shock value – the touristic equivalent of our more prurient and basic tabloid newspapers. Looking at some 'heritage' sites and facilities one has sympathy with their concern. But often these places actually have little to do with heritage, history and least of all education. Hot interpretation has to be undertaken responsibly if it is not to be merely sensational.

Interpreters are generally willing to claim credit when visitors leave a heritage site having had a stimulating and enjoyable educational experience. Should they not also take responsibility for other effects, particularly those which are intended? How does one cater for those for whom the interpretation provides a powerful, evocative and emotional experience? What responsibility do interpreters have for the reactions of people who may have found the interpretation moving or even traumatic? Such visitors need to be catered for, as well as those for whom a place or experience is simply an intellectual encounter with the past – one which evokes little or no emotional connection.

Some may be concerned that hot interpretation might be used for propaganda purposes – to indoctrinate ideas, reinforce stereotypes, incite and encourage fear. This is not being advocated here. Hot interpretation, like all interpretation, should present perspectives on the world which encourage visitors to question and explore different understandings, values and viewpoints. Truth is, after all, contestable. Is it the fact that hot interpretation openly admits that information is by its nature value laden and attempts to engage the whole person, rather than restricting itself to a knowledge-based approach, which opens it to the criticism of not being 'objective' or 'balanced'? Surely, however, no interpretation is values free? For instance, simply to ignore the emotions and ethical issues surrounding armed conflict or to fail to represent the impact of air pollution on people's health and development is to exhibit a very real values position. It might be hidden from the visitor, but it clearly represents a values standpoint. It could be argued that at least a hot interpretation approach alerts the visitor to the critical approach and stance being employed. One is reminded of the words of Martin Luther King:

> History will have to record that the greatest tragedy of this period of social transition was not the vitriolic words and violent actions of the bad people but the appalling silence and indifference of the good people.

Surely we are not questioning whether interpreters should nail their colours to the mast and 'shout' a warning to society on certain issues. This was Tilden's motivation, after all. The issue is not whether, but how. For this reason, we have argued that hot interpretation has potentially positive roles to play in society. In particular, we have outlined by two examples how, when used as part of community development, it can bring peoples together rather than be used as an instrument of division.

References

Ballantyne, R. R. (1995) 'Interpreters' conceptions of Australian Aboriginal culture and heritage: implications for interpretive practice', *Journal of Environmental Education*, 26(4): 11–17.

Ballantyne, R. R. and Uzzell, D. L (1993) 'Environmental mediation and hot interpretation: a case study of District Six, Cape Town', *Journal of Environmental Education*, 24(3): 4–7.

Bandura, A. (1977) *Social Learning Theory*, Englewood Cliffs NJ: Prentice Hall.

Dudley, R. (1990) 'Forced removals: the essential meanings of District Six', in S. Jeppie and C. Soudien (eds) *The Struggle for District Six – Past and Present*, Cape Town: Buchu Books.

Hartley, L. P. (1953) *The Go-Between*, Harmondsworth: Penguin.

Janis, I. L. and Mann, L. (1979) *Decision-Making: a Psychological Analysis of Conflict, Choice and Commitment*, New York: Free Press.

Jeppie, S. and Soudien, C. (1990) *The Struggle for District Six – Past and Present*, Cape Town: Buchu Books.

McGuire, W. J. (1985) 'Attitudes and attitude change', in G. Lindzey and E. Aronson (eds) *Handbook of Social Psychology*, vol. 2, 3rd edn, New York: Random House, pp. 233–346.

Pawlik, K. (1991) 'The psychology of global environmental change: some basic data and an agenda for co-operative international research', *International Journal of Psychology*, 26(5): 547–63.

Tilden, F. (1957) *Interpreting Our Heritage*, Chapel Hill: University of North Carolina Press.

Uzzell, D. L. (1989) 'The hot interpretation of war and conflict' in D. L. Uzzell (ed.) *Heritage Interpretation: Volume I: The Natural and Built Environment*, London: Belhaven, pp. 33–47.

Uzzell, D. L. (in preparation) 'The psycho-spatial dimension to global environmental problems'.

11 Contested heritage in the former Yugoslavia

MARIJA ANTERIĆ

Introduction

All interpretation is mediated by cultural values. This applies to the critique of interpretation as much as to its generation and provision. Interpretative theory, like interpretative practice, involves contested values. It is the very fragility and local particularity of our past, the inevitable decay and change, which provide for history – for evaluation and interpretation, re-interpretation and re-evaluation. Sixty years ago in Dubrovnik, Rebecca West commented on 'the appalling lack of accumulation observable in history, the perpetual cancellation of human achievement, which is the work of careless and violent nature' (West 1943: 244). It also provides for an uneasy and ambiguous relationship with ancestry, collective identity and heritage. Irish writer Colm Toibin, contemplating New Grange, a 5,000-year-old burial site near Dublin remarks wistfully:

> But I like the idea of coming from this race of Neolithic people who took their bearings from the European mainland, were concerned with problems of angle and elevation, weight and stress, and made cold, abstract art and a passage that the sun would enter only on the shortest day of the year. This is easier to live with somehow than the wild excesses of the Celtic imagination, and the general recklessness with which Ireland is often associated.
>
> *Toibin 1993: 38*

If the local with its ambiguous nature is contentious, the global is also not without problems. There are two faces of globalisation. One is the collective realisation of our shared, human identity, our responsibility for the planet and for each other. The other is the levelling down of cultural identity beneath inexorable market forces and Coca-Cola/Karaoke culture. People are not passive consumers: they do not merely buy, they also sing along.

Exotic states and Balkan intrigues

'Coca-Cola' interpretation is not a new phenomenon and the regions of former Yugoslavia have been as subject to it as anywhere. Shakespeare makes his parochial Welshman, Fluellen, say of Macedonia:

> I think it is in Macedon where Alexander is porn. I tell you, captain, if you look in the maps of the 'orld, I warrant you shall find, in the comparisons between Macedon and Monmouth, that the situations, look you, is both alike. There is a river in Macedon, and there is also moreover a river at Monmouth: It is called Wye at Monmouth; but it is out of my prains what is the name of the other river; but 'tis all one, 'tis alike as my fingers is to my fingers, and there is salmons in both
>
> *Shakespeare*, King Henry V, *Act IV, Scene VII*

Generations of British tourists to the area doubtless share Fluellen's views. By contrast, pre-1945 Yugoslavia held a particular attraction for the educated European middle class for its history of cultural, religious and ethnic diversity, as well as its perceived 'wild' peoples (Alcock and Young 1991).

The Balkan peninsula and the eastern Adriatic were seen as the exotic 'other' face of civilised Europe, a window into the East as well as the origin of classical and neo-classical virtues from the birthplace of Alexander the Great to the architecture of Robert Adam. Adam's architectural 'import', which greatly influenced Georgian architecture, originated from his visit in 1757 to the Roman Emperor Diocletian's Palace (built *c.* 305AD) in Split (Bryant 1992).

Struggles against the Ottoman Empire and the eternal permutations of the 'Eastern question' caught the imagination of many in Western Europe. Much of the romantic support for Serbia and Greece and perceptions of their heroic and noble heritage stem from their successful liberation from the Ottomans in the 19th century.[1] The 'Balkan attractions' of Postojna, Split and Dubrovnik as well as the exotic areas of previously Turkish Balkans became a part of Central and Southern European travelogues. Sites, peoples and history were often presented as elements of a coherent pattern of growth and change of European civilisation. During the 1920s and 1930s many European travellers and tourists came to Yugoslavia, especially to Dalmatia – a much preferred area of cultural, natural and geological interest (Ball 1932; Tyndale and Brown 1925).

1. In 1941 Olive Lodge dedicated her book *Peasant Life in Jugoslavia* to 'the Spirit of Kosovo'.

Many visitors' interpretations have influenced governments and international policy. Count Marsigli travelled as the Habsburg imperial boundary commissioner in the late 17th century and collected information about the natural and cultural heritage (Stoye 1994). Rebecca West (1943) in the influential *Black Lamb and Grey Falcon*, an account of her journey through Yugoslavia in 1937, offers an extraordinary study of 'Yugoslav' ethnic character, geography, history, morals and politics. Although many of her observations were acute, her perceptions were coloured by a very particular idea of Yugoslavia and the Slav character.

Many travellers to the Balkans, then as now, became enmeshed in nationalist politics and often championed particular peoples. The following view of the partisanship of 'outsiders' rings as true today as it was then:

> English persons, therefore, of humanitarian and reformist disposition constantly went out to the Balkan Peninsula to see who was in fact ill-treating whom, and, being by the very nature of their perfectionist faith unable to accept the horrid hypothesis that everybody was ill-treating everybody else, all came back with a pet Balkan people established in their hearts as suffering and innocent, eternally the massacree and never the massacrer.
>
> *West 1943: 22*

Landscapes of war and peace

> The history of the Balkans is the history of migrations – not just of peoples, but of lands. The original Serbia was far from the Danube, the political centre of Croatia was on the Adriatic, the 'little land of Bosnia' (to Khorion Bosona) of Constantine Porphyrogenitus was a small canton at the source of the Bosna River, and the term Slovenia emerged as a geographical and national designation only in the nineteenth century.
>
> *Banac 1984: 33*

Long before the South Slavs arrived on the Balkan peninsula and the eastern Adriatic, these lands were fought over, inhabited and occupied by many diverse peoples, from the local Liburni to the major colonial powers of Greece and Rome. After the fall of the Roman Empire and the invasions of Avar and Slavs between the 5th and 7th centuries, a number of South Slav medieval states emerged, varying in duration and size but none lasting beyond the 15th century. The eastern Adriatic and the Balkans for much of medieval history became the battleground of the three-cornered struggle for power by the Hungarians, Carolingians and Byzantines. The territories were also divided religiously between the spheres of influence of the Catholic and Orthodox Churches. Catholic Croatia became subsidiary to Hungary in 1102, while Orthodox Serbia developed into a large czardom in the first half of the 14th century to be completely subsumed together with Bosnia and Herzegovina into the Ottoman Empire by the 15th century. With the arrival of the Turkish Empire in the 14th century and for five centuries hence, most of the South Slav lands became a constantly shifting frontier between Christendom and Islam. While the eastern territories were part of the Turkish Empire the western territories were held, at various times, by the Hungarians, Austrians, French and Venetians. Only Dubrovnik Republic remained independent until its occupation by the French in 1806.

The great powers did not take much notice of the needs of native populations. The present-day borders between Croatia and Serbia and Croatia and Bosnia-Herzegovina are largely a result of the borders established following the Carlowitz treaty of 1699 between Austria, Turkey and Venice. Equally the military border (Krajina) in Croatia, a locus of recent disputes, was firmly established by Austria in the 17th century to guard against Ottoman attacks. The borders thus created were purely political and no importance was attached to ethnic origins of the inhabitants. Continuous changes of frontier as empires peaked and waned often resulted in shifts in religious, ethnic and political allegiances. Vagaries of economic, cultural and political changes, coupled with a sense of native impotence, were responsible for much economic and social impoverishment, disease and famine.

2. In 1809 following a defeat of a Serbian rebellion, Turks built a tower in which they embedded skulls of almost a thousand dead Serbian insurgents. Today there are only a few dozen skulls left on this strange monument.

People and religions often migrated in the wake of victories or defeats of great powers in the region (Babić 1991; Difnik 1986). Territories comprising the Austrian military border at times lay abandoned for decades; the areas of Plitvice Lakes and Krka National Parks, Slavonia and Vojvodina suffered from intermittent depopulation and repopulation from the 15th to the 18th century. Many remnants and symbols of the imperial occupations survive: from the Roman ruins and the stark fortresses of Klis, Dravograd and Smederevo to the carved lions of St Mark. In these often inaccessible and ungovernable lands there was also much rebellion, lawlessness and banditry. The macabre Cele Kula[2], in southern Serbia, the corsair fortifications at Senj and near the mouth of the Cetina River in southern Croatia are a lasting testament to the area's turbulent history.

For thousands of years the territories have been a crossroads of vital trade and communication routes between the Mediterranean and the Balkans, between Southern, Central and Eastern Europe and between Europe and Asia. In many crucial periods of history they have been as important for the diffusion of ideas and cultures as for the movement of goods and people. The remains of Greek settlements and Roman villas, the monasteries and churches of the eastern Adriatic, southern Serbia and Macedonia, the medieval stecci,[3] the civic institutions and palaces of the maritime cities, as well as the progressive laws of Dubrovnik are an equally lasting testament to the area's successive colonisations and its substantial cultural and urbane heritage.

3. Scattered throughout much of the region of central Dinaric Alps and extending south-east to Macedonia are late medieval stone monuments and tombstones of great beauty. Their origin is unknown although they have been associated with the medieval dualist sect the Bogumils, spiritual siblings of Cathars and Patarenes.

Throughout the centuries of division and strife the South Slavs retained and developed distinct regional and national identities and an awareness of shared origins. In spite of the turbulent history Slav languages and customs not only survived but were firmly established. During the 19th century a number of movements and political parties were established promoting national awakening among Croats, Serbs and Slovenes. The national movements were, however, overshadowed by demands for the cultural unification of South Slavs, the most important being the Croatian Illyrian movement of the 1840s. The greatest proponent of the idea of cultural unity was the Catholic Archbishop Josip Strossmayer, a philanthropist and a founder of the Yugoslav Academy of Sciences and Arts in Zagreb, Croatia.

In 1918 the Kingdom of Serbs, Croats and Slovenes was established after the demise of the Austro-Hungarian empire. Yugoslav affinities and affiliations flourished in the first years of the new state, but its autocratic nature disappointed many people and revived Croatian and Serbian nationalism. The country suffered from a host of economic and political problems related to its chequered past, uneven development and divergent national aspirations. The 1930s world economic crisis proved devastating for this largely agricultural land in which mineral and industrial resources were mainly owned by international companies. Large numbers of its citizens suffered poverty, ill health and illiteracy.

4. Ustashe were the Croatian élite fascist troops in the service of the Independent State of Croatia, 1941–5, a creation of the German and Italian occupying forces. The Chetniks were mainly composed of the Serbian and Montenegrin nationalists, Royalists and fascists, although they were in the service of the Yugoslav government in exile. They originally had the support of the Allies until 1943 when the support was switched to the Partisans.

Many of the roots of the most recent conflicts can be traced to the events of World War II and the civil war between the Fascist and nationalist armies, Ustashe and the Chetniks, and the multi-ethnic, communist-led and ultimately victorious Partisans.[4] A number of US and British officers were sent among the Chetnik and Partisan forces of whom the best known were Sir Fitzroy MacLean, William Deakin, Michael Lees and Franklin Lindsay.

Their accounts and allegiances inform and colour to this day our perceptions of Yugoslav conflicts (Deakin 1971; Lees 1990; Lindsay 1995: Maclean 1949).

Post-1945 Yugoslavia

In territories with diverse ethnic, religious, linguistic, economic and social factors within historically unstable geopolitical contexts, peoples and communities often have great difficulty in adapting themselves to modern state structures. In the eastern Adriatic and the Balkans two lasting legacies of living in disputed territories and military borderlands have been a deep suspicion of state and centralised power and a propensity to look for intrigue and conspiracy. In the past these were often useful tools for survival but have proved quite unproductive in the modern world. The Yugoslav Communist Party, which formed the post-war government of supranational unity, established Yugoslavia as a federal and socialist state. It emphasised the unifying factors in the federation: self-liberation and the partisan struggle, economic progress through self-management and socialist independence. An oft-quoted slogan of the former Federation was that it 'has seven neighbours, six republics, five nations, four languages, two scripts, and one goal: to live in brotherhood and unity' (Crnobrnja 1994: 15).

Yugoslavia, I submit, considered itself a country of political and economic pluralism promoting global peace, non-alignment and co-operation. Post-war reconstruction, urbanisation and industrialisation transformed a largely agrarian rural country into a modern state. The economic development also brought with it a myriad of environmental and social problems. The rapid expansion in educational institutions led to a high regard for culture and arts even if hampered by political dogma.

The history of oppression and subjugation was perceived to have been redeemed by the Partisan victory. Many monuments were erected commemorating victims of Fascism and Partisan heroism, and President Tito became the symbol of new Yugoslavia. When he died, on 3 May 1980, the football match between Hajduk (Split) and Crvena Zvezda (Red Star Belgrade) halted and the players wept while the public sang a Tito song.

The diversity of peoples and cultures of the former Yugoslavia was matched by the physical diversity of its landscapes: the often inaccessible mountain ranges of the Alpine regions, the high plateaux and ravines of the karst areas, the fertile plains of Pannonia intersected by the great river basins of Danube and Sava, numerous lakes and the Adriatic with its narrow littoral and hundreds of islands.

The natural and cultural heritage of Yugoslavia was actively promoted. Numerous national parks, nature reserves and areas of special cultural interest were created mainly under local administration. Tourism was encouraged and became economically very important, although uncontrolled growth often resulted in neglect or even destruction of the heritage. Yugoslavia was depicted as a country of great geographical, natural and cultural variety, where both unity and local traditions were valued. However, the new Yugoslavia was not to everyone's liking. Modernisation appeared to have destroyed not only the poverty but also much of the mystique. One person most upset by the new Yugoslavia was Rebecca West for whom the Slav character, exemplified by Macedonian peasant values, was no longer represented in socialist Yugoslavia. 'She did not merely love Yugoslavia … she believed in it – and she never forgave it for being other than she believed it was' (Alcock and Young 1991). Felicity Rosslyn, following in the footsteps of West, is disappointed with Lake Ohrid, and declares that 'Macedonia was as spiritually vacant as a car park' and complains of 'a rapacious brand of tourist exploitation' (Alcock and Young 1991: 112).

Break-up of Yugoslavia, contested interpretation and dilemmas for the future

The collapse of Yugoslavia has allowed ethnic and national divisions – real or imagined – to be used as the pretext for the assertion of power by new political forces: 'Yugoslavia was never only a state. It has been and remains a geographical region interwoven with numerous geographic, economic, cultural and family links. It has also been an idea, a vision, and a political objective' (Crnobrnja 1994: 265). Those links and that vision were the first victims of conflict as cultural monuments were destroyed or damaged deliberately to obliterate the material presence of unwanted peoples. In the worst affected areas, in Croatia and Bosnia-Herzegovina, attempts at destruction included the savage shelling of Dubrovnik. Many irreplaceable treasures have gone, such as the famous bridge at Mostar which Henry Moore described as a 'moon over the river'.

The natural heritage has suffered too. Plitvice has been described in many modern travelogues as a natural wonder: 'Three or four hours short of Zagreb, we left the train and spent a day at the Plitvitse Lakes, the most laughing and light-minded of natural prodigies. Here the creative spirit is as far from the normal as at Niagara or the Grand Canyon or the Matterhorn;

5. In August 1995 following a military intervention the region was again incorporated into Croatia.

but it is untouched by the tragic or terror, it is solely dedicated to gaiety and loveliness' (West 1943: 464). From 1991 to 1995 the national park was inaccessible to all but the Serbian nationalists.[5] Sadly, by the time it reopened it had been greatly touched 'by the tragic' and 'terror' and much of the area subject to looting and destruction. Many of the staff and inhabitants of the Plitvice Lakes National Park have become refugees, others were killed or suffered imprisonment and torture.

Vukovar, a baroque Slavonian city where the Yugoslav Communist Party was founded in 1920, and the surrounding area became a site of the most appalling devastation after a long Serbian nationalist siege which left the town in ruins and most of its surviving citizens refugees. Within the Croatian national mythology Vukovar is now the symbol of resistance and martyrdom and a permanent reminder of the Serbian betrayal.

Reconstructing and reinterpreting the past

The break-up of Yugoslavia, the demise of socialism and the ensuing conflicts have precipitated interpretation and reinterpretation of past, history and heritage. In many places the names of historic streets and sites, some long predating the socialist period, have been changed. Monuments have been removed or destroyed, and institutions purged of their historical connections to conform to the new political agendas, items of an 'excluded past' (Stone and Mackenzie 1989). (See Plate 11.1.)

The Yugoslavism of both Archbishop Strossmayer and Ivo Andric are now uncomfortable reminders of the shared history and vision, ignored or vilified. The Gavrilo Princip bridge in Sarajevo, named after the young Bosnian nationalist whose fateful shots defined the beginning of the World War I, is again Latinski Most (Latin Bridge). The past presents dilemmas for interpretation. An example is the Sutjeska National Park in Bosnia and Herzegovina. Cuddon's *Companion Guide*, one of the most popular guides to Yugoslavia describes the area thus:

> South of Foca lie the Zelengora Mountains and the Sutjeska Gorge. East of the gorge rise the peaks of the Maglic, Studenci and Vlasulja – all nearly eight thousand feet high. It was in this region that another epic legend was created by the Partisans ... They fought their way across the Sutjeska to the north and escaped with the loss of nearly half their men.
>
> *Cuddon 1968: 324*

At present, like most national parks and protected areas of Bosnia-Hercegovina, it is out of bounds to visitors. Although an area of immense natural and scenic interest, Sutjeska is of significance principally as the site of the battle, a monument housing the bones of 3,301 fighters and the resting place of the Yugoslav hero Sava Kovacevic.

Inevitably much historical and heritage interpretation has focused on the conflicts of the World War II, the role of the Partisan army and the emer-

Plate 11.1
Monument to the fallen local Partisans, Trogir, Croatia, vandalised following the break-up of Yugoslavia. The monument was completely removed in 1997 by the municipal authorities
Source: Marija Anterić

gence of socialist Yugoslavia. In Sarajevo city centre a large plaque honours and commemorates the 1945 liberators of Sarajevo (Plate 11.2). Following the recent conflicts it was proposed that the names of Serbian and Montenegrin Partisan brigades should be removed from the monument. The proposal did not meet with much popular approval. In post-conflict areas reinterpretation is often perceived as an undemocratic, politically motivated process by which the past is rewritten without people's participation or agreement.

In Croatia reinterpretation of past conflicts is central to a wider political project of national reconciliation. Retroactive 'hot interpretation' (Uzzell 1989) has included calls for the establishment of common graves for the fallen Partisans and Ustashe in the name of reconciliation. One such proposal, supported by the Croatian president, Franjo Tudman, envisages a shared Croatian memorial grave at Jasenovac, the notorious Ustashe concentration camp in which tens of thousands of Jews, Serbs, Gypsies and Croats perished. The monuments commemorating victims were damaged during the 1995 military operation to recover the territories under the con-

Plate 11.2
The controversial 1946 plaque to the 1945 liberators of Sarajevo
Source: Marija Anterić

trol of Serbian rebels. The proposals have been met with consternation by the survivors of the Fascist terror, the partisan veteran organisations and the Jewish community.

Since the establishment of sovereign Croatia, interpretations of Croatian history have been characterised by an extensive use, both pictorially and narratively, of the imagery of suffering and salvation directly borrowed from the Catholic faith. The recent war and selected events from the past are often presented as the Croatian 'Stations of the Cross'. Bleiburg, a small place in Austria, has become its foremost symbol. It was here that the British Army handed over the remnants of the Croatian and Serbian nationalist and Fascist troops to the Yugoslav Army in 1945. In 1975, a black marble monument commemorating the event was unveiled depicting a grieving mother of Croats bemoaning the fate of the vanished Croatian army.

Conclusion

It has been argued that heritage creation is a positive and even a necessary process: 'people often have to recreate a more suitable past for themselves'(Nairn 1995: 4). But it is also a problematic and contentious process. Uncritical interpretations of heritage tend to ignore both its 'dark' side and its fictional nature. 'Heritage is not the same as history. Heritage is history processed through mythology, ideology, nationalism, local pride, romantic ideas or just plain marketing, into a commodity... When history has been processed into heritage, scientific evidence has lost its case, for "heritage" creates its own reality' (Schouten 1995: 21–2).

The past and its remains never speak by themselves. Their discovery and exploitation involve a process of interpretation and mediation which not only transforms them but also endows them with contemporary meanings. For instance, half a millennium ago in 1389, Prince ('Czar') Lazar was killed in the battle of Kosovo Polje in which the Serbian army was defeated by the Ottoman Turks. Both the battle and Lazar became the central emblem of the later Serbian national mythology, symbols of suffering and stoical heroism. In 1989, under the auspices of Slobodan Milosevic, his bones were taken from his tomb and toured around Serbia as a sacred relic of the Serbian nation. By the autumn of 1991 Yugoslavia was engulfed in the internecine war.

It has been claimed that: 'Large numbers of people are quite prepared to sacrifice their lives for the recognition of their national identities and the restoration of their "historic" lands' (Smith 1986: 2). Ambiguity and questionable historical veracity inherent in such 'hot interpretation' is common. As can be easily observed in the former Yugoslavia and elsewhere, the banal and sad truth is that the supporters of a nationalist cause cloaked in 'historical' justifications are certainly prepared to kill for it. As a character in a Sean O'Casey's play says: 'I believe in the freedom of Ireland, an' that England has no right to be here, but I draw the line when I hear the gunmen blowin' about dyin' for the people, when it's the people that are dyin' for the gunmen. With all due respect to the gunmen, I don't want them to die for me' (O'Casey 1967: 111).

References

Alcock, J. B. and Young, A. (1991) *Black Lambs and Grey Falcons: Women Travellers in the Balkans*, Bradford: University of Bradford.

Babić, I. (1991) *Prostor izmedu Trogira i Splita, Kastel Novi*, Split: Zavicajni Muzej Kastela.

Ball, O. H. (1932) *Dalmatia*, London: Faber & Faber.

Banac, I. (1984) *The National Question in Yugoslavia: Origins, History, Politics*, Ithaca and London: Cornell University Press.

Boskovic-Stulli, M. (1991) *Pjesme, Price, Fantastika*, Zagreb: Nakladni Zavod Matice Hrvatske.

Bryant, J. (1992) *Robert Adam: Architect of Genius*, London: English Heritage.

Cosgrove, D. and Daniels, S. (1988) *The Iconography of Landscape*, Cambridge: Cambridge University Press.

Crnobrnja, M. (1994) *The Yugoslav Drama*, London: I. B. Tauris.

Cuddon, J. A. (1968) *The Companion Guide to Jugoslavia*, Glasgow: Collins.

Deakin, W. F. (1971) *The Embattled Mountain*, New York: Oxford University Press.

Denecke, D. (1982) 'Applied historical geographies of the past: historic–geographical change and regional processes in history', in A. T. Baker and M. Billinge (eds) *Period and Place: Research Methods in Historical Geography*, Cambridge: Cambridge University Press, pp. 127–35.

Difnik, F. (1986) *Povijest Kandijskog Rata u Dalmaciji*, Split: Knjizevni krug Split.

Kuzic, K. (1997) *Povijest Dalmatinske Zagore*, Split: Knjizevni krug Split.

Lees, M. (1990) *The Rape of Serbia*, New York: Harcourt Brace Jovanovich.

Lindsay, F. (1995) *Beacons in the Night: With the OSS and Tito's Partisans in Wartime Yugoslavia*, Stanford: Stanford University Press.

Maclean, F. (1949) *Eastern Approaches*, Edinburgh: J and J Gray.

Nairn, T. (1995) 'Nationalism is not the enemy', *Observer*, 12 November.

Nikolic, V. (1993) *Bleiburska tragedija hrvatskoga naroda*, Zagreb: Knjiznica Hrvatske revije.

O'Casey, S. (1967) 'The shadow of a gunman', *Three Plays*, London: Macmillan.

Schouten, F. F. J. (1995) 'Heritage as historical reality', in D. T. Herbert (ed.) *Heritage, Tourism and Society*, London and New York: Mansell.

Smith, A. D. (1986) *The Ethnic Origins of Nations*, Oxford: Blackwell.

Stone, P. and Mackenzie, R. (1989) 'Is There an "excluded past" in education?' in D. Uzzell, (ed.) *Heritage Interpretation, Vol. 1: The Natural and Built Environment*, London: Belhaven, pp. 113 –20.

Stoyanov, Y. (1994) *The Hidden Tradition in Europe*, London: Arkana/Penguin Books.

Stoye, J. (1994) *Marsigli's Europe: the Life and Times of Luigi Ferdinando Marsigli, Soldier and Virtuoso*, New Haven and London: Yale University Press.

Toibin, C. (1993) 'Miracles in stone', *Independent on Sunday*, 3 January: 38–44.

Tyndale, W. and Brown, H. F. (1925) *Dalmatia*, London: A & C . Black.

Uzzell, D. (1989) 'Interpretation of war and conflict', in D. Uzzell (ed.) *Heritage Interpretation, Vol. 1: The Natural and Built Environment*. London: Belhaven, pp. 33–47.

West, R. (1943) *Black Lamb and Grey Falcon*, 2nd edn, London: Macmillan.

12

Strategic considerations and practical approaches to the evaluation of heritage and environmental interpretation

DAVID UZZELL

Introduction

Although interpretation is a relatively new field, the honeymoon period is now over. The learning curve for heritage organisations has been steep; some have mastered it, some have not. Interpreters, however noble their motivations and intentions, are operating in an environment that is highly competitive. It is not only competitive in terms of the leisure pound, dollar or yen, or even the leisure hour and day, but is also operating in an environment that is competitive for the hearts and minds of the visitor. The public is assaulted on all sides for their attention and support for compelling ideologies, causes and campaigns, all highly worthy and defensible. Interpreters have to deliver.

As we approach the millennium, one priority for heritage and environmental management and interpretation is research and evaluation. In Britain, twenty years after the building of the first visitor centres and other large-scale investment in interpretive facilities and services, we are still designing exhibitions and spending millions of pounds on interpretations without any clear idea as to whether they work or have the kind of short-, medium- or long-term effects commensurate with their goals or level of investment. If interpretation is to achieve the objectives to which most interpreters aspire, then simply throwing money at exhibitions, leaflets or staff has at best an uncertain outcome and at worst is profligate. Coming to grips with 'doing it' has taken precedence over standing back and questioning whether 'it' is actually working. The pressure to provide interpretive facilities and services because they are seen as important elements of conservation education with a direct impact on management and protection, or perhaps because they are seen as an essential income stream ensuring financial viability, means that reflection and review have taken a back seat. It is understandable, but not desirable, condonable nor wise.

There is considerable experience and knowledge around the world such that interpretive managers, planners and practitioners can draw on best practice (see Chapter 14). But interpretation, like the heritage itself, is place specific. The type of interpretive solutions adopted ought to reflect the particular opportunities and constraints inherent in the heritage and its location. If we regard knowledge as socially constructed, then there is a dynamic relationship between the interpretive content, the place, the visitor and the social group to which people belong and the meanings which are generated as a consequence of that interaction (Chapter 2). Consequently, understanding the visitors and the social group to which they belong is a vital part of interpretive planning and provision.

Of course, experience provides interpreters and heritage managers with an intuitive or evidential understanding of their visitors. While this can be useful, it can also be incomplete and misleading. The only way really to understand the visitor is to carry out research and evaluation. We know from evaluation studies what visitors like and whether they feel they have learnt something from their interpretive experiences. We have only scraped the surface in determining how effective interpretation is in enhancing people's understanding of environmental issues, in changing their attitudes and behaviour, and in increasing their action competence (Chapter 13).

Evaluation or research

There is a distinction to be made between research and evaluation. They are frequently treated as if they are synonymous (Barrow 1993). This is understandable because the methods used in evaluation and research may be the same – observation studies, surveys, focus group discussions, controlled experiments. The objectives are, however, different. Evaluation is always context specific. It seeks to provide specific and prescriptive information that can lead to performance improvement. Robson (1993) defines an evaluation as 'a study which has a distinctive purpose ... to assess the effects and effectiveness of something, typically some innovation or intervention: policy, practice or service'. It might be a subsequent goal of evaluation to contribute to the improvement or increased effectiveness of that which is being evaluated. Evaluation studies often try to address issues of change, the barriers to implementing change and how these may be overcome. Evaluation tends, however, not to look beyond itself and does not try to generalise its findings to other situations.

Research, on the other hand, is often concerned with understanding processes, explaining how variability in one factor can lead to variability in another and from there creating generalisations and models. Essential to this iterative process is the generation of theory: a body of data is collected in order that we can theorise about the phenomenon under investigation. At a formal scientific level, hypotheses are established in order to test theories. Interpretation has not been well served over the years because those responsible for its development have failed to ask questions which are driven by theoretical considerations. These would undoubtedly provide new insights into the function and effectiveness of interpretation.

Miles (1993) suggests that there are at least six differences between evaluation and research. For example, one aim of evaluation is to gauge how well something works, whereas in visitor research the aim is to explore empirical generalisations about visitors and exhibits. However the most important differences, Miles suggests, concern the purpose and approach of the exercise. Is the work carried out to make judgements or to develop generalisations? Is the work pragmatic, as in the case of evaluation, or rigorous as with controlled research studies? Miles argues that research results can be used for the purpose of evaluation, but rarely can the results of evaluation studies inform research other than at a descriptive level.

The value of research is readily demonstrated. For example, interpreters often talk about enhancing the visitor's sense of place and creating place identity. A considerable amount of research has been undertaken in environmental psychology on defining a sense of place so that it can be operationalised as a meaningful and testable proposition (Lalli 1992; Twigger-Ross and Uzzell 1996). Research by the author examining the effectiveness of a museum to communicate a sense of place was informed by place theory (Uzzell 1995). The results were surprising and in some respects counter-intuitive, but enabled as a consequence specific suggestions to be made as to what aspects of the town story would be most effective in enhancing place identity, thereby truly having an effective impact. The amount of research which has been undertaken on interpretation is lamentably little to the ultimate detriment of the development of the sub-discipline and profession.

Evaluation

This chapter will concentrate on examining evaluation. Evaluation is one of those activities more honoured in the breach than the observance. Everyone agrees that it is a good thing, but when it comes down to it there is always a reason why it cannot be done: a lack of time, money, expertise or simply a view that it is not worthwhile. Unfortunately evaluation studies are usually the last thing to be considered in the planning, design and management of interpretive facilities and services. This usually means that inadequate resources are set aside from the outset, so that if it is suggested that the interpretive material is tested there is insufficient money available (formative evaluation). As will be seen later, evaluation can and should be carried out at every stage in the implementation of an interpretation programme. Evaluation studies can be undertaken to find out the size and nature of the anticipated audience for the interpretation and how many different types of audiences there are for the facility or service. What do these different audiences know about the subject matter to be interpreted and what kind of interpretive and recreational experience are they seeking? Likewise in the design of the interpretation, whether it is exhibition panels, an audio-visual programme, or a self-guided walk leaflet, evaluation studies can be carried out to test whether the interpretive material is clear and understandable. Have visitors found the interpretive guide friendly, approachable and stimulating? Do visitors come away with the key concepts? After the interpretive programme is in place evaluation can be undertaken to ascertain visitors' level of satisfaction with the service provided. Do they think the interpretation has been interesting and stimulating? What else would they like to know about? What have they learnt?

It is important to examine the non-educational arguments for undertaking evaluation studies. These need to be articulated because they can be used as part of an advocacy case in support of an application for funding or other resources to monitor and assess interpretive provision. Paradoxically, evaluation exercises are considered by some to be a luxury only to be afforded during periods of economic prosperity. However, it is when budgets are limited that such studies are necessary. At a time when the financing of interpretive provision is a major element in any discussion of interpretive planning, it is appropriate that economic arguments are deployed in support of evaluation studies. While it is sometimes difficult to determine the economic value of an educational benefit, as heritage and environmental interpretation cannot always be assessed by the more conventional indicators of the marketplace, methods have to be found to demonstrate to politicians, government administrators and the public that there is a cost-effective return on public expenditure. In short, there is a need for resource managers to measure and quantify the costs and benefits of their facilities and programmes. It will be on those sites which are least cost effective, or where the costs and benefits cannot be demonstrated, that public investment will be reduced or even terminated. On a more positive note, when evaluation studies demonstrate that interpretation is educationally and financially effective, the findings can be used by interpreters to support their case for increased financial investment in their work.

The cost of evaluation studies has to be assessed in the context of the capital and recurrent costs of the interpretive facility and service. Some facilities such as visitor centres are extremely expensive to build, fit out and staff. Over the lifespan of an exhibition and on-site interpretation the costs of evaluation will amount to an extremely small proportion of the total facility costs. The financial costs of an evaluation study should be assessed against questions such as:

- Given the amount of money that is and will be spent on interpretive facilities, is the interpretive material communicating site values and getting planned messages across to visitors?

- Do the public understand the exhibition material?

- Is it pitched at their level of comprehension?

- Could interest and comprehension be increased by different routing or by other means of physical management?

- Do the public find the interpretation stimulating?

- Who is visiting the site and which market segments are not being reached?

- Which of the media used is most successful?

Set in this context, the benefits of evaluation studies are out of all proportion to their costs. Clearly the financing of an evaluation study should not be regarded as a once and for all item of expenditure, but should be seen as an annual or biennial budget item if constant monitoring is to take place. While it is easy to minimise the financial burden of evaluation studies, it is recognised that for managers with a limited budget even several hundred pounds can be out of the question. Evaluation does not have to be expensive: it is an attitude of mind that says a way must be found to monitor performance and effectiveness.

To senior administrators, interpretation may be a desirable but not necessarily essential service. It may not be the primary function of the organisation. It is ironic, as Roggenbuck and Propst (1981) point out, that although professional interpreters are experienced in the ways of persuasive communication, they have only been moderately successful in convincing senior management in their own organisations of the value of the service they provide. In order to secure greater intra-organisational support it is essential for interpreters to evaluate and demonstrate to senior decision-makers, in terms understandable to that group, that interpretive services can play a vital role in fulfilling the organisation's overall objectives.

Two reasons why evaluation studies may be expensive to undertake is that they can be both labour-intensive and require skilled design and subsequent analysis. One can, of course, buy in these skills. However, it is possible with a small amount of training to design, undertake and analyse basic evaluation data that will provide considerable information about the visitors and their interaction with the heritage and the interpretation.

The remainder of this chapter examines different types of evaluation studies, the different ways of asking similar questions depending on the type of information one is trying to obtain, six common sources of error and bias in data collection and finally six different research and evaluation methodologies.

Front-end, formative and summative evaluation

Evaluation can be implemented at all stages of exhibition and interpretation development. Miles (1993) distinguishes among three major types of exhibition evaluation: front-end, formative and summative evaluation, corresponding to before, during and after implementation (Table 12.1).

TABLE 12.1. FRONT-END, FORMATIVE AND SUMMATIVE EVALUATION

	Before	During	After
Plans	Front-end evaluation		
Mock-ups		Formative evaluation	
Completed exhibit or programme			Summative evaluation

Front-end evaluation

Drawing on Miles's (1993) definitions, front-end evaluation is carried out in the early stages of the planning process. This might take the form of undertaking surveys of potential visitors to ascertain whether they would be interested in the introduction of new interpretive stories or new interpretive techniques. Front-end evaluation might also draw on pre-existing visitor surveys to understand the kind of visitors which comprise the current audience. The data collected from a front-end evaluation study might then be used to assess the appropriateness of an interpretive solution to a particular situation. Front-end evaluation is essential if you know little or nothing about your current or potential audience:

- Who are your visitors and where do they come from?

- What facilities and services do they require?

- How do visitors perceive the museum or interpretive site?

- What made them visit the museum in the first place?

- What do visitors know about the interpretive theme of the exhibition?

- How interested are visitors in industrial buildings compared with domestic buildings?

- Do different types of visitors visit different types of museums?

- What is their attitude to wildlife or architectural conservation?

- What kind of interpretation do they prefer?

Formative evaluation

Formative evaluation is typically undertaken at the design stage in order to test the efficacy of a particular design or communication solution. Mock-ups or prototypes of exhibition panels, leaflets or audio-visual programmes can all be tested. For example, if there is an exhibition on the Battle of Trafalgar, it may be the intention of the interpreter and designer to explain that the significance of Nelson's leadership in the Battle of Trafalgar was not that he was a dashing commander who led the British fleet despite having one arm and one eye; rather, it was that he employed audacious and revolutionary battle tactics against the French fleet. Do visitors understand and appreciate this having seen the exhibition panel or read the leaflet which tells this story? If they do not, then the panel or leaflet should be rewritten and then tested again. Formative evaluation is a means of testing by trial and error whether a piece of interpretation works. Questions typically posed in formative evaluation include:

- Does the visitor understand the key concepts which the interpretation tries to communicate?

- Are there any words which the visitor does not understand?

- Is the text written at an appropriate reading age?

- Do the illustrations help or hinder understanding?

- Should the text have accompanying photographs or diagrams?

- Is the text size written using a point size that enables it to be be read with ease from a distance of 1 metre?

Summative evaluation

Summative evaluation is, as Miles points out, 'carried out on real exhibits in real exhibitions under real conditions ... and almost always involves real visitors' (1993:25). Having planned, designed and implemented an exhibition or piece of interpretation, summative evaluation is used to assess what visitors think about it. Usually the evaluator will be interested in the answers to a particular set of questions, such as:

- Does the visitor think that the exhibition is interesting or informative?

- What do visitors learn as a consequence of seeing the audio-visual programme?

- What would encourage visitors to return for a repeat visit?

- Which interpretive media do visitors prefer?

- Which themes and stories did visitors find most interesting?

- Was there anything the visitors saw in the exhibition that encouraged them to explore the site or area more fully?

- Did the visitor talk to a member of staff?

If the principal concern is to assess how effective an exhibition has been in terms of facilitating learning, this falls largely within the sphere of summative evaluation. Of course, the findings may be implemented subsequently in the formative stages of other exhibit planning. The methods used in summative evaluation are dependent on the kinds of questions one is seeking to answer. These are concerned not only with learning but also relate to which displays and type of media visitors prefer and why. The visitor centre management may also be interested in which displays are most effective and what kind of person is attracted to the centre. Interpretation, like marketing, has to be targeted to particular audiences. Front-end and summative evaluation are essential parts of this process.

It should be stressed that if one undertakes an evaluation study and it is found that the interpretation is deficient in some respect, the evaluation itself may suggest ways in which it can be improved. Revising the interpretation will not necessarily mean that the interpretation will now be effective. The revisions themselves need to be subject to some form of testing. Evaluation will tell you whether or not something works. It might also suggest where any deficiencies occur and how they might be addressed. But one will still not know whether the problems have been solved – indeed new problems may now appear – until further testing has been undertaken.

Questionnaires are fairly common instruments in summative evaluation. Any standard textbook in research methods (Breakwell *et al*.1995) will describe in detail the criteria which are essential to consider in the design of a questionnaire. There is usually more than one way of asking questions. The way questions are phrased can have a crucial impact on the type of analysis subsequently undertaken and ultimately the value and practical usefulness of the information obtained. This can be illustrated by the following simple example to ascertain visitors' opinions about a particular trail leaflet, one could ask the question illustrated in Table 12.2:

TABLE 12.2 QUESTIONNAIRE INVITING YES/NO RESPONSE

Did you find the Chalk Downlands Trail leaflet easy to understand?

1	☐ Yes
2	☐ No
3	☐ Don't know

Apart from not providing us with very much information, this is a fairly insensitive measure requiring either a 'yes' or 'no' response, when our feelings about the trail may have been more mixed. The data generated by this answer are called nominal or categorical level data. They are the most basic form of data and permit very little mathematical manipulation. For example, one cannot obtain a mean or average score across a sample of visitors; one can only say x per cent responded 'yes' and y per cent responded 'no'. This also means that one can only use a limited range of statistical procedures in order to test whether, for example, there is a gender difference in response to the answer.

Alternatively, one could ask the question in the way shown in Table 12.3.

TABLE 12.3 QUESTIONNAIRE INVITING COMPARISONS

Please rank the following trail leaflets in terms of how informative you found them:

1	Chalk Downlands Trail leaflet
2	Heathland Trail leaflet
3	Nuts and Berries Trail leaflet
4	Fur and Feather Trail leaflet

Questions phrased like this allow one to draw comparisons between the different trail leaflets and ascertain which is seen as the best, the second best and so on. Asking people to rank order such a list results in ordinal level data. A wider range of more powerful statistical procedures can be used for analysing ordinal data including tests of correlation and difference. One limitation with this approach, though, is that the answer does not tell us how good, in absolute terms, the leaflets are regarded. The Chalk Downlands Trail leaflet may be evaluated as the best, but it may be the best of a poor bunch.

We can overcome this shortcoming by asking the question in the manner shown in Table 12.4.

TABLE 12.4 QUESTIONNAIRE TO OBTAIN SCALE RESPONSE

How informative are the following leaflets? Please rate each leaflet on a scale from

1 (very informative) to 5 (very uninformative)

1 Chalk Downlands Trail leaflet	1_____2_____3_____4_____5
2 Heathland Trail leaflet	1_____2_____3_____4_____5
3 Nuts and Berries Trail leaflet	1_____2_____3_____4_____5
4 Fur and Feather Trail leaflet	1_____2_____3_____4_____5

Asking the question this way, we can not only find out how highly regarded each leaflet is relative to the others, but also how highly regarded each leaflet is in absolute terms. While this data is not strictly at interval level in statistical terms, it is often treated as such by social scientists. This allows the use of an even wider and more powerful group of statistical tests.

Lies, damned lies

There are many considerations to be taken into account and pitfalls to be avoided in the planning and design of evaluation studies and instruments. Six issues are briefly discussed here: validity, reliability, bias, vagueness, ambiguity and the need for the systematic sampling of visitors.

Validity

A valid instrument is one that measures what it sets out to measure. Unfortunately, operational definitions of validity often end up being circular and self-fulfilling. A good example from psychology is intelligence tests. Does the concept of intelligence have an independent existence outside the means used to test its existence? There is an obvious danger that intelligence is what intelligence tests measure. For this reason, it is useful to have a second independent measure against which the evaluation instrument can be assessed in order to ensure that it explains what it claims to explain. We know, for example, that a ruler is a valid instrument for measuring distance because it measures what it claims to measure in terms of our understanding and concepts of distance.

Reliability

Reliability is more straightforward. An evaluation instrument is reliable if it gives consistently similar results when applied on a number of occasions under the same conditions. If visitors have been properly sampled from a 'parent' population, then drawing another sample by the same means and asking the same questions should, within a certain degree of error, lead to a similar set of results. There may be a small difference in, say, percentages, but this should not be significantly different from the previous sample.

Bias

Designing a questionnaire that does not have 'loaded' questions which result in biased responses is a skilled task, as is the subsequent analysis of the collected data. It is possible, though, for someone with little previous experience to acquire the skills in questionnaire design that will permit the collection of basic but highly useful information.

Bias may take the form of only interviewing visitors under 30 years of age, visitors who are walking by themselves, or visitors who look 'friendly'. Of course, if you are only interested in the views of visitors under 30 years of age that's fine, but if you want the responses to be as representative as possible of all your visitors then you need to sample across the whole range. There may be special interest groups who have to be specifically targeted in order to ascertain their views because they comprise a small but nevertheless important subgroup of visitors, e.g. disabled people.

Bias occurs not only in the sampling of visitors to be interviewed, but also in the way questions are phrased. The following question may seem acceptable: 'Which of the displays did you find the most informative?' The respondent, however, may have found none of them informative, but you are forcing them to agree with the basic assumption of the question that the displays are informative and one is more informative than another.

Vagueness

It is important that any questions asked are not vague. Vague questions are those which generate responses that are difficult to interpret and even more difficult to act upon. A question commonly asked in evaluation questionnaires is: 'Have you enjoyed the exhibition?' At one level, this can be a useful question as it provides some kind of measure of overall satisfaction with the interpretation. But if one thinks about the question more closely, one can see it is rather vague and difficult to subsequently operationalise. For example, if a large proportion of visitors say that they did enjoy an exhibition, what does this really mean? If one wanted to design another exhibition that generated similar levels of enjoyment, precisely what is it about the exhibition that visitors enjoyed? What is the actual aspect of the exhibition that contributed to their enjoyment?

Ambiguity

Ambiguous questions should also be avoided. An example of a double-barrelled question would be: 'Did you find the audio-visual programme and exhibition interesting?' It could be that the audio-visual programme is interesting, but the exhibition is boring.

Systematic sampling

Another important consideration is the requirement to be systematic. Being systematic means interviewing people at the same place (e.g. at the end of the trail) and at the same time (e.g. weekday afternoons), because the kinds of visitor you receive at weekends may be different from those you get on weekdays. Likewise, the response visitors give you at the end of the trail may be different from the response they give while only halfway around. In this way the conclusions you can draw will be more specific: that is, you will be able to say something fairly precise about the type of visitors who complete the trail during weekday afternoons. Their views may be very different from visitors who do not complete the trail at weekends. If you want to come to some general conclusions about the trail, then make sure you interview people systematically across the whole length of the trail and at various times throughout the week. You must recognise though that within these results there will be a mix of visitors who have different needs, preferences and reactions.

All research methodologies involve a trade-off between level of detail, generalisability, cost and effort as well as many other factors. Only by examining individual needs, constraints and resources will it become apparent where emphases must be given.

Evaluation techniques

Various methods are used in evaluation studies: questionnaires, interviews, focus groups, observation studies, experiments and readability tests. Each of these is described briefly, but it is not possible to discuss them in any detail here. Nor is it possible to discuss how to design and analyse questionnaires, or how to conduct an observation study. Specific guidance on these and other evaluation techniques can be found elsewhere (Breakwell and Millward 1995; Breakwell *et al.* 1995; Miles *et al.* 1988; Robson 1993).

Questionnaires

Questionnaires can be used for both front-end and summative evaluation. They are particularly useful for collecting large amounts of data, where visitors are sampled according to demographic and group characteristics or how often they visit, the catchment area of the facility and service, other types of recreational destinations they visit and the reasons for their visit. Questionnaires can also be useful for collecting information on visitors' assessment of an exhibition or guided walk: Was it easy to understand? Which exhibits did they find most interesting? Are they now encouraged to explore the countryside or forest further as a consequence of learning about wildlife in the visitor centre? Questionnaires can be used for assessing learning in a fairly rudimentary way: for example, by asking visitors a series of 'quiz questions' about things they have seen in an exhibition. These kinds of data have to be treated with some caution though as they are really only a measure of recall, not learning (Chapter 13).

One advantage of questionnaire surveys is that they permit the collection of a substantial amount of standardised data, but coding this information numerically and analysing it by computer is usually the only effective way of dealing with the large amount of information that surveys generate. This is, however, at the expense of a detailed insight into the complex and often contradictory ways in which people think about issues. A questionnaire channels responses along a predetermined route with little opportunity for the individual to say 'Yes, but', to elaborate on exactly what they mean or to contextualise their responses. The meaning and significance of the world being investigated is defined by the researcher, not the respondent.

Interviews

Interviews are an important component in the evaluator's set of tools. They can be used at any stage in the evaluation process: in front-end evaluation to explore visitors' understanding and attitudes towards a subject; at the formative evaluation stage to assess visitors' reactions to a mock-up display; and at the summative evaluation stage to discuss visitors' detailed reactions to the interpretive provision. Furthermore, interviews can also inform the design of questionnaires or be used following a survey or behavioural mapping study in order to learn in more detail about issues which respondents have raised or why visitors were attracted to and their attention held by particular exhibits. Structured interviews are based on asking a set number of questions in a fixed order. In unstructured interviews, the interviewers have a number of issues which they wish to discuss and skilfully manage the interview to cover each of them while at the same time allowing the discussion to develop as naturally as possible.

Focus groups

The focus group is a discussion-based interview conducted among a small group of people. In many ways it is similar to a structured interview except that it will involve between 6 to 12 participants, with 6 to 8 being an ideal number (Millward 1995). Normally one would convene a minimum of three groups of this size in order to ensure variation either within or between groups. It is important to have a clear idea from the outset as to the composition of the focus groups. The findings generated by focus groups are not meant to be generalisable to the rest of the population. The groups should be chosen, therefore, to reflect those sections of the population whose views are most relevant in terms of the goals of the evaluation study (e.g. special interest groups, young families, the disabled). The discussion is led by a moderator who ensures that it remains focused on particular issues. As a technique it has wide currency in the advertising and marketing world where it is used among consumer groups to answer the question: why do consumers behave the way they do? In some circles it is seen as something of a 'quick and dirty' approach to accessing consumer thoughts and opinions, but it is a legitimate and cost-effective approach that has considerable potential in front-end and formative evaluation.

Observation studies

What people say they do and what they do in practice can be two very different things. Furthermore, we know from research that attitudes are not always a predictor of behaviour. What people think about something is not always a predictor of what they will do. For example, they may have negative attitudes to fast food, but one cannot assume that they will never buy fast food. If one wants information about people's behaviour the surest way of collecting accurate information is not to ask them what they do, but actually to observe them. Observations of visitor behaviour in exhibition environments involve reports of how people move and interact and how long they stay. This type of study has a long history (Melton 1972). For many years studies of visitor behaviour have focused on the 'attract' and 'hold' power of exhibits: that is, the ability of an exhibit initially to attract people's attention and then to retain their interest. This has been achieved either by discretely tracking visitors in person, by using video cameras or by time sampling at intervals to record the number of visitors at each exhibit. Behavioural mapping exercises like this use a plan of the exhibition or site to mark visitors' progress around the interpretation. The subsequent analysis provides a measure of the routes taken and the discrepancy between the route intended by the designer and the routes actually followed by the visitor, as well as the attract-and-hold power of individual exhibits.

Experiments

The essence of the experimental method is that, in its simplest form, two groups of subjects are treated in exactly the same way except one variable is different (e.g. age, sex, educational background, first time or repeat visitor). If a difference in performance is noted between the two groups then this is attributable to the one factor which differentiated the groups. Experiments usually conjure up an image of studies taking place in a laboratory. While this may occur, the experimental approach can be used in a field setting. For example, an experimental paradigm is employed when the performance of a group of visitors to an exhibition is compared with a control group of people who have not visited the exhibition. One can therefore assess whether learning has occurred if the experimental group scores significantly higher than the control group. Other kinds of experiments which can be undertaken in interpretive settings include examining the effect of different independent variables such as labelling, lighting or orientation systems on a number of dependent variables such as attention, learning or attitude change. When conducting evaluation studies with an experimental design, it is important not to infer causality from a correlation. Just because two variables may correlate closely, this does not necessarily mean that one is a cause of the other.

Readability tests

All of the techniques previously described involve interacting with members of the public in one form or another. One technique which can be very useful, is inexpensive, easy to undertake and can be carried out in less than an hour, is a readability test. This involves taking a piece of text, such as a leaflet or interpretive guide, and subjecting it to an analysis of its basic structure in order to estimate the age at which the average person could understand it. Usually this involves counting the average number of words *per se*ntence and the average number of syllables per word over a piece of text of about a hundred words. Normally one would take three samples of approximately a hundred words each in order to improve the accuracy of the test. These figures are then incorporated into a formula, the result of which is a readability or reading ease score. This figure can be translated into a school grade or age level. Typically, text should be written for a reading age of 12 to 14. Tabloid papers usually have a reading age of about 13–16; the reading age of broadsheet papers is higher. The most commonly used test is the Flesch Reading Ease Test. Some word processors now come with built-in text analysis programs. For example, one can analyse the reading age of text using the Flesch Reading Ease Test (and others) in Microsoft Word.

Generally, interviews, focus groups, surveys and observation studies concentrate on describing the kinds of people who visit museums and the preferences and attitudes which they hold. Experimental studies and some types of questionnaire survey are often concerned with assessing both preferences and learning.

Conclusion

This chapter has sought to put forward the case for undertaking evaluation studies. Evaluation is not just a fancy 'extra' but should be seen as a vital and integral part of interpretive provision and heritage management. I have tried to provide an overview of evaluation studies – the different forms they can take and the different stages in interpretive planning, implementation and use when they can be employed.

Any incipient profession needs to develop and maintain high standards. Stevens (1989) has argued that heritage has been sucked in by tourism, public relations and marketing professionals, redefined, reconstituted and repackaged to become an exercise in trivia. If heritage and environmental interpretation and management is to be more than simply a value-added component on the menu of tourism opportunities and a force for public education and change, then it will need to pursue and maintain the highest standards and be subject to constant monitoring and evaluation. It becomes impossible to improve interpretive facilities and plan future interpretive services unless one knows what is effective and why. Equally, if some aspects of interpretive provision fail, it is important to know why; otherwise future investment and changes can only be at best random.

References

Barrow, G. (1993) 'Environmental interpretation and conservation in Britain', in F. B. Goldsmith and A. Warren (eds) *Conservation in Progress*, Chichester: Wiley, pp. 271–79.

Breakwell, G. M., Fyfe-Schaw, C. and Hammond, S. (1995) *Research Methods in Psychology*, London: Sage.Breakwell, G. M. and Millward, L. (1995) *Basic Evaluation Methods: Analysing Performance, Practice and Procedure*, Leicester: British Psychological Society Books.

Lalli, M. (1992) 'Urban related identity: theory, measurement and empirical findings', *Journal of Environmental Psychology*, 12: 285–303.

Lee, T. R., Uzzell, D. L. and Henderson, J. (1980) *Forestry Commission Visitor Centres: An Evaluation Package*, internal report, Edinburgh: The Forestry Commission.

Melton, E. (1972) 'Visitor behaviour in museums: some early research in environmental design', *Human Factors*, 14(5): 393–403.

Miles, R. (1993) 'Grasping the greased pig: evaluation of educational exhibits', in S. Bicknell and G. Farmelo (eds) *Museum Visitor Studies in the 1990s*, London: Science Museum, pp. 24–33.

Miles, R. S., Alt, M. B., Gosling, D. C., Lewis, B. N. and Tout, A. F. (1988) *The Design of Educational Exhibits*, 2nd edn, London: Unwin Hyman.

Millward, L. (1995) 'Focus groups', in G.M. Breakwell, C. Fyfe-Schaw and S. Hammond, *Research Methods in Psychology*, London: Sage, pp. 27–92.

Robson, C. (1993) *Real World Research: A Resource for Social Scientists and Practitioner Researchers*, Oxford: Blackwell.

Roggenbuck, J. W. and Propst, D. B. (1981) 'Evaluation of interpretation', *Journal of Interpretation*, 6(1): 13–24.

Stevens, T. (1989) 'The visitor – who cares? Interpretation and consumer relations', in D. L. Uzzell (ed.) *Heritage Interpretation: Volume I: The Natural and Built Environment*, London: Belhaven, pp. 103–7.

Twigger-Ross, C. and Uzzell, D.L. (1996) 'Place identity and place attachment', *Journal of Environmental Psychology*, 16(2): 205–20.

Uzzell, D. L. (1992) 'Les approches socio-cognitives de l'évaluation sommative des expositions', *Publics et Musées*, 1(1): 107–23. An abbreviated version in English is published in D.L.Uzzel (1993) 'Contrasting psychological perspectives on exhibition evaluation', in S. Bicknell and G. Farmelo (eds) *Museum Visitor Studies in the 1990s*, London: Science Museum, pp. 125 –9.

Uzzell, D. L. (1995) 'Creating place identity through heritage interpretation', *International Journal of Heritage Studies*, 1(4): 219–28.

13

Evaluating the effectiveness of heritage interpretation

TERENCE R. LEE

Introduction

All interpretation should confront the issue of accountability. Can we be sure that, having clearly defined our objectives, we are actually achieving them? Are we communicating? Few professional interpreters can answer these questions convincingly, but more seriously, they do not see the point of them. To them it is obvious they are doing good.

The whole political and social climate has moved strongly in the past two decades towards quality assurance. This requires first the formation of a 'mission statement'. This may sound self-conscious, but it is simply a declaration of shared values and goals. Well-run organisations then assess their effectiveness by the use of performance indicators and the setting of targets. Quite apart from the moral obligation to provide value for money, there is the superordinate aim of achieving continuous operational improvement. This is hard to achieve unless we can make reliable and valid evaluations, not only of the total operation but also of its constituent elements.

In the contemporary scene, where the budgets of interpretive services are constantly under review by sponsors who are driven by hard-headed accountants, this issue is becoming critical. If cut-backs have to be made, services that cannot justify their usefulness are bound to be vulnerable. Professional judgement is no longer a sure defence. There has been a steep decline in the deference accorded to experts. Evidence is now what counts.

It remains a fact that the majority of interpretive centres rely for performance indicators on nothing more than 'face validity'. This means that the message should look as if it gets across – or is logically related to the desired outcome. The question is whether the human sciences can help in achieving more reliable and valid data as a spur and guide to focused action. It cannot be assumed that effectiveness is assured by employing a highly professional exhibition designer. This is exemplified by an evaluation study undertaken for the UK Atomic Energy Authority which sought to assess their exhibition stand at the annual Ideal Home Exhibition in London (Lee and Uzzell 1984). The exhibition attempted to persuade people to see nuclear power in a more favourable light. Three sets of visitors were intensively interviewed:

- visitors who passed the stand without entering;

- those who entered;

- those who were leaving.

The stand was apparently effective in one respect. It tended to attract those who were less favourably disposed towards nuclear power than the average. However, the group leaving the exhibition was even less favourably disposed than those 'matched' visitors who were interviewed on entering.

This expensive exhibition was found to be largely ineffective both in providing information and in changing attitudes in the intended direction. For example, despite a massive sign above the exhibition stand which blazoned the main message – 'Electricity from Uranium' – only about a third of the visitors could answer the simple question: 'What is the fuel used to make electricity in nuclear power stations?' This is about the same percentage that we have found in a national survey of attitudes to nuclear power. Simply providing information via wallboard displays and a film show was not enough. The fault was a lack of contact with staff, lack of a coherent thematic layout, and overuse of pictorial and textual material on beautifully designed panels which conveyed very little information, as distinct from 'real' exhibits. Most important, it concentrated on technical issues at the expense of the particularly sensitive human interest problems of nuclear safety, health effects and the disposal of radioactive waste. Many interpreters would confidently dismiss this result as exceptional because of the issues involved, but it is likely that many similar exhibitions and visitor centres would fail to stand up to this kind of close scrutiny. It follows that there is sometimes a reluctance to evaluate because it appears to undermine the professional role as well as causing extra work.

Failure to provide a clear statement of goals and values before embarking on evaluation means that sponsors, designers and managers may not be pulling in the same direction. It is generally acknowledged that the aims of interpretation are to inform, to persuade, to provide enjoyment and, ultimately, to modify behaviour. But in what proportions? To quote Lee and Balchin (1996)

The balance between learning and persuasion in this mode of communication is variable. The interpretation of an historical site may involve mainly learning; mapping the past and our place within it. A Forestry Commission Visitor Centre may do the same for the natural environment but in addition may alter our attitude towards countryside conservation or towards trees as an economic crop. The interpretation of a Second World War battlefield or a concentration camp may change one's attitude towards war. A step further brings us to the interpretation of whisky distilleries, chocolate factories or the nuclear industry. Here we are at the opposite pole on several dimensions from the museum curator – and coming close to public relations.

Lee and Balchin 1996

The issue is complicated by the fact that the various objectives of interpretation are interrelated. All rely on voluntary involvement; the visitor must first be attracted by the prospect of enjoyment. In some cases, this may be provided by the prospect of learning something new, but enjoyment of the trip normally dominates the decision to visit. A further interaction is that the enjoyment derived from scanning exhibits provides the positive reinforcement that consolidates learning. Learning is not a simple accretion of facts. The stream of information is selected, interpreted and organised to form the cognitive structures that we shall refer to as 'schemas'.

Some schemas may be neutral, free of emotional or motivational implications, but this is rare. Even railway timetables or insurance policies can attract, if only for their usefulness. Such schemata may also comprise the knowledge base of attitudes. This occurs when some environmental object or issue has become important in a person's life, whether it is liked or disliked, approached or avoided. An attitude also includes a range of possible ways of reacting to the object, ready to be selected, according to circumstances. The ultimate test in evaluating interpretation is whether attitude change has led to measurable changes in, for example, countryside conservation behaviour. Following the visit is the visitor more likely to gather up litter, keep to footpaths and close farm gates? There is only sparse evidence available on this point (McDonough and Lee 1990).

This chapter will be organised around the following important objectives of interpretation:

- attracting and holding attention;

- visitor enjoyment;

- knowledge gain;

- knowledge restructuring

- attitude change.

It will discuss each of these facets of evaluation in different settings. The author and colleagues have been associated with most of the studies referred to and are representative of the field but without aspiring to a comprehensive review (see McDonough and Lee 1990, for a review).

Attracting and holding attention

We know far too little about how to attract and hold visitor attention. Some interpreters and designers favour a hands-off and free-range approach on the grounds that people will select according to their needs. They are instinctively averse to anything that might savour of social engineering. Others prefer strict visitor control (even to the point of involuntary transport) through a sequentially evolving theme. The choice obviously depends on the subject matter. Also, one end of this continuum probably favours enjoyment and the other learning. We should not underestimate the overall effects of learning without awareness, but efforts must surely be made to increase learning with awareness.

What is certain is that many exhibits do not attract or hold very successfully. In museums, many displays are skipped altogether (Beer 1987; Ham and Shew 1979). Audio-visual displays attract, but few stay to see them through (Beer 1987; Landay and Bridge 1981; Lee *et al*. 1980). Viewing times for exhibits across a wide range of studies vary from 10 to 40 seconds (McDonough and Lee 1990). Shiner and Shafer (1975) found that visitors spent from 15 to 64 per cent of the time actually needed to read through a wallboard text.

Two simple measures are critical. The first, to use Melton's terminology (1972), is 'drawing power', i.e. how successful a display is in attracting attention. The second is 'holding power', i.e. having succeeded in attracting, for how long does it hold the attention? These indices rely on tracking visitors or time sampling the number attending to each display at, say, fifteen-minute intervals. This quantified approach is most effective if it is combined with interviews, questionnaires or attitude scales that elicit reac-

Figure 13.1 Behaviour mapping of the Queen Elizabeth Country Park Visitor Centre, Hampshire

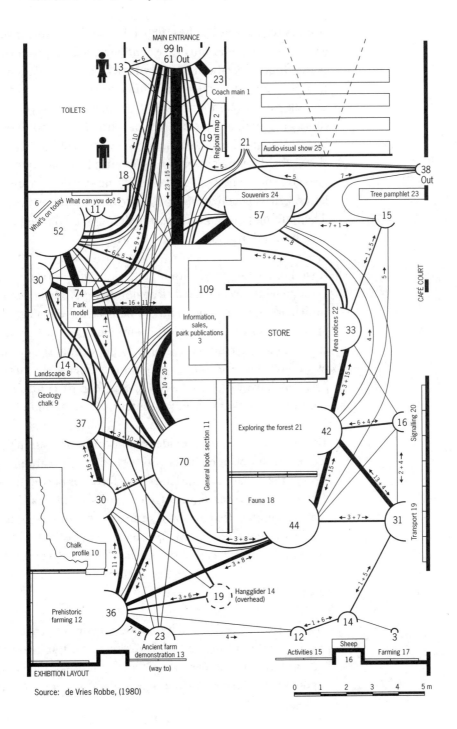

Source: de Vries Robbe, (1980)

tions to the displays and to different aspects of the overall experience, i.e. measurements of cognitions, feelings and attitudes. These techniques are subsumed as 'behavioural mapping' by environmental psychologists.

A study by de Vries Robbé (1980) is a model study of movement patterns in a visitor centre. The aim of the centre was to interpret an extensive country park (Queen Elizabeth Country Park), partly in relation to its history, but mainly relating to its flora and fauna, conservation and recreational potential. Visitors were unobtrusively tracked as they moved around the exhibition. This made it possible to plot traffic flows and to represent these by lines of proportional thickness, as shown in Figure 13.1. This plot also shows the drawing power of each exhibit by the frequency of stops shown at each exhibit and by the corresponding size of the viewing segment. The latter data were collected by separate time sampling every fifteen minutes. The holding power, i.e. the mean duration of viewing at each exhibit was also recorded (not shown in the figure).

It would have seemed natural to design a clockwise circuit because reading, in our culture, proceeds from left to right. However, in this as in many similar cases, the physical and thematic layout encouraged the reverse and 88 per cent of visitors proceeded anti-clockwise. Interestingly, 39 per cent of these dropped out – while only 17 per cent of the clockwise visitors fell by the wayside. We should not infer too much from this because the samples may have varied in other respects (e.g. percentage of repeat visitors) and sequential thematic development was not prominent in this centre.

The author found little evidence for 'museum fatigue' after correlating sequential order of exhibits with drawing power frequency and ascribed most of the variance in the latter to differences between visitors' interest in the various activities depicted. However, secondary analysis shows that the data are a better fit to the 'hard centre' model discussed below. This would mask a linear correlation coefficient. It was already found (as is clearly visible from Figure 13.1) that the mean drawing power for the second half of the exhibition (mean = 25.7) was substantially lower than the first half (mean = 42.7).

The exhibits were divided into those that oriented the visitor to the interpretive themes, those that were directly related, and those that were irrelevant. Observation showed that 30 per cent of the total drawing power was devoted to the 25 per cent of the exhibits that were judged to be irrelevant.

A measure of 'required viewtime' was derived for nineteen of the displays that included textual material. This was based on reading time at 300 words per minute, plus 5 seconds for scanning each illustration or object. These estimates are inevitably somewhat arbitrary but are none the less likely to be adequate for comparative purposes. A substantial correlation (r = 0.80; p <0.001) was found between required and observed mean viewing times. It is encouraging that visitors respond to increased quantity of information with extended attention and this seems at first sight to contradict the frequent admonitions to keep displays simple in order to encompass the low mean reading age. However, Wittlin (1971) has described how visitors focus first at a distance that allows the whole exhibit to form a gestalt and then move closer in order to break up this Gestalt into smaller ones. Hence, an extended 'required viewing time' may simply reflect attention to a series of discrete panels, objects, or labelled subtexts.

Figure 13.2 Differences in comprehension between pre-visit and post-visit respondents

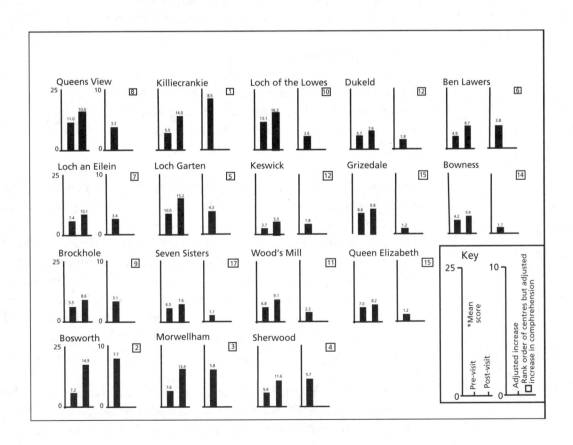

This suggests that panels should be clearly delineated and arranged stepwise so that viewers can (a) select information that is congruent with existing schemata; (b) select information at an appropriate level; and (c) elaborate and differentiate their schemata. This progression is the quintessence of learning.

De Vries Robbé (1980) found that on average visitors viewed exhibitions for only 15.6 per cent of the time required to perceive them. He then computed an actual–required time ratio to index the effectiveness of each one. The aim was to compare this measure of 'holding power' with a number of predictor variables. Using canonical correlation, he explored whether the effectiveness indices of the various exhibits that aimed to guide and interpret 'walking in the park' were related to (a) the intended behaviours; and (b) the intended locations of those leaving the centre. No relationship was found. The measures of effectiveness were then correlated with the departing visitors' descriptions of exhibits which had been of greatest interest. This was significant ($r = 0.84$; $p < 0.02$) but only in relation to the two historical exhibits with highest holding power, confirming the finding of Fothergill *et al* (1978) that historical themes are most effective.

Visitor enjoyment

The prospect of enjoyment dominates the decision to visit. Even visitors to an institution as academically oriented as the British Museum of Natural History see it as a 'place of entertainment' (Miles *et al.* 1988). It obviously behoves the interpreter to maximise this anticipation – for without visitor flow all other objectives are obviously weakened.

Unfortunately, it is difficult to study those who stay away. A visitor profile, as well as showing who has responded, can identify subgroups that are absent. Even more helpful, however, is to survey visitors' reasons for coming and determine what they have most enjoyed. Two studies in the literature have shown that the activities and exhibits that interpretation staff consider to be most enjoyed by visitors are not the ones reported by visitors themselves (Ham and Shew 1979). Roth and Hodgson (1977) were able to demonstrate that prior training on how to perceive an exhibition increased both learning (in the sense of increased cognitive complexity) and enjoyment.

It is not a safe assumption that because people enjoy themselves on the visit they will necessarily learn more. An extensive study was carried out on seventeen visitor centres in all parts of England and Scotland by a combined team from Dartington Amenity Research Trust and the University of Surrey Department of Psychology (Fothergill *et al.* 1978). The centres were deliberately chosen to be varied, because it was the effect of these differences upon visitors that we aimed to explore. For example, some were historic, e.g. Killiecrankie and Bosworth Field; some were natural-history based, e.g. Woods Mill and Brockhole; others mainly concerned with conservation and landscape, e.g. Loch of the Lowes and Seven Sisters. Sizes varied from 40 square metres up to 232 square metres of exhibition space. Some included guided walks or trails, others had observation hides and all used a variety of display techniques.

Almost 3,000 visitors were interviewed; about a third pre-visit and two-thirds post-visit. The interview covered biographical data and then three main objectives: knowledge gain, enjoyment and motivation. Analysis of the data enabled the provision of detailed visitor profiles for each centre as well as aggregate-level data to facilitate comparisons between centres. Thematically, the top three centres for enjoyment in the study of seventeen visitor centres (Fothergill *et al.* 1978) were of the comprehensive kind, where least learning occurred. Also, there were seven centres which had guided walks or trails associated with them and the experience was that these were also high in enjoyment. The size of the centre appeared to influence enjoyment positively, although it too was inversely related to learning.

The original analysis of this study was univariate, i.e. it looked at the influence of variables one at a time. Moscardo and Pearce (1986) carried out a further interesting analysis of the published data set, using partial correlation analysis. The knowledge gain/enjoyment partial correlation became even more negative ($r = -0.508$) when the demographic characteristics of visitors (i.e. age, education, size of group) were added to the equation. Younger people learned more, but older, less well-educated people in larger groups enjoyed themselves.

We do not find the negative correlation to be surprising; indeed, it is more plausible than a zero relationship. This is because the construction and extension of schemata is an active, seeking process; it is hard work. It may be perceived as satisfying but not necessarily as enjoyable. The latter is associated more with relaxation.

The concept of schema has been introduced because it is recognised as a more valid model than the layman's assumption that learning is a process of passive osmosis, in which the nature of the stimulus and the length of exposure are the main determinants. On the contrary, pre-existent knowledge and attitudes are extremely important in governing both what is attended to, how it is construed, whether it is assimilated to an existing package of knowledge and, if so, to which one.

Interestingly, Moscardo and Pearce (1986), in the secondary analysis of the Seventeen Visitor Centres research, while acknowledging the relevance of the schema model, used a partial concept called 'mindfulness' (Bandura *et al.* 1984; Langer *et al.* 1978). They described this as an indication of an active mental state combining measures of knowledge gain, subjective assessment of new learning, wanting more information on the topic and wanting more from the centre. This index was moderately correlated ($r = 0.402$) with enjoyment. Moscardo *et al.* have further developed its application to visitor responses. Its relevance to interpretation and visitor centres is that it is 'characterised by detailed attention to a task or activity and analytic processing of material resulting in changes to cognitive structures' (Moscardo and Pearce 1986). This distinction is now more widely recognised in the scientific literature on attitude change or persuasion as one between central and peripheral cognitive processing. The former is hard work but its effects are more enduring (Eagly and Chaiken 1993).

Knowledge gain

Whether it is called 'informing', 'educating' or 'increasing understanding', the dominant aim of most visitor centres is to add to the knowledge of visitors. This is usually evaluated by questioning them on what they recall of the exhibits they have seen. Such approaches can be derided as 'quiz questioning'. Taken alone, they certainly do not comprise a depth of understanding. But they can be valuable indicators, especially if carefully chosen to require comprehension of concepts as well as facts.

In the study of Seventeen Visitor Centres (Fothergill *et al.* 1978), we devised a set of six questions about the most recognisable and prominent displays in the exhibition. In addition, mounted colour photographs of some of the distinctive artefacts or illustrations were shown and the visitors were asked if they could name them and describe briefly the point they appeared to be making within the theme. These 'recall' and 'recognition' items were combined to make a scale with a maximum score of 30. Every effort was made to match the difficulty across centres, but of course the diversity made this difficult and any comparison is approximate.

A correlation between the 'raw' scores and the percentage gain before/after showed no relationship. Hence, the results shown in Figure 13.2 are based on raw score increases. The expected substantial difference (i.e. an increase) in knowledge gain was found with social class and years of education but not with the relevance of subjects studied at school. Those who had made previous visits to the centre tended to have a higher pre-score and to gain more from their visit. It would appear that there is some evidence here that the effects are enduring, but of course those who show sufficient interest to visit more than once are a special group. Holidaymakers learned more than day-trippers, possibly because they had more time and were more relaxed. With regard to type of party, those visiting with both family and friends learned least, followed by those who visited alone; those who visited with friends had the highest gain. The latter are more likely to be adults (less distracting and more patient than children), but it is also of interest that those who visit in a family group are probably prompted by each other or by a parental need to supplement and reinforce the message with their own interpretive efforts.

Turning to type of centre, the material in historical centres, as distinct from that concerned with the countryside, led to a greater knowledge gain among visitors. Also, there was a clear difference between those centres where the 'museum' influence was pre-eminent, (i.e. with a large assortment of artefacts and more scholarly aims), and those presenting a clear *theme* with a sequential development and one through which the visitor was steered through, instead of being 'let loose'. The latter centres showed significantly more knowledge gain.

Knowledge restructuring

It was earlier noted that quiz questions may provide quantitative indicators of knowledge gain, but more sophisticated measures are required if we are to assess understanding. This was attempted in a study of three Farm Open Days (Lee and Uzzell 1980). Although it is usually a one-day event, organised by volunteers, the farm open day is typical interpretation. Its explicit aim is to 'educate' townspeople about the agricultural industry in order to ensure their continuing support. This means not only enhancing their knowledge but also changing their attitudes towards farming as an occupation and a lifestyle. It is also hoped to encourage townspeople, when using the countryside for leisure, to recognise the need both to preserve the heritage and to respect its role as a means of production.

The theory of schema and its relevance to perceptual learning in visitor centres had already been broached retrospectively as a model in the Seventeen Visitor Centres study. In the Farm Open Day study it formed the main rationale, although 'quiz questions' were not entirely abandoned. I quote here the original description of the schema approach:

> It is assumed that, in their many transactions with the environment, people construct cognitive 'images' in the mind; structured, organised 'inner representations' of the countryside. The farm, for example, is a complicated pattern of social working relationships mapped on to a geographical setting of fields, farm buildings, dwellings and roads, etc. The image of the farm that people form integrates all this information. An accepted term that we shall use to describe such an image is the 'schema'.

> The process by which people learn about farming is one of constructing, through repeated experiences, a corresponding schema in the mind. Learning is emphatically not the acquisition of a small and random proportion of presented 'facts'. On the contrary, it is a dynamic development. The schema assimilates new material selectively, absorbing information that is compatible with what is there already; it also modifies itself in order that certain information that would otherwise be incompatible can be accommodated or 'locked on' to the relevant schema.

> This is the way in which people divide up their experiences of things and events. It is by constructing schemas that they give meaning to their perceptions and it is their schemas that are consulted when they have to act.

> *Fothergill et al. 1978: 8–9*

In the earlier study (Fothergill *et al*. 1978), the schema had been invoked to explain the fact that displays and artefacts are likely to be found interesting and to be remembered better if they form easy connections to the visitors own experiences and emotions. For example, historical items were found more likely to stay in the memory than natural history items – unless the latter are given some human immediacy. This may be achieved, for example, by emphasising the relevance of the natural environment to life style to food, or to manufactured items such as furniture or clothes. The best remembered of all displays in the study of seventeen visitor centres was the 'soldier's leap' at Killiecrankie – the legendary, superhuman leap across the gorge by a highlander escaping from the pursuing troops of the king, following a battle. Conversely, the information associated with cross-sections of named trees to reveal their grain, often seen in natural history and forestry centres, is hard to retain. The same applies to exhibition panels that illustrate the undoubted beauty of fifty butterflies or the mysteries of geological events in the Pleistocene period.

This socio-spatial cognitive model is described in some detail because it has governed the methods of research we have adopted and because these methods are fairly radical. The quiz question approach, referred to previously, is a useful device but it is only a crude index of the enhancement in understanding that may have taken place. People's attitudes and judgements may have been changed by a learning experience although they may be unable to recall specific facts.

What we therefore attempted to measure in this study is not only facts but the form and complexity of the structure in which these facts are embedded – the schema of farming. In attempting to do this we used two different questionnaire approaches and subjected the results to sophisticated computer analyses. The schema of the farm is relatively stereotyped for the town dweller. For some, 'a farm is a farm is a farm'. Children's story-books (e.g. *Blackberry Farm*) convey the prototypical farm. The essence of learning is to construct a more differentiated, complex schema from successive inputs that are actively organised into a structure. (See Plates 13.1 and 13.2.)

Differentiation of farm schemata

Our first approach to the measurement of this process was to use the tool known as a 'repertory grid' (Fransella and Bannister 1977; Kelly 1955). This assumes that different types of farm are perceived to possess different attributes (Kelly referred to different elements being evaluated by different constructs – the principle is the same). The 'difference between farms' form presents a grid with the schemata as rows and the attributes as columns. The respondent is asked to say how accurate the attribute is as a descriptor of each of his/her schemata by using a 7–point scale. The schemas were four different types of farm: dairy, livestock, cropping , market gardening. The attributes are listed in Table 13.1. The study was carried out in three very large (i.e. over 1,400 acres) mixed farms. A sample of 82 visitors was interviewed as they arrived and (a different) 62 on departure.

TABLE 13.1: MEAN CONSTRUCT SCORES AND STATISTICALLY SIGNIFICANT CHANGES IN 'BEFORE' AND 'AFTER' SCORES: DAIRY FARMING

	Before	After	Before/After
Cleanliness is vital	6.79 (1)	6.82 (2)	
Seven-day working week	6.25 (2)	6.87 (1)	t = -3.00 (p <0.001)
Requires a lot of capital	5.84 (3)	6.17 (3)	t = -1.81 (p <0.05)
Skilled labour is required	5.39 (4)	5.79 (4)	t = -1.72 (p <0.05)
Good quality land needed	5.37 (5)	5.67 (5)	
Highly scientific approach used	5.30 (6)	5.64 (6)	
Needs lots of land	4.96 (7)	4.81 (9)	
Uses lots of machinery	4.82 (8)	5.50 (7)	t = -2.71 (p <0.005)
Needs sheltered land not too exposed	4.68 (9)	5.10 (8)	t = -1.75 (p <0.05)
Weather is important	4.60 (10)	4.69 (10)	
Financially risky	4.41 (11)	4.61 (11)	
Large profits made	4.41 (11)	4.51 (12)	
Employs many workers	3.78 (13)	4.03 (13)	
Nine to five working day	2.01 (14)	1.74 (14)	

n = before 82, after 62; rank order in brackets

Plate 13.1
A demonstration of sheep shearing at a Farm Open Day in Scotland
Source: David Uzzell

Despite the relatively small samples and the fact that these were independent (i.e. not 'repeat' measures), there were enough statistically significant changes to be sure that real changes in understanding had occurred. Of the fourteen attributes, significant differences (before/after) were found in seven of the attribute scales for dairy farming, seven for Livestock, four for General Cropping and five for market gardening. It should also be noted that all three of the farms included in the programme which the visitors actually experienced, were mixed farms. The results for dairy farming are shown in Table 13.1 as an example. Two of the significant changes (not shown) occured on single open days.

By analysing the relative size of the variances for each of the attributes, it is possible to deduce their perceived importance for distinguishing between farms – and whether their use is modified as a result of the interpretive experience. (Variance is the degree of dispersion of scores from the mean (average) score.) It is possible to express the total variance for all 14 attributes and then to calculate the percentage of this that is due to each one. This showed that five of the attributes were found particularly relevant for discriminating between farms by the pre-visit sample. 'Uses lots of machinery' was the most important and it remained so. Thereafter, four further

Plate 13.2
A tractor and trailer ride around a farm, East Sussex
Source: David Uzzell

attributes were called upon about equally, dealing respectively with the importance to farming of good quality land, sheltered land, good weather and cleanliness.

However, our main interest here is in change, and it was found that the attributes were used differently following the interpretive experience. The need for good quality land and sheltered land were now seen as less critical – because they are essential, it seems, for all farms. Weather became a more important discriminator because it matters less for dairy and livestock than for general cropping and market gardening. There was also greater discrimination by the characteristics of the work pattern. This is the extent to which it is true that farming imposes a nine to five working day and/or a seven-day working week. This, again, depends on the type of farm, i.e. they are most accurate as, respectively, positive and negative descriptors of dairy farming and, to a lesser extent, livestock. whereas general cropping and market gardens are seen in reverse.

The same kind of analysis applied to the four farm types showed that pre-visit, people's schemata were dominated by livestock and general cropping, i.e. these were closer to their stereotype, but on departure the visitors had widened their range to perceive all four types more equally. Ideally, we would have liked to measure the schemata of a sample of experienced farmers and to confirm whether the public had moved closer to these 'expert' views. Our subjective impression was that all the changes were in this direction.

The image of farming: attributes of the farming schema

Another technique used at the three Farm Open Days was to present samples of 'before' and 'after' visitors with twenty-four 'statements' about the financial, occupational and social aspects of farming, i.e. attributes of farming. The respondents were asked to assess the accuracy of these statements, i.e. how well they described the industry. The twenty-four statements, together with the mean before/after scores, are shown in Table 13.2. It will be seen that six of the statements (19–24) refer to 'countryside' as distinct from farming in an attempt to tap into people's schemata of this wider socio-spatial schema and its recreational/leisure aspects.

TABLE 13.2 MEAN SCORES FOR IMAGE OF FARMING STATEMENTS (ALL FARMS)

		Before	After	t value	p <
1.	Farming is a seven-day-a-week activity	6.62 (1)	6.71 (1)		
2.	Farming is a major British industry	5.88 (2)	5.75 (5)		
3.	Farming has changed over the years	5.85 (3)	5.95 (2)		
4.	Farming is physically hard work	5.84 (4)	5.89 (3)		
5.	Farming is subject to government involvement	5.84 (4)	5.64 (7)		
6.	Farmers feel close to nature	5.63 (6)	5.40 (8)		
7.	Farming is highly mechanised and scientific	5.51 (7)	5.89 (3)	-1.73	0.05
8.	Farming is highly organised	5.41 (8)	5.67 (6)		
9.	Farming is subject to modern day stresses	5.04 (9)	4.98 (10)		
10.	Farming is a family business	5.03 (10)	4.42 (16)	2.25	0.01
11.	The countryside is working farmland	4.85 (11)	4.71 (12)		
12.	Farmers experience problems from visitors to the countryside	4.84 (12)	5.08 (9)		
13.	Farming is financially rewarding	4.79 (13)	4.96 (11)		
14.	In the countryside old-fashioned values still exist	4.66 (14)	4.57 (13)		
15.	Farming is subject to trade union involvement	4.41 (15)	4.44 (15)		
16.	In the countryside life is slow, peaceful and quiet	4.12 (16)	4.46 (14)		
17.	Farmers have contact with holiday makers/day trippers	4.09 (17)	4.00 (18)		
18.	Farming is a man's world	4.03 (18)	4.23 (17)		
19.	Farms are like factories	3.67 (19)	3.61 (20)		
20.	In the countryside children and dogs can play	3.59 (20)	3.59 (21)		
21.	Farming is easy for outsiders to join	3.54 (21)	3.62 (19)		
22.	In the countryside you can picnic in green fields	3.20 (22)	2.93 (23)		
23.	The countryside is the playground of the city	3.14 (23)	3.27 (22)		
24.	Farming is only a nine to five day	1.36 (24)	1.71 (24)	-1.61	0.05

n = before 100; after 59

Only three of the changes reach statistical significance, but overall they show clear trends that were consistent with the organisers' aims. The perception that farming is highly mechanised and scientific, already quite well established at the pre-visit stage, was strongly reinforced, as was the evaluation that farming is highly organised, financially rewarding and has changed over the years. At the more political level, agriculture had, and continues to have, a high profile due to the public perception of government protection and control. However, this direct contact with the more entrepreneurial side of the industry resulted in quite a marked reversal, reflected in lower scores on 'farming is a major British industry' and 'farming is subject to government control'.

From the sponsor's point of view, changes in the visitors' attitudes towards the use of the countryside for recreation were cause for encouragement. The idea that 'children and dogs can play' and that 'you can picnic in green fields' received slightly less support and the statement 'the countryside is working farmland' slightly more.

In attempting to look at the overall patterns, pre and post, we applied a 'multi-dimensional scaling' procedure known as 'smallest space analysis' (SSA) (Shye 1978). This uses the correlations between sample responses to each and all of the twenty-four statements, to arrive at an optimal distribution of the statements in two–dimensional space. This 'solution' is governed by the prescription to locate those 'statements' that are perceived as similar close together – and those seen as different far apart.

The resulting 'plots' for the pre- and post-visit responses are shown in Figures 13.3 and 13.4. It will be seen that there is a significantly more orderly pattern for the post-visit sample. It is more structured than the pre-visit plot. The arrows in Figure 13.4 show some of the most important 'readjustments' in the space resulting from the visit. Much of the movement makes 'farming as an industry' more coherent. What is also impressive is that the statements referring to farming as countryside with potential for leisure were scattered quite widely in the 'pre' plot. Five of the six moved to form a coherent and close-knit group after the visit. We can summarise this by saying that people appeared to have clarified their ideas about farming and the countryside. Methodologically, this is a far cry from an improvement in the scores on a set of quiz questions. But this kind of learning also took place. Ten questions based on the factual information provided at each farm showed significant before/after improvement.

Probably uniquely, this evaluation study included a follow-up to see whether the effects of the visit survived for two months or more. Addresses were obtained from a children's competition in which prizes had been promised. The respondents were contacted in advance and fifty from an area of about forty miles from the farms were visited. The 'difference between farms' questionnaire was readministered, as well as the 'quiz' test. Much was retained from the conceptual reorientation that had taken place two months before and, in the case of dairy and livestock farming, some of the shifts had been reinforced. Many of the answers to 'quiz questions' had been lost, but there was still a small but significant improvement over the pre-visit knowledge.

Attitude change

The Sellafield plant of BNFL (British Nuclear Fuels Ltd) in Cumbria is primarily concerned with the reprocessing of spent nuclear fuel, not only from the UK but also from Japan, Germany and other countries. It is a huge complex employing over 7,000 people. It is involved also in fuel manufacture, waste management, decommissioning, electricity generation and, increasingly, high technology research and development. It is a major icon in the industrial culture of the UK, for it was here in 1946 that the world's first civil nuclear reactor (Calder Hall) generated electricity for domestic consumption. At that time, the public was strongly supportive, excited by the project of limitless cheap energy. However, it is well known that the Sellafield site and nuclear power generally have become chronically controversial issues.

The company felt that its poor public image, partly due to its inextricable link with nuclear weapons and the Cold War, was being amplified by the media and the unremitting opposition of environmentalist groups. This tarnished reputation, the company felt, was not justified by its record in health and safety. The charges that radioactive emissions were the cause of a leukaemia cluster in the local population and, later, the cause of inherited defects in the children of workers were not substantiated by the scientific evidence and eventually withdrawn. However, there remains the enduring criticism that emissions (despite dramatic reductions over the years) are polluting the Irish Sea.

The decision was made to invest considerable sums of money in a publicity campaign. The explicit aim of this was to 'educate' the public. The major planks in the campaign were a 'nothing to hide day trip' tour of the site and an ambitious visitor centre, recording over 130,000 visitors each year. However controversial the issue, this mix of teaching, persuasion and enjoyment is quintessential heritage interpretation. (See Plates 13.3 and 13.4.)

Outline of the study

What we wanted to know about the exhibition was (a) whether people's knowledge of the nuclear industry and its technology is enhanced by the interpretation; if so, (b) what contribution is made by the various displays; and (c) whether attitudes towards nuclear power change and, if so, in respect of which aspects: environmental, health related, economic etc.

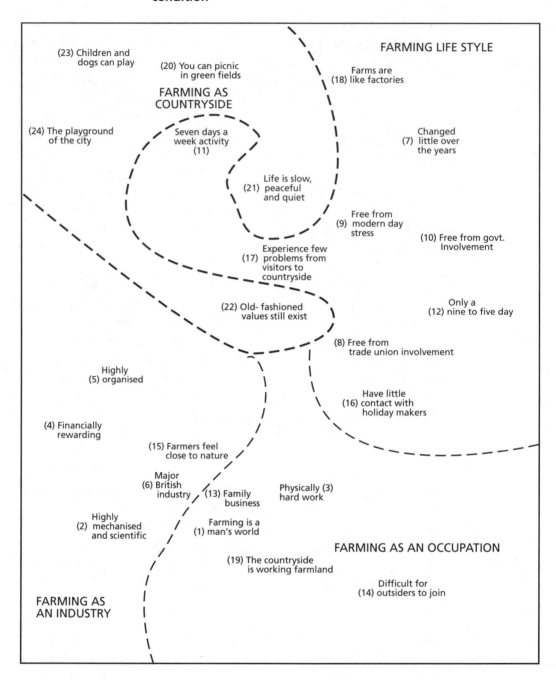

Figure 13.3 Smallest space analysis (SSA) of farm data for 'before' condition

FARMING LIFE STYLE

(23) Children and dogs can play

(20) You can picnic in green fields

Farms are (18) like factories

FARMING AS COUNTRYSIDE

(24) The playground of the city

Seven days a week activity (11)

Changed (7) little over the years

Life is slow, (21) peaceful and quiet

Free from (9) modern day stress

(10) Free from govt. Involvement

Experience few (17) problems from visitors to countryside

(22) Old-fashioned values still exist

Only a (12) nine to five day

(8) Free from trade union involvement

Highly (5) organised

Have little (16) contact with holiday makers

(4) Financially rewarding

(15) Farmers feel close to nature

Major (6) British industry

(13) Family business

Physically (3) hard work

Highly (2) mechanised and scientific

Farming is a (1) man's world

FARMING AS AN OCCUPATION

(19) The countryside is working farmland

Difficult for (14) outsiders to join

FARMING AS AN INDUSTRY

Figure 13.4 Smallest space analysis (SSA) of farm data for 'after' condition

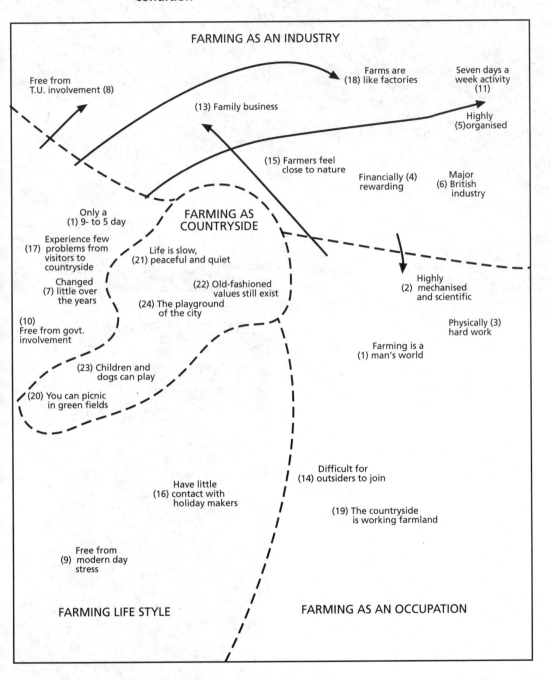

FARMING AS AN INDUSTRY

Free from
T.U. involvement (8)

Farms are
(18) like factories

Seven days a
week activity
(11)

(13) Family business

Highly
(5)organised

(15) Farmers feel
close to nature

Financially (4)
rewarding

Major
(6) British
industry

Only a
(1) 9- to 5 day

FARMING AS
COUNTRYSIDE

Experience few
(17) problems from
visitors to
countryside

Life is slow,
(21) peaceful and quiet

Changed
(7) little over
the years

(22) Old-fashioned
values still exist

Highly
(2) mechanised
and scientific

(24) The playground
of the city

Physically (3)
hard work

(10)
Free from govt.
involvement

Farming is a
(1) man's world

(23) Children and
dogs can play

(20) You can picnic
in green fields

Difficult for
(14) outsiders to join

Have little
(16) contact with
holiday makers

(19) The countryside
is working farmland

Free from
(9) modern day
stress

FARMING LIFE STYLE

FARMING AS AN OCCUPATION

Plates 13.3 and 13.4
Sellafield Visitor
Centre
Source: Terence R. Lee

(Lee and Balchin 1996). Three instruments were designed – a nuclear knowledge questionnaire, a pictorial knowledge test and a nuclear attitude scale. All were applied to pre- and post-visit samples. In addition, a time sampling method was used to measure the 'attract/hold' effectiveness of different displays.

The knowledge questionnaire included a series of seventeen multiple choice and open-ended questions, based on the eight sections of the exhibition. For example: 'The most penetrative form of radioactivity is …?' and 'The rate at which fuel is converted to energy in the reactor core is …?' This was augmented with a pictorial test in which sets of four photographs showing individual displays were randomly selected from a total of eighteen for showing to each respondent. These items were relatively unfamiliar to visitors, so it was not difficult to determine from the responses whether they had studied the displays and if their function was understood.

The attitude questionnaire comprised a thirty-item Likert scale on various aspects of nuclear power. It was found to have good reliability (Cronbach's alpha = 0.888). Most of the statements were cognitive, i.e. concerned with beliefs about nuclear power. Respondents were asked to agree/disagree on a 5-point scale. Examples are: 'Britain can safely manage the long term storage of radioactive wastes'; 'Nuclear power is good for the progress of scientific and technical research'; and 'Nuclear power seriously threatens people's health.' However, a proportion of explicitly emotional items was included, for instance: 'The thought of nuclear flasks being transported across the country gives me a slightly sick feeling'; 'When I think about nuclear power I experience mild feelings of anxiety.'

The data were subjected to principal components analysis (PCA). The aim of this is to identify groups of items that go together and clearly underlie the overall responses. These are 'factors' derived from the full matrix of intercorrelations between each item and every other. The outcome was a set of five subscales, each measuring a different aspect (component) of people's attitudes: economic and technological; health and safety; emotional feelings; environmental; passive acceptance aspects.

Display effectiveness was assessed by means of behaviour mapping. This involved a sample count of the number of visitors in the vicinity of the eight main sections and seventeen display groupings of the exhibition. Since movement through these sections is controlled, the sequential order remains the same for each visitor, which enabled us to test the effect of this spatial variable.

The results

The two knowledge tests (i.e. pictorial and questionnaire) were moderately correlated (rho = 0.580) and this was useful confirmation of their validity. On the questionnaire there was a substantial gain in knowledge across a sample of 245.

The use of 'analysis of variance' allows us to examine the relationships between knowledge and attitude scores and to break the data down by different types of respondent. For example, it was found that men knew more than women initially, as did those with higher educational experience. Age groups did not differ. However, all these groups made about the same knowledge gains from the visit. In attitude terms, those who began with relatively greater knowledge were those who also brought with them more positive attitudes towards the environmental effects of nuclear power; those with little prior knowledge were more likely to have brought an attitude of passive acceptance. Other relationships between knowledge level and attitudes were non-significant.

The predicted effect of spatial position was found. This was rather uneven because the 'attract' and 'hold' strength of a display is obviously affected also by its intrinsic interest. Notwithstanding this, if the two sections at the beginning and two at the end are compared with the four middle sections, the predicted difference is clearly demonstrated (Chi-squared = 249.13; p <0.001). This effect was put down to 'museum fatigue' in early studies, but this does not explain the 'end spurt' very well, unless we add a feeling of guilt (at the lack of concentration) that builds up as the exit approaches. The effect is also found, however, in the learning of poetry and prose, where more complex explanations have been advanced, i.e. the 'bowed serial position curve' (Deese and Hulse 1967).

The critical importance for interpretation is that the 'hard centre' effect has to be taken into account in any attempt to compare the intrinsic effectiveness of displays. If the layout is thematic, displays cannot be rotated in order to isolate the effects from those of spatial positioning.

It is worth noting that the knowledge gain for different displays varies over a wide range and the effects of 'human interest' were once again heavily confirmed. For example, the most effective exhibit, in learning terms, was an exhibition panel demonstrating the barriers needed to protect against different types of radioactive particle.

Turning to attitudes, the single question put to 'arrival' visitors: 'Are you generally in favour or against the use of nuclear power for generating electricity?' yielded 62 per cent in favour, 20 per cent against and 18 per cent uncommitted. This is similar to BNFL's own findings and those from other sources. The aggregate score on the attitude scale showed a significant difference between the 'before' and 'after' samples ($F = 1.245 - 3.57$, $p < .001$) in the direction of more 'pro' nuclear.

More revealing are the changes recorded in the subscales and these are summarised in Table 13.3. There were positive attitude changes across the board ('main effects') for two of the subscales and changes that were limited to part of the sex or age range ('interactions') for two other subscales. It is particularly notable that the Visitor Centre makes no impact on the emotional feelings about nuclear power, except for a negative change in younger visitors. Health and safety attitudes are changed in the direction of reduced anxiety, but only for males, who are least worried to begin with.

TABLE 13.3 ATTITUDE CHANGE RESULTING FROM SELLAFIELD VISITOR CENTRE

Attitude subscale	Change
General economic and technical value	Positive change for all
Health and safety	Positive change for males only
Emotional feelings	Negative change: young, less educated only
Environment	Positive change for all
Passive acceptance	No change

Note: ANOVAs were computed in each of the five scales in a 2 x 2 x 4 design. All changes shown are significant at $p < 0.05$.

Conclusion

Evaluation should be an essential part of the original design and subsequent improvement of exhibitions and visitor centres. The methods and tools of interpretive evaluation are not new. They may be considered as part of a wider field known as 'visitor studies', the origins of which can be traced to the classic studies of visitor behaviour in museums and art galleries during the 1930s (Melton 1933, 1935, 1972; Robinson 1930, 1931). This had led to a very important distinction between 'formative evaluation' and 'summative' or 'post hoc' evaluation (Miles *et al.*1988). In the former, exhibits are constructed as 'mock-ups' which a sample of visitors is asked to view and discuss. This leads to progressive modification until the display is judged to be both understandable and interesting. In the latter, evaluation is carried out on existing exhibitions and embraces both visitor movement patterns and responses to displays.

Effectiveness should not be taken for granted. In particular, there is an undoubted tendency for professional designers to aim for visual impact devoting, for example, too much of the budget to displays that may be eye-catching but which do not carry a message of much substance. The converse of this – the Achilles heel of the expert informer (or persuader) – is to extend and enrich the written text to a degree that makes it redundant at best and discouraging at worst.

Attitude change has been the subject of considerable research in social psychology (Lee 1986). The main variables influencing the process fall into four groups:

- the perceived credibility of the message source, e.g. expertise, honesty, attractiveness;

- the message itself, e.g. clarity, comprehension, argument ordering;

- the media used for transmission; and

- the characteristics of the target audience.

They obviously interact: for example, although there are important principles that apply to all messages, the message also needs to be adjusted to the particular target audience.

The aim of changing visitor attitudes is usually implicit in visitor centres. In a study of Forestry Commission visitor centres Lee *et al.* (1980) found that even the staff in the centres, when asked what themes were being presented, found it difficult to formulate an answer. They tended simply to describe the exhibits. This is patently less true of the visitor centres provided by the nuclear industry. While not neglecting enjoyment, the explicit aim is to change public attitudes towards nuclear power by providing information on its scientific and technical basis. The important point is that the exhibition designer should be aiming to optimise these four variables when setting up a visitor centre or exhibition.

Heritage and environmental managers and interpreters will need to become considerably more mindful of the type of research described here if they are to meet the challenge of accountability. At present, most interpreters rely on 'face validity' when challenged in respect of effectiveness. The clients trust their 'expertise', but in future are increasingly likely to ask for evidence that all four of the major communication variables (credibility of the communicator, the message, the media, the characteristics of the target audience) have been systematically considered. Next, the clients will ask for evidence that visitors have comprehended, can recall the message and have understood it conceptually; also, where relevant, that their attitudes have been modified in the intended direction. This confirmation will be required not only for the 'experience' as a whole, but for its component parts, so that these can be refined where necessary.

References

Aldridge, D. (1975) *Guide to Countryside Interpretation: Principles of Countryside Interpretation and Interpretive Planning*, London: HMSO.

Bandura, M. M., Langer, E. J. and Chanowitz, B. (1984) 'Interpersonal effectiveness from a mindlessness/mindfulness perspective', in P. Trower (ed.) *Radical Approaches to Social Skills Training*, London: Croom Helm.

Beer, V. (1987) 'Great expectations: do museums know what visitors are doing?', *Curator* 30(3): 206–15.

Bitgood, S. C. and Loomis, R. J. (1993) 'Environmental design and evaluation in museums', *Environment and Behaviour*, 25: 683–97.

Deese, J. and Hulse, S. H. (1967) *The Psychology of Learning*, 3rd edn, New York: McGraw Hill.

de Vries Robbé (1980) 'Countryside interpretation: the interaction between countryside visitors and interpretive displays', unpublished MSc thesis in Environmental Psychology, University of Surrey.

Eagly, A. H. and Chaiken, S. (1993) *The Psychology of Attitudes*, London: Harcourt, Brace and Jovanovich.

Falk, J. H. and Dierking, L. D. (1992) *The Museum Experience*, Washington DC: Whalesback Books.

Fothergill, J., Binks, G., Dower, M., Lee, T. R. and Stringer, P. (1978) *Interpretation in Visitor Centres* (CCP115), Cheltenham: Countryside Commission.

Fransella, F. and Bannister, D. (1977) *A Manual for Repertory Grid Technique*, London: Academic Press.

Ham, S. H. and Shew, R. L. (1979) 'A comparison of visitors' and interpreters' assessments of conducted interpretive activities', *Journal of Interpretation*, 4(2): 39–44.

Kelly, G. A. (1955) *The Psychology of Personal Constructs* (vols 1 and 2), New York: W. W. Norton.

Landay, J. and Bridge, R. G. (1981) 'Video vs. wall-panel display: an experiment in museum learning', *Curator*, 25(10): 41–56.

Langer, E. J., Blank, A. and Chanowitz, B. (1978) 'The mindlessness of ostensibly thoughtful action', *Journal of Personality and Social Psychology*, 36: 635–42.

Lee, T. R. (1986) 'Effective communication of information about chemical hazards', *The Science of the Total Environment*, 51: 149–83.

Lee, T. R. and Balchin, N. (1996) 'Learning and attitude change at British Nuclear Fuel's Sellafield Visitors Centre', *Journal of Environmental Psychology*, 15: 283–98.

Lee, T. R. and Uzzell, D. L. (1980) *The Educational Effectiveness of the Farm Open Day*, Countryside Commission for Scotland.

Lee, T. R. and Uzzell, D. L. (1984) *Visitors to the UKAEA Exhibition 'Electricity From Uranium'*, London: report to the UKAEA.

Lee, T. R., Uzzell, D. L. and Henderson, J. (1980) *Forestry Commission Visitor Centres: An Evaluation Package*, internal report, Edinburgh: The Forestry Commission.

McDonough, M. H. and Lee, T. R. (1990) 'Evaluation of interpretive services: What do we know in 1990?', in *Proceedings of National Interpreters Training Workshop*, Charleston SC, November–December.

Mahaffey, B. (1969) *Relative Effectiveness and Visitor Preference of Three Audio Visual Media for Interpretation of a Historic Area*, Department Information Report no. 1, College Station TX: Department of Recreation and Parks, Texas A & M University.

Melton, A.W. (1933 'Studies of installation at the Pennsylvania Museum of Art', *Museum News*, 10: 5–8.

Melton, A.W. (1935) *Problems of Installation in Museums of Art*, Washington DC: American Association of Museums.

Melton, A.W. (1972) 'Visitor behaviour in museums: some early research in environmental design', *Human Factors*, 14: 393.

Miles, R. S., Alt, M. B., Gosling, D. C, Lewis, B. N. and Tout, A. F. (1988) *The Design of Educational Exhibits*, 2nd edn, London: Unwin Hyman.

Moscardo, G. and Pearce, P. L. (1986) 'Visitor centres and environmental interpretation: An exploration of the relationships among visitor enjoyment understanding and mindfulness', *Journal of Environmental Psychology*, 6: 89–108.

Robinson, E. (1930) 'Psychological problems of the science museum', *Museum News*, 8: 9–11.

Robinson, E. (1931) 'Exit the typical visitor', *Journal of Adult Education*, 3: 418–23.

Roth, C. Z. and Hodgson, R. W. (1977) 'The contribution of perception training to interpretive effectiveness: an experiment', *Journal of Environmental Education*, 9(1): 23–30.

Sheppard, D. (1960) 'Methods for assessing the value of exhibitions', *British Journal of Educational Psychology*, 30: 259–69.

Shiner, J. W. and Shafer, E. L. (1975) *How Long Do People Look at and Listen to Forest Oriented Exhibits?*, research paper NE-325, Upper Darby PA: US Department of Agriculture, Northeastern Forest Experimental Station, p. 16.

Shye, S. (1978) *Theory Construction and Data Analysis in the Behavioural Sciences*, London: Jossey-Bass.

Wittlin, A. S. (1971) 'Hazards of Communication by Exhibits', *Curator*, 14(2): 138–50.

14

Planning for interpretive experiences

DAVID UZZELL

The opening paragraphs of Freeman Tilden's book *Interpreting our Heritage* begin:

> The word interpretation as used in this book refers to a public service that has so recently come into our cultural world that a resort to the dictionary for a competent definition is fruitless.
>
> Yet every year millions of Americans visit the national parks and monuments, the state and municipal parks, battlefield areas, historic houses publicly and privately owned, museums great and small – the components of a vast preservation of shrines and treasures in which may be seen and enjoyed the story of our natural and man-made heritage.
>
> In most of such places the visitor is exposed, if he chooses, to a kind of elective education that is superior in some respects to the classroom, for here he meets the Thing Itself – whether it be a wonder of Nature's work, or the act or work of Man.
>
> *Tilden 1957: 3*

These three paragraphs, written over forty years ago, raise many different issues. The only real clue to the fact that they were not written recently is the gender discriminating language which assumes the creator of, as well as the visitor to, the heritage is male. Taking the first paragraph, could one resort to the dictionary now for a competent definition? Can we say with confidence even in 1998 that people readily understand the word 'interpretation'? Do all interpreters readily agree among themselves as to the meaning of the word? The answer is 'no' to all three questions.

We may be much more sophisticated now in our interpretive techniques and use the latest computer simulations, but the real innovation in interpretation lies not in a computer chip but in the minds of imaginative interpreters who can fire and inspire the visitor. Rereading Tilden's book one cannot fail to be struck by the words he uses to communicate to the reader the power and the importance he attached to interpretation in the conservation of the natural and built heritage – 'beauty', 'wonder', 'inspiration', 'spiritual elevation', 'treasures', 'discovery', 'provocation', 'inspired', 'experience'. These appear in the first chapter alone.

Tilden was moved to write his book because while he was aware that there were many excellent interpreters who, although they were not necessarily aware of any principles, through natural ability and inspiration could bring heritage sites alive, there were also many who could not. Tilden had to admit that 'if there were enough pure inspiration in the world to go round, this might be the best way to perform the service. But we are not so cluttered with genius as all that' (1957: 4). One might add as a postscript that since the number of interpreters throughout the world has increased manyfold since 1957, if the proportion of geniuses has remained the same the absolute number of uninspired and uninspiring interpreters must also have risen manyfold. This would clearly support the need for a set of principles to encourage and guide good practice.

One suspects that very few trainee interpreters now read Tilden as it is 'out of date' and superseded by 'training manuals', 'interpretation delivery modules' and all the other corporate management-speak accessories of the 1990s. I have heard it said that Tilden is 'old hat' and what we need is a new set of principles or guidelines. Although his style of presentation is at times rather whimsical, and while some of his ideas and principles rest on questionable assumptions (Chapter 2), the general thrust and tenor of his approach remains as valid today as it ever was.

In these days of virtual experiences (e.g. 'The London Experience'), phoney experiences (e.g. 'The Dinosaur Experience') and tacky experiences (e.g. 'The Smugglers Experience'), Tilden reminds us that an essential role of interpretation is to promote encounters with real objects and experiences. Interpretation should not be a surrogate experience for the very heritage that attracts visitors from 10, 100 or 1,000 miles away. An important objective of interpretation is to encourage people to explore the real environment. One should never underestimate the power of the real object or experience itself (Plate 14.1). However well-meaning and convincing our efforts to simulate through some form of virtual reality the feeling of overlooking the Grand Canyon, seeing the sun set at Uluru (Ayers Rock) or grasping the corporate imagination that built cities like Florence or Venice, such attempts will ultimately be inadequate and dishonest (Plate 14.2).

Plate 14.1
The 'real thing':
French tourists walk
across the 50m high
Pont du Gard
aqueduct in southern
France, built by the
Romans 2,000 years
ago
Source: David Uzzell

Plate 14.2
Can virtual reality ever
adequately capture
through interpretation
the corporate
imagination that built
cities like Venice?
Source: David Uzzell

Interpretation can, however, be the door through which one walks to understand 'the meaning and significance' of such places. Unfortunately, too often the door remains locked and the person holding the key is off doing something else.

In the light of these observations, the intention of this chapter is to address Tilden's challenge – to develop a set of interpretive principles which will lead to coherent, educationally stimulating and beneficial experiences of the heritage. The remainder of this chapter can be divided into three parts. The first part outlines a holistic approach to the provision of interpretation which seeks to provide a framework for incorporating within one model all the significant inputs and outputs required to plan a successful interpretive experience. So often the end point of interpretive plans is the identification of interpretive themes or stories and the techniques which can be used to communicate them. These are, however, only a means to an end. One ought to be planning to achieve particular cognitive, affective and behavioural interpretive experiences. The second part, by means of a case study of a forestry interpretation centre and site in south-east England, illustrates how this model was used in the creation of an interpretive planning experience. The final section attempts to synthesise these ideas drawing on the findings of research and evaluation with a view to providing a set of principles and guidelines which will ensure that interpretive projects do provide high quality learning experiences.

Constructing an interpretive experience

The themes–markets–resources model
The success of too many heritage projects is jeopardised because insufficient attention is given to the planning stage. As suggested above, there is often a confusion between means and ends. Most interpretive plans follow the traditional planning model that was developed by Patrick Geddes and has been taught in planning schools since the 1920s. This proposes that there are three essential stages in the planning process – survey, analysis and plan. A survey involves collecting all the relevant information about the resource to be developed – in this case interpreted. This information is then analysed with a view to projecting the data into the future in order to better understand how the resource might be developed. Finally a plan is devised which attempts to incorporate all the information and analyses within the context of good planning and interpretive practice. An elementary way of thinking about interpretive plans is to use a variant on Lasswell's (McQuail and Windahl 1981) communication model of 'who

says what to whom, where, when, why and how', where 'who' could be designers, interpreters, rangers, volunteers; 'what' are the themes and stories which are to be told; 'to whom' are the actual and potential audiences such as day visitors, tourists, specialist interest groups, children; 'where' and 'when' refer to the precise locations and times at which interpretation will take place; 'why' addresses the aims and objective of the interpretation; and 'how' refers to the techniques to be employed.

A characteristic feature of most interpretive plans is that the planning process is treated linearly. In practice, however, the process is necessarily more recursive and iterative. Furthermore, there is a much greater interaction between all the different elements that make up a plan; change one component and this will inevitably have an impact on another. Too often, owners and managers of sites have a preconception as to what they want without giving full consideration to all the factors, and their interaction, which need to be taken into account in the planning, design, management and use of a heritage or environmental site.

There are three key elements in any heritage development – the themes, market and resources. The starting point for the creation of successful interpretive programmes and facilities can be conceived as the product of the interaction and synergism between these three elements, as exemplified in Figure 14.1. In some cases the quality and quantity of individual factors will be unknown, for example at a new heritage site. Where a heritage site or museum is being redeveloped or extended then much of this information will be available. It is the synthesis of this knowledge which results in a successful plan, so that not only will supply meet demand (which is essential if the site is to be financially successful) but supply can also lead demand (which is important if one is concerned about the educational development of the public in respect of environmental conservation).

Resources Each of the three circles in Figure 14.1 represents inputs related to resources, markets and themes. In the case of resources, this includes the essence of the valued heritage which is the object of the interpretation and the site itself, which includes any additional recreational and aesthetic value as well as space for buildings and parking. Resources also include: interpretive media and programmes; the staff (full-time, part-time, professional, ancillary, volunteer); the associated management structure; promotion and marketing programmes; the financial base of the organisation (the different sources and stability of capital and revenue finance). There are also intangible but no less important resources upon which to build such as track record and reputation, as well as good practice gleaned either from past experience or in related organisations and sites.

Market The market includes all aspects of the visitor base, including the size of the market (actual and potential); the spatial extent of the catchment area from which visitors will be drawn (typically in drive time rather than distance); visitor social, economic and cultural characteristics as well as their interests, purchasing power, recreational, environmental and cultural needs. An important input factor in relation to markets is the identification of market gaps – where visitor needs are not being met. A common problem with interpretation is that much of it is highly influenced by market factors. That is, interpretation is geared more to what providers think visitors want to hear rather than the story they should be telling. Typically this happens at sites where authentic heritage may be in short supply and where the principal motivation is not heritage conservation but tourist income generation.

Figure 14.1: The themes–markets–resources model

Resources
The Heritage
Site characteristics
Staffing and
   management
Infrastructure
Funding and financing
Promotion and
   marketing
Interpretive media
Good practice
Intrinsic value

Markets
Scale
Catchments
Characteristics
Spending power
Gaps
Access
Interests
Needs

Themes
Stories
Message
Strength
Variety
Relevance
Availability
Uniqueness

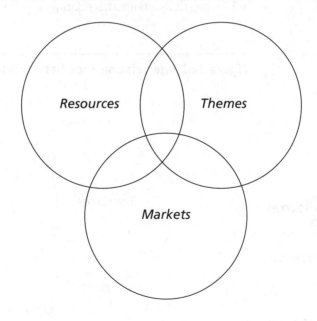

Themes Theme factors are more than just the themes, stories and messages which the interpreters wish to communicate to their audience. They are also the means by which the theme is operationalised. Ham (1992: 21) suggests that the major difference between themes and stories (which Ham calls 'topics') is that the topic is merely the subject matter of the presentation, whereas the theme is the main point or message that the interpreter is attempting to communicate. For example, the theme might be global warming and long-term climate change. Within this theme there can be any number of topics or stories such as the increasing incidence of desertification in Southern Europe and the effect of sea level rises on Pacific islands.

Interrelationships between themes, markets and resources Although individually each of the input elements is important, it is the interaction between the elements that defines interpretive outcomes (Figure 14.2). The overlapping parts of the circles between any two elements (themes/resources, themes/markets, markets/resources) mark the relationship which must necessarily exist between those two elements. Each of the three elements should only be seen in the context of their relationship to the other two elements. For example, the overlapping circles related to themes and markets raise questions about the relationship between the chosen themes and

Figure 14.2 Interrelationships between themes, markets and resources

Themes/resources
Presentation
Interpretive media

Market/resources
Location
Access
Capacity
Transport
Marketing/promotion

Themes/markets
Appeal
Understandable
Market creativity

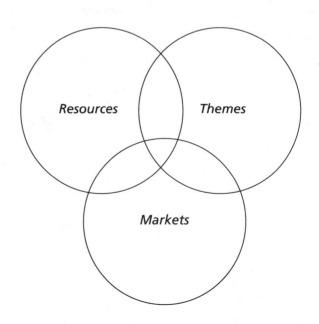

messages and the markets at which they are targeted. This includes issues such as will a particular audience be interested in a particular theme, e.g. the seriousness of global environmental change. It may be felt or even known from formative evaluation that a sizeable proportion of the visitors to the centre are not interested in abstract issues concerning environmental change. If one suspects that this theme may not appeal to visitors, how can it be approached so that it will attract and hold their attention? If one knows about the visitors' educational levels, interests and prior learning, certain features of environmental change can be focused on and certain types of interpretive media used which will particularly appeal or will allow easier assimilation of information. On the other hand, the development of a particular theme may attract social groups who previously would not have considered visiting the site or museum.

The second relationship is between the two elements, themes and resources. This can pose questions such as: given the chosen themes, what are the most appropriate media to interpret those themes? If the preferred means is people-based interpretation, is there the financial capacity and managerial structure to support this? Similarly, if it is considered that an environmental education programme would be desirable or beneficial, for educational and financial reasons, what resource implications does this have in terms of staffing, classroom facilities, the development of interpretive material and work packs?

The relationship between the final combination of elements – market and resources – raises questions such as: is the location, access and marketing appropriate given the intended markets? What is the competition for certain markets? Is there an appropriate provision and mix of facilities and services for the intended markets? A simple example will illustrate the point.

We know from research that approximately 20 per cent or more of visitors to many heritage attractions are schoolchildren. This therefore represents a significant income stream. If the financial planning requires that 100,000 visitors come through the turnstiles in the first year, and one anticipates that 20 per cent of the visitors will be schoolchildren in school groups (not children coming with their parents at the weekends or in the holidays), then it is known that one needs to attract approximately 20,000 schoolchildren. If one further assumes that there are thirty- two weeks available through the year for school visits (excluding holiday periods, examination periods and bad weather) then this implies that, on average, one will need to attract approximately 625 children a week, or 125 children a day. If one then assumes they will be arriving in buses which take approximately fifty children per bus, then the consequence of this is that one has to plan for three buses per day. This in turn raises important resourcing questions. Is there adequate staff to manage three busloads of children a day? Are there adequate wet weather facilities and/or classroom facilities for three groups at a time, or do the visits have to be staggered? Is there adequate parking for three buses at the same time that will not seriously reduce the parking available for other visitors? Will three parties of children impact on other visitor groups to the detriment of all? If so, what can be done to separate the two groups, and what resources will be needed to successfully achieve this?

Of course, any good planner will go through this process as a matter of course, but this simple example illustrates how the themes–markets–resources model suggests important questions which need to be asked in relation to these three essential elements in interpretive planning.

It is the resolution of the three elements of themes, market and resources where all three circles overlap that comprises the interpretive experience,

Figure 14.3 The creation of an interpretive experience and consequent benefits

Output benefits
Profitability
Employment potential
Social and cultural bene-
  fits for the local com-
  munity
Environmental benefits
Tourism generation ben-
  efits
Catalyst for further
  development
Public relations and
  image promotion
Community pride
educational benefits for
  schools and colleges

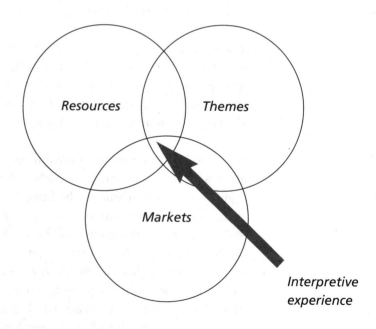

such as the range of intended cognitive and affective responses to the heritage or the anticipated or desired behavioural outcomes (Figure 14.3). Furthermore, from the interaction between the three factors, one can begin to identify some of the outputs or benefits, including employment potential, additional educational resources for local schools, the social and cultural benefits to the local community through additional educational facilities and tourism income, and environmental benefits through to less tangible but no less important benefits such as enhanced community pride and a sense of place.

Planning an interpretive experience

Visitors – whether they are day-trippers, tourists, members of the local community, specialist interest groups, school groups – visit countryside sites, museums, national parks, historic houses, nature reserves and all the other different types of heritage attractions for a multitude of reasons. There is one thing, however, that they are all looking for – an experience. They either want to experience 'the Thing Itself' as Tilden phrased it – to see it, to touch it, to hear it, to be in its presence – or they wish the experience to be centred on themselves or the social group of which they are a part. In the first instance – *the heritage experience* – the experience is located outside the person, the pleasure come from being in proximity to the heritage. In the latter – the *psychological experience* – the experience focuses on the individual who seeks to satisfy personal and social needs, wishes and preferences. There is, of course, an interaction between the heritage and the psychological experiences. In practice, one cannot separate the two because one does not exist without the other. They can be distinguished on the plane of analysis, but on the plane of experience they are indivisible.

The emphasis in interpretive planning has been directed, quite understandably, towards the heritage experience. How can a psychological experience be provided for visitors? Planning interpretive facilities to create and satisfy both a psychological and a heritage experience was the objective of a project undertaken for the UK Forestry Commission at Bedgebury National Pinetum in Kent in south-east England. Bedgebury National Pinetum comprises a commercial forest area, the Pinetum itself and the Forest Plots. The commercial forest which covers the largest proportion of the land is used for the planting and harvesting of both broadleaf and coniferous trees. The Pinetum is, in essence, an outdoor tree museum and resembles a traditional English parkland in which fine specimens of coniferous trees collected from all of the world since the early decades of the 20th century are set in closely mown greensward. The Forest Plots is a comparatively small experimental research area in which various species of coniferous trees are grown under different planting conditions. An interpretive plan was written for the development of a visitor centre and exhibition as well as on-site interpretation which would make use of all three sites (Uzzell and Parkin 1987).

It was decided that the focus of the interpretive plan should be the development of a variety and a sequence of experiences to hold the visitors' attention from the moment they arrived until the time they left. Formative evaluation undertaken with staff and visitors as well as research on the likely visitor profile of the new interpretive facilities resulted in the identification of a number of different experiences. These ranged from simple relaxation, because formative evaluation had shown that many current visitors to the Pinetum valued the peace and quiet and the opportunity to enjoy a pleasant stroll among the autumn colours, through to more active interpretive pursuits. (see Table 14.1.)

TABLE 14.1 PLANNING FOR THE VISITOR EXPERIENCE

Experience	Concept	Theme	Audience	How	Location
Relaxation	Peace and tranquillity	Historic Bedgebury Bedgebury NP	Adults, family groups	Trails, leaflets, walks, wayside signs	Pinetum, plots, forest
Activity and excitement	Wind-down	Introduction	Children	Play equipment	Vicinity of visitor centre
Education Interpretation Living history	A sense of the past	Victorian botanists, crafts/industries, forest products	Adults, schools, specialist groups, coach parties	Actors, AV, demonstrations, temporary exhibits	Pinetum, forest
Activity and fantasy	'If you go down to the woods today...'	Trees	Children under 10	Tree house trail	Forest
Education Interpretation	Caring for nature	Conservation, Bedgebury plots, forest products	Children, schools	Environmental education, summer playschemes	Pinetum, plots, forest
Excitement and awe	A walk among the tree tops	Historic Bedgebury, Bedgebury NP, Victorian botanists	Adults, family groups, schools, coach parties	Tree Top Trail wayside signs, AV, leaflets	Pinetum
Learning Sensory experience	Anatomy of a tree	Bedgebury plots	Schools, family groups	Acclimatisation, demonstration	Plots

On the basis of the identified experience, a concept was developed to capture the essence of that experience. An example is the concept developed for the experience of 'activity and fantasy'. Forests and woods have a significant place in folklore and children's fairy stories which it was felt important to draw on as one valuable way of interpreting forests. Consequently, the concept of 'If you go down to the woods today...' was developed. This was intended to immediately signal this line of thinking and also fitted within one of the eight themes which had been identified as central to the Bedgebury story. The audience for this interpretation were children under the age of 10. This raised the question of how the experience was to be delivered. It was decided that many fairy stories involve houses or cottages in woods and forests, so it was proposed that a trail of child-size forest cottages would be built, each having the name of a well-known fairy story, e.g. Red Riding Hood Cottage, The Three Bears Cottage, Hansel and Gretel Cottage. The cottages would be simple, timber-framed constructions containing bench seating for four or six children and a table. It was not felt necessary to provide elaborate interpretation, maybe a small amount of text giving the outline of the story. The name of the cottage above the door would be the most important element because this would act as a trigger for the children's imagination. These stories are familiar to all children and encouraging them to interpret the forest themselves in an imaginative way was seen as the key to interpretation.

Another experience was one of 'excitement and awe' as a consequence of viewing the forest from the top of the trees. This is not so unusual, but we wanted to make this experience available to all visitor groups, including the disabled. Taking advantage of a fall in the land away from the site of the proposed visitor centre, a walkway was to be built comprising ramps and gentle slopes that would enable visitors in wheelchairs to pass among the tree tops. This walk would be augmented by wayside signs and leaflets and pre-trail interpretation in the visitor centre. Further examples of the way in which a variety of experiences were identified and the means by which they were to be achieved for particular groups in particular parts of the forest are provided in Table 14.1. The Bedgebury case study illustrates that the interpretive process is not linear. There is an interaction between the various components so that the themes–markets–resources mix is appropriate to create a unique experience.

By way of a postscript, the visitor centre and other on-site interpretive facilities were never built. As the project was moving through the last few stages of approval in October 1987, a freak hurricane hit southern England and destroyed 10 per cent of the Pinetum, 30 per cent of the forest, and 90 per cent of the Forest Plots. It took almost three days for the foresters to get into the forest, such was the extent of the devastation, and several years for forestry operations to return to a modicum of normality. Consequently, all interpretive proposals were immediately abandoned.

Creating high-quality psychological, social and contextual experiences

Having identified the necessary infrastructure for constructing environmental and heritage experiences, what do we know from research and evaluation studies that can help interpretive planners and designers as well as environmental and heritage managers provide visitors with satisfying, stimulating and lasting experiences? Notwithstanding the analytical distinction drawn earlier between a heritage experience and a psychological experience, the remainder of this chapter attempts to synthesise some of the principal findings from research in order to identify guidelines for creating high-quality psychological, social and contextual experiences for the visitor.

Psychological issues

The first conclusion that one can draw from research and evaluation studies is that interpretation must be situated in the visitor's own experience. It is only in this way that the heritage or the environment and its interpretation will be made meaningful and can be used as a resource on which the visitor can draw to understand further information and interpretation and guide future action. Visitors need a framework with which to structure and make meaningful what they can see and relate it to their own experience. This is what Lee refers to as a schema (Chapter 13). It is too easy for managers of museums and heritage sites to assume that the visitor can 'read' and understand their site in the same way that they do. Too often, managers make unreasonable assumptions about the visitors' knowledge levels and experience. This may result in interpretation starting from where the manager is or where s/he thinks the visitor is, rather than from where the visitor actually is. Interpretation should build on pre-existing experience and knowledge. If we do not know how visitors perceive and understand a heritage site then we need to do some research to find out. This will ensure that the interpretation is relevant and meaningful and builds on (or corrects) existing perceptions and information.

Some visitors will arrive at the site with pre-existing knowledge which will enable them to assimilate and accommodate new information. For others,

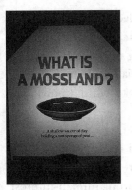

Plate 14.3
'What is a Mossland?'
Risley Moss Visitor
Centre, Warrington
Source: David Uzzell

the subject matter will be unknown and they will require help with forming a new schema for understanding the interpretive material. This is usually best achieved by drawing an analogy with something already familiar. The exhibition at Risley Moss Visitor Centre in Warrington New Town provides an excellent example. The exhibition tells the story of the mossland and how its existence has influenced wildlife, conservation, industry, agriculture, transport and the lives and livelihoods of the people who lived on or near it. The exhibition opens with a simple but effective panel that asks the question: 'What is a Mossland?' It then gives the answer which provides the concept central to an understanding of the site: 'A shallow clay saucer holding a wet sponge of peat'. Underneath this panel is a clay saucer with peat in it. This image is used as a leitmotiv throughout the exhibition to reveal the relationship between the geomorphological structure of the area and its social, economic and cultural development (Plate 14.3). If the visitor can understand this concept, then the remainder of the exhibition becomes that much more interpretable and meaningful.

Several years ago Uzzell *et al.* (1988) wrote an interpretive strategy for Ironbridge Gorge Museum, a World Heritage Site. Ironbridge Gorge Museum comprises at least seven museums or significant sites. Although the visitor can get a great deal out of the interpretation of any one site, the whole is much greater than the sum of the parts. The true significance of the site – the 'keynote' as Tilden terms it (1957: 60) – only becomes apparent if the visitor can appreciate it in a larger context. Consequently, it was suggested that the types of key concepts necessary to communicate to visitors are:

> The existence of coal or iron ore or clay on any one site during the 18th century would have been significant. But in Ironbridge, they all existed and in abundance, along with water and the imaginative and entrepreneurial skills of the early industrialists.

> Ironbridge Gorge went through three phases of industrial development: an iron-smelting period from 1709–1818: decorative porcelain from 1795–1926: decorative tile-making from 1850–1960s. Each of these phases is represented by three major industrial and now visitor sites – Coalbrookdale, Coalport and the Jackfield Tile Works. In each of these areas it was internationally important. For one small river valley to achieve this pre-eminence must surely be unparalleled.

> *Uzzell et al. 1988: 54*

Visitors need to be told what is unique about the place they are visiting. Why is it significant and worthy of interpretation? Visitors cannot be assumed to recognise the significance and meaning of objects or places from the objects or places themselves. This is especially true for overseas visitors who may arrive with a different cultural background, knowledge base and set of expectations.

Tilden argued forcefully that 'interpretation should relate to something within the personality or the experience of the visitor'. The most effective way this can be achieved is if the interpretation has strong human-interest themes. These are themes for which visitors already have pre-existing cognitive structures enabling them to assimilate new information. People are interested in people. Generally, they are less interested in subjects such as geology, architecture or ceramics. If it is felt important to tell the story of the architectural history of a place, then it should be told through the people who were involved in the commission, design, construction or use of the buildings.

Visitors need orientation to the site they are visiting in order to give them a mental map and to appreciate its structure, whether it is a museum, historic house, dockyard or national park. This can be done by line drawings, axonometric drawings, artists' impressions, models and all the other imaginative techniques at the designer's disposal. Orientation also enables visitors to understand the scale of the site and to pace their visit more effectively and enjoyably so that they can choose what they want to see, when they want to see it and how much time they need to allocate to each element of the visit. If the site is very large, visitors can see from the outset that they will not be able to visit it all. They can plan which parts they will concentrate on and then visit the remainder on another occasion. This will ensure that they do not hurry through the interpretation and leave out some parts of the story because they have left insufficient time.

Visitor comprehension is enhanced if there is a relationship between the subject matter and the spatial layout. Historical themes have an obvious advantage here as material is often chronologically presented. This should be reflected in the spatial layout of the exhibition so that each idea develops from the previous one. The spatial organisation of displays that minimises competing claims on the visitor's attention, such as exhibitions that route people along a corridor, is also more successful than those that allow uncontrolled and often random movement between displays. An exhibition that is thematically organised can still benefit from a layout which suggests to visitors the linkages and relationships between themes so that the cognitive organisation required for understanding the concepts and their associations is mirrored by the spatial layout. It should not necessarily be assumed that the most appropriate chronological sequence is from the past to the present. If understanding is enhanced by relating the interpretation to the visitor's experience, it may be more appropriate to start in the present and work chronologically backwards.

So much interpretation is little more than books on the wall. Of course it is important to provide written information. Just because interpretation is available, however, this does not mean that visitors will necessarily notice or read it. Text should be presented in ways which people will be able to assimilate more easily. It has been found in evaluation studies undertaken in museums that large amounts of information provided in exhibitions are educationally redundant. Visitors to one (probably not exceptional) visitor centre spent less than 15 per cent of the time necessary to read the exhibition panels (de Vries Robbé 1980). Visitors have to be attracted to the interpretive material and once there their attention has to be held. Exhibition text should be presented in hierarchical levels to reflect the interests and comprehension abilities of different visitor groups.

There is a limit to how much the visitor can absorb. It is better that one key feature is interpreted well and the visitor understands its meaning and significance than that ten aspects of the heritage are interpreted which the visitor just ignores. What do the visitors need to know (in an interpretive sense) about the heritage site to make their visit more interesting, stimulating, enjoyable and memorable? What one or two pieces of interpretation can visitors be given to convey the essence of the heritage such that they begin to appreciate its uniqueness or its special quality? Tilden's second principle of interpretation is: 'Information, as such, is not interpretation. Interpretation is revelation based upon information. These are entirely different things. However, all interpretation includes information.' How often is information confused with interpretation? When the task is to interpret the domestic architecture of the county or state, so often this ends up as a chronological account of changing styles.

The emphasis here has been on addressing the cognitive dimension of learning. It has been argued elsewhere (Chapter 10) that the affective dimension of interpretation is no less an important component of any interpretive experience. As Tilden advocated: 'The chief aim of interpretation is not instruction, but provocation.'

Social issues

People visit museums and interpretive centres as part of a social experience. They do not always go to learn – they visit to be entertained, to be with friends and relatives, to have a relaxing and enjoyable time. This does not mean that interpretation should just be a form of entertainment or exhibitions just a frivolous backdrop to a social encounter. We know from research that exhibits with which visitors can physically interact are more effective for learning, providing that the physical interaction is part of the learning experience itself, than static exhibits such as exhibition panels. Research (Uzzell 1993) has shown, however, that the most effective exhibits for learning encourage social interaction between visitors, i.e. those which encourage visitors to talk to each other about the exhibits, what they mean and how they relate to their lives. Not only does the social-interactive exhibit encourage much more discussion among family members, but this interaction is qualitatively different to that prompted by exhibits which do not encourage social interaction. Interpretation should be an interactive and involving experience. It should encourage visitor groups, especially family groups, to interact and learn from each other. There are a growing number of countryside and heritage sites that provide interpretation which encourages precisely this type of response. Adults and children are given interpretive material that enables them to learn from each other. In this way not only do children learn from adults but adults learn from children. Therefore, it is not the interpretation *per se* which leads to learning but rather the interactions and discussion encouraged by the interpretation (Chapter 5).

Interpretation can draw on a variety of techniques. These include permanent and temporary exhibitions, audio-visual presentations, demonstrations, costumed interpreters, trails, events, wayside panels, a guided walks and talks programme, themed catering, themed children's play equipment and leaflets. The decision about which techniques to use should be determined by considerations such as what is being interpreted, to whom and for what purpose. Too often, interpreters decide that they want to use certain interpretive techniques prior to deciding what they are going to interpret. In other words, the interpretation should be appropriate for the setting, the particular type of audience, the theme of the interpretation and the experience one is trying to create in order to ensure educational effectiveness and the integrity of the site, its artefacts, buildings and setting and the conservation work of the management.

There is no such body as 'the general public'. The so-called 'general public' is made up of different audiences with different needs and different expectations. These should be acknowledged and planned for in order to ensure effective interpretation and conflict avoidance. Different groups (e.g. the elderly and children) will be looking for different types of interpretive experiences than singletons or visitors with a specialist interest. Research undertaken by Lee and Uzzell (1984) found that an exhibition on forestry which was designed for children using the medium of cartoons was not only perceived and understood differently by children as compared with adults, but that the children picked up different messages and learnt different things about forestry than the exhibition designers intended and assumed they would learn. In other words, while the designers thought they were designing for a child audience, they failed to base the interpretation within the child's view and understanding of forestry. This supports Tilden's sixth principle that: 'Interpretation presented to children should not be a dilution of the presentation to adults, but should follow a fundamentally different approach. To be at its best it will require a separate program.'

Research is an essential part of any interpretive development. Too often though, most of the energy is expended on researching the subject matter, with neither time nor resources left to research the actual or potential visitors. Even worse, it is assumed by the management that they know all they need to know about the visitors without any research or evaluation. The distinction between research and evaluation and the different types of evaluation studies (front-end, formative and summative) are discussed in detail elsewhere (Chapter 12).

Contextual issues

The context of interpretation is as important as the interpretation itself. One cannot consider the provision of a visitor service in isolation from all the other factors that contribute to the visitor experience. So it is for interpretation. If the interpretation is excellent, but other facilities such as car parking, signposting, catering and lavatories are poor, this will have a detrimental effect on the visitors' image of the place. Apart from having an unsatisfactory experience, they will not recommend a visit to their friends, they will not make a repeat visit themselves and, most importantly, they will not be in a receptive frame of mind to grasp the concepts and meaning of the exhibition or site and leave with an enhanced understanding of the heritage. Unfortunately good interpretation will not compensate for poor facilities, but good facilities will enhance the appreciation and reception of the interpretation.

Selling a ticket to a heritage attraction is selling an experience. One duty of the heritage owner or manager is to plan and provide a sequence of interpretive experiences to interest, entertain and inform visitors from the moment they arrive until the time they leave. In this way, the whole visit can be considered as a potential interpretive experience from the themed restaurant to themed children's play areas. Even ancillary services such as catering can be themed using 'authentic' meals (e.g. reflecting contemporary cooking and diets). In this way, the restaurant becomes a genuine part of the interpretive experience and adds an important dimension to the visit.

Any interpretive strategy must be sympathetic to the needs and interests of local residents for whom the visitors' heritage site may be their home, such as an historic village or even a landscape. Many people in such communities resent this open-house invitation as tourists peer in through windows, have a presence in every public place and disregard the social, spiritual and symbolic spaces that assume meaning and significance for the inhabitants and their ancestors but are little more than scenic backdrops to a family photography for the tourist. Contrary to the notion that travel broadens the mind and brings people from different cultures and backgrounds together, leading to greater intercultural empathy and understanding, most research evidence suggests that antipathy and resentment are often all that is exchanged (Krippendorf 1987). Everything should be done to ensure that any expected increase in visitors and tourists has a minimal negative effect on local people's daily lives. Interpretation can be used for visitor management as much as visitor education, and advantage should be taken of the various interpretive devices to reduce the less acceptable consequences of tourism.

Conclusion

Interpretation has seen many developments since Tilden first wrote *Interpreting Our Heritage*. These include: the proliferation of training courses and qualifications run by heritage management organisations, universities and colleges; the establishment of international and national professional membership organisations such as Heritage Interpretation International (HII), the National Association of Interpretation, the Society for the Interpretation of Britain's Heritage and the Interpretation Australia Association; periodicals produced by these organisations as well as independent publications such as the *International Journal of Heritage Studies* and *InterpEdge*; the heritage mailing list operated by Keith Dewar at Massey University on behalf of HII. Most of these initiatives have successfully attempted to raise standards of interpretive provision and enhance the skills and professionalism of interpreters.

There have also been major advances in interpretive technique, most notably in the development of first-person interpretation and the introduction of technology – the tough and tender side of interpretation. Battle re-enactments and scenes of medieval domesticity may have a persuasive air of verisimilitude, but when they become the 'Thing Itself' rather than a means to understanding and appreciating what they are actually meant to be representing, then all is not well. Likewise, computers, animatronics, artificial smells and simulations have all sought to attract and hold the visitors' attention and inspire them to understand and appreciate the heritage such that they will want to support its conservation. But interpretation is no more amenable to 'technological fix' solutions than other areas of our lives, and there is always a danger that their indiscriminate use will reduce interpretation to the level of a tricksy sideshow. Technology by itself cannot replace an inspiring and imaginative interpreter: it can at best only be an aid to good interpretation. It can educate, entertain and divert, but it will never nor should it try to be the 'Thing Itself'.

There is no doubt that the kinds of techniques briefly referred to here have served to make interpretation more attractive and appealing to a wider audience with the prospect, hopefully, of reaching and educating groups who a few years ago would not have seen themselves as consumers of heritage or informal environmental education. But one does wonder whether visitors to heritage sites feel as close to the heritage – and along with that closeness an identification and sense of responsibility – that Tilden sought to advocate forty years ago. Reference was made at the beginning of this chapter to the words Tilden uses in the opening pages of *Interpreting Our Heritage*: 'beauty', 'wonder', 'inspiration', 'spiritual elevation', 'treasures', 'discovery', 'provocation', 'inspired'. These are the kind of words that come out of an experience of the 'Thing Itself'. If interpretation is to be effective, leading to conservation education and the development of global citizenship, then we must plan for interpretive experiences that provide nothing less than an enhanced appreciation and understanding of the 'Thing Itself'.

References

de Vries Robbé (1980) 'Countryside interpretation: the interaction between countryside visitors and interpretive displays', unpublished MSc thesis in Environmental Psychology, University of Surrey.

Ham, S. (1992) *Environmental Interpretation*, Golden CO: North American Press.

Krippendorf, J. (1987) *The Holiday Makers: Understanding the Impact of Leisure and Travel*, Oxford: Heinemann.

Lee, T. R. and Uzzell, D. L. (1984) *Interpretive Provision in Forestry Commission Visitor Centres: Strathyre Visitor Centre*, report to the Forestry Commission, University of Surrey.

McQuail, D. and Windahl, S. (1981) *Communication Models for the Study of Mass Communications*, London: Longman.

Tilden, F. (1957) *Interpreting Our Heritage*, Chapel Hill: University of North Carolina Press.

Uzzell, D. L. (1993) 'Contrasting psychological perspectives on exhibition evaluation', in S. Bicknell and G. Farmelo (eds) *Museum Visitor Studies in the 1990s*, London: Science Museum, pp.125–29.

Uzzell, D. L., Blud, L. M., O'Callaghan, B. and Davies, P. (1988) *Ironbridge Gorge Museum: Strategy for Interpretive and Educational Development*, report to the Leverhulme Trust, Ironbridge Gorge Museum Trust, February.

Uzzell, D. L. and Parkin, I. (1987) *Bedgebury National Pinetum: Interpretive and Development Plan*, report submitted to the Forestry Commission, Edinburgh.

Index

aborigines/aboriginal, 30, 31, 49, 158,
   168–9
accountability, 108, 203, 228
action competence, 186
affect (*see* emotion)
Africa, 33, 34
   see also South Africa
aims/purposes of interpretation, 2, 10,
   67, 78–82, 105–108, 137, 140, 143,
   147, 153–4, 158, 167, 168, 185,
   204–5, 207, 212, 213, 228, 236,
   247, 248
ambiguity, 196
America (*see* USA)
apartheid, 21, 165–8
art galleries, 16, 149, 227
   see also museums
Asia, 34, 116, 120, 134, 176
attitudes, 11–13, 18, 19, 57, 60, 66, 68,
   77–97, 98, 101, 103, 106, 161, 162,
   191, 198, 199, 200, 204–5, 212,
   221–9
attitude change, 12–13, 77–97, 103, 105,
   153–4, 186, 200, 204–6, 212, 213,
   215, 220, 221–9
attract and hold measures (*see* drawing
   power; holding power)
audience, 17–18, 70, 81–2, 83, 86, 87,
   90, 91, 158, 186, 188, 191, 193,
   228–9, 236, 237, 238, 248
Australia, 14, 16, 17, 30, 31, 125, 159,
   162–3, 168–9, 250
Australian War Memorial Museum, 16
Ayers Rock Resort Visitor Centre, 169
   see also Uluru

Bandura, 65–6, 163, 212
BBC, 159
Bedgebury National Pinetum, 241–3
behaviour, 12–13, 58, 61, 66–9, 77–97,
   103, 106, 108, 199, 205, 210

   see also visitor behaviour
behaviour change, 12–13, 66, 77–97,
   103, 105, 106, 153, 186, 204, 205,
   227
   see also visitor behaviour
behavioural mapping, 198–9, 207, 225
   see also visitor behaviour
beliefs, 13, 19, 39, 69, 152, 153, 168, 225
   see also attitudes; values
bias, 32, 47, 49, 195–6
Bosnia, 20, 27, 159, 174–80
Britain/British, 14, 26–30, 41, 48, 49,
   139, 148, 159, 173, 176, 182, 185,
   191, 210, 225, 250
   see also BBC, England, UK
built environment (*see* environment,
   built)

Canada, 51, 125
casual interpretation, 145
centres, 16, 19, 22, 47, 50, 56, 60, 68, 77,
   82, 83, 84, 90, 92, 93, 141, 149,
   169, 185, 189, 193, 197, 203, 204,
   207–8, 210–13, 221, 227–8, 235,
   238, 241, 243, 244, 246, 247
charging policies, 104, 138
children, interpretation for, 58–61, 64–6,
   70–1, 91, 236, 239–40, 242–3, 248
   see also families
citizens/citizenship, 16, 45, 79, 82, 107,
   130
   see also global citizenship
Clifford's Tower, 156
cognitive conflict/dissonance, 84, 87–9
Cold War, 14, 161–2, 221
community development, 165–70
conceptual change, 87–93
conservation, 11, 12, 13, 20, 22, 81, 98,
   101–5, 108, 122, 127–9, 133,
   139–42, 145, 147, 148, 185, 205,
   207, 211, 233, 236, 250, 251

constructivism, 83–90

consultation, 91, 168

contested heritage, 125–6, 172–84

controversial issues, 37, 50–2, 151–71, 221

country parks, 207

Croydon, 149

crusades, 31–2, 124, 156

Cuban Missile Crisis, 15

cultural identity (*see* identity, cultural)

cultural psychology (*see* psychology, cultural)

culture/cultural, 15, 16, 19, 21, 22, 31, 34, 37–40, 45, 48, 49, 57, 64, 68–72, 100–8, 113, 114, 116, 119–21, 124, 126, 127, 130, 137, 140, 147, 149, 154, 168–9, 172–8, 249

  see also popular culture

data collection (*see* focus groups, interviews, observation studies, questionnaires, surveys)

decision-making, 77, 78, 107–8, 122, 152, 158, 161

deforestation, 162–3

  see also forests

Diana, Princess of Wales, 148, 157–8

displays, 16, 27, 31, 41, 48, 50, 62, 77, 84, 91, 134, 142, 156, 193, 196, 198, 206–8, 211–12, 214, 221, 225–8, 246

District Six Museum, 167–8

docents, 60–2

drawing power/attraction, 193, 198, 199, 206–10, 225, 226, 246, 250

  see also holding power

ecotourism/ecoutourist, 98–111

  see also tourism

Egypt, 27, 32–3

Elgin Marbles, 29, 114

emotion/affect, 7–8, 13, 63, 66, 68, 81, 103, 105, 107, 152–71, 205, 214, 225, 227, 235, 240, 247

emotive issues, 7–8

empowerment, 41, 80, 81, 130

England/English, 16, 26, 28, 30, 46, 49, 135, 140, 156, 174, 183, 210, 235, 241, 243

  see also Britain, UK

enjoyment, 56–60, 78, 83, 101, 103, 106, 159, 169, 196, 204–6, 210–12, 221, 228, 246–7

entertainment, 41, 78, 100, 103, 105, 122, 126, 139, 159, 160, 165, 210, 247, 249, 250

environment, built, 37–40, 116–18, 121, 124, 127, 130, 133–51

  see also interpretation of urban environment

environmental conceptions/beliefs, 13, 84–9, 91, 93

environmental education, 19, 77–97, 98, 104, 105, 107, 162, 239, 250

environmental heritage, 31, 38

environmental interpretation, 5, 16, 19, 77–97, 98–109, 165, 244

environmental issues/problems, 11, 14, 77, 81, 82, 86, 88, 99, 103, 147, 153, 162–5, 177, 186, 221, 226, 238

environmental psychology (*see* psychology, environmental)

ethical issues, 2, 11, 170

ethnic cleansing, 156, 159

Europe/European, 11, 14, 21, 27, 31, 49, 112–32, 173, 176, 238

evaluation, 8–9, 86, 108, 185–202, 203–31, 235, 243, 248–9

  formative, 190–2, 198–9, 238, 241, 242, 227

  front-end, 190–91, 193, 197–9

  research and, 186–7

  summative, 192–5, 197, 198, 227

exhibit design/designers, 17–19, 70, 71, 78, 83–93, 137, 152, 158, 185, 187, 188, 191, 192, 196, 199, 203, 204, 206, 227, 228, 235, 236, 243, 246, 248

experiments, 199–200, 241

face validity (*see* validity)
families, 18, 49–50, 56–9, 62, 63, 67,
    69–72, 155, 165, 213, 247
    see also children, interpretation for
Farm Open Day, 213–4, 218
feminism, 34, 37–55
    see also gender
First World War (*see* World War I)
Flesch Reading Ease Test, 200
focus groups, 86–7, 146, 186, 198–9
    see also interviews, observation
        studies, questionnaires, surveys
Forestry Commission, 205, 228, 241
forests, 31, 108, 163, 235, 241–3, 248
    see also deforestation
formative evaluation (*see* evaluation,
    formative)
France/French, 26, 29, 45, 154
front-end evaluation (*see* evaluation,
    front-end)
future (*see* interpretation of future)

gender, 22, 37–55, 194
    see also feminism
Gestalt, 64, 208
global citizenship, 12, 251
global heritage, 29, 31–34, 117–8, 127
global warming, 31, 89–90, 162, 163, 238
globalisation, 114, 119, 149, 172
Greece, 31, 32, 46, 173, 174
greenhouse effect, 89–90
group identity (*see* identity, group)
group members/membership, 21–22,
    57–9, 63, 65, 67, 70, 186
guides, 71, 98, 105–6, 108, 155, 188
guidebooks, 91, 155, 179, 200
guided walks, 188, 197, 211, 248

Ham, 81, 99, 206, 237
heritage industry, 11, 26, 122, 126
heritage interpretation, 11, 20–3, 40, 47,
    50, 52, 112–32, 152–3, 180
High Street management, 143

holding power, 198–9, 206–10, 225, 226,
    241, 250
    see also drawing power
holocaust, 119, 125, 126, 168
hot interpretation, 13, 152–71, 181, 183

identity theories, 22
identity, 21–3, 34, 39, 40, 112–5, 117,
    120, 124, 128, 172
    cultural, 22, 49, 116, 117, 119, 121,
        172
    group, 21
    place, 21–3, 112–3, 116, 119, 127,
        128, 187
    self, 68, 70
    social, 21–2
    urban, 22
information, 12–14, 17, 20, 59–61, 64,
    67, 68, 70, 78, 84–7, 89, 91, 105–7,
    138–9, 143, 148, 152–3, 158, 170,
    204–5, 208, 210–12, 214–15, 220,
    228, 236, 244–7
Interpretation Delivery Modules, 233
interpretation of
    future, 15–16, 19, 93, 133, 141–50
    objects, 16–18, 20, 26, 29, 32, 50, 63,
        64, 70, 77, 81, 83, 84, 86, 114, 140,
        153, 233, 245
    past, 11, 12, 14–16, 19, 28, 37, 48, 50,
        52, 99, 114, 117, 120, 122, 124–8,
        130, 133, 136, 142, 169, 172,
        179–82, 205
    place, 14–16, 18, 20–1, 133, 137, 139,
        140, 144, 145, 148, 157–61, 245
    urban environment, 22, 127–9,
        133–51
    war, 13, 45, 125–6, 153–9, 142, 161–2,
        164–5, 180–2, 205
    see also environmental interpretation;
        heritage interpretation
interval level data, 195
interviews, 86, 168, 196–7, 198, 206, 211
    see also focus groups, observation
        studies, questionnaires, surveys

Ireland/Irish, 48, 113, 172, 183, 221
Ironbridge Gorge Museum, 245

Jews/Jewish, 156, 181–2
    see also holocaust

Killiekrankie, 211, 214
knowledge, 13, 17–19, 77–9, 85, 103,
    106, 140, 170, 186, 205, 212, 221,
    244
knowledge gain, 17, 59, 206, 211–13,
    226
    see also learning
knowledge organisation/restructuring,
    84–5, 87, 205–6, 213–15
    see also meaning construction, social
    construction of knowledge

landscape, 37–9, 51, 98, 113, 126, 130,
    133, 140, 143, 146, 153, 154, 177,
    211
layering, 113–14, 116, 130, 139–41, 146
leaflets, 136, 139, 145, 155, 191, 193–5,
    200, 243
learning, 18, 58–60, 63, 65–7, 70, 72,
    77–8, 82–91, 102, 103, 106, 107,
    144, 163, 188, 192, 198, 200, 205,
    206, 210–12, 214, 215, 220, 226,
    235, 247, 248
    see also knowledge gain; knowledge
    organisation; meaning
    construction; social construction of
    knowledge
linkage, 143, 148–9, 246
Local Agenda 21, 146, 163
Lockerbie, 159

Malta, 46, 119
market/marketing, 28, 32, 40, 82, 98,
    100–2, 108, 113, 115, 118, 120,
    126, 139, 140, 164, 172, 182, 189,
    193, 199, 235–40, 243, 251
mass media, 14, 64, 67, 72, 142, 143,
    153, 163, 221

meaning construction/meaning-making,
    18, 19, 56–72, 83–5, 214
    see also knowledge organisation;
    social construction of knowledge
media, 147–8, 150, 153, 164, 189, 192,
    193, 228, 229, 236, 239
    see also mass media
mediation (*see* social mediation)
memories, 14, 16–18, 46, 50, 68, 116,
    124, 126, 134, 142, 145, 152, 153,
    156, 158, 168, 214
mindfulness, 212
mission statement, 203
mock-ups (*see* prototypes)
modelling, 59–63, 65, 66, 71–2
monuments, 41, 45, 115, 117, 118, 123,
    166, 177–82, 232
motivation/reasons for visit, 14, 21, 57,
    68, 70, 78, 82, 84, 197, 205, 210,
    211, 241
movement patterns, 207, 227, 246
multidimensional scaling, 220
multimedia, 91
museum fatigue, 208, 226
museums, 15–19, 22, 26–34, 41, 48–50,
    52, 56, 59–62, 67, 69–72, 77, 82,
    84, 90, 93, 117, 126, 141, 144, 149,
    155, 156, 167, 168, 187, 191, 200,
    205, 206, 210, 213, 227, 232, 236,
    239, 241, 244–7
    see also art galleries

nation building, 21, 116–17, 125, 165
National Parks, 38, 47, 108, 178–80, 232,
    241, 246
nature, 12, 13, 31, 49, 98, 100–1, 139,
    140, 232, 241
nature-based tourism, 101–2, 105
    see also ecotourism
New York, 41, 44, 45, 47, 136
New Zealand, 31
nominal level data, 194
North York Moors, 16
nuclear industry, 31, 153, 204–5, 221,
    225, 226–8

objects (*see* interpretation of objects)
observation studies, 199–200
    see also focus groups, interviews,
        questionnaires, surveys
Oradour-Sur-Glane, 154–8
ordinal level data, 194
orientation, 60, 200, 246
ownership, 26, 30, 32–4, 80–1, 107, 108,
    114–15, 118
ozone layer, 31, 32, 162, 163

participation, 16, 19, 69, 79, 106, 143,
    145–6, 148, 181
past (*see* interpretation of past)
perceptions, 14, 18, 64, 68–70, 78, 82,
    85, 92, 101, 107, 147, 154, 214,
    219
    see also environmental conceptions
performance indicators, 203
place (*see* interpretation of place;
    identity, place)
place theory, 187
planning, 13, 16, 78, 84, 85, 90, 117,
    121, 127–9, 143, 145, 149, 186–8,
    190, 193, 195, 201, 232–51
pollution, 31, 79, 89, 162, 165, 170
popular culture, 100–1
    see also culture
Port Arthur Historic Site, 159–60
prior knowledge/experience/learning,
    57, 58, 63, 84, 85, 86, 100, 106,
    152, 212, 226, 239, 244, 245
promotion, 138, 149, 164
propaganda, 19, 161, 170
prototypes/mock-ups, 190–1, 198, 227
psychology, 12–14, 64, 91, 195, 211,
    244–7
    cultural, 68
    environmental, 14, 22, 187, 207
    social, 22, 56, 63–7, 228
public image, 221
pubs, 134, 135, 137
purposes of interpretation (*see* aims of
    interpretation)

quality assurance, 203
questionnaires, 86, 193, 195–8, 200, 206,
    215, 220, 225, 226
    see also focus groups, interviews,
        observation studies, surveys)
quiz questions, 197, 212–5, 220

railways, 134, 136, 137, 149
readability tests, 200
reasons for visits (*see* motivation)
reconciliation, 126, 165–7, 181
reliability, 195, 225
repertory grid, 215
research, 21, 22, 71, 72, 108–9, 134,
    185–7, 248
    see also evaluation
Risley Moss Visitor Centre, 244

sampling, 195–7, 206, 207, 225
schema, 205, 211–12, 214–8, 244
school students/groups, 59–61, 70–1,
    78–82, 83, 89–93, 239, 241
Scotland/Scottish, 30, 41, 46, 49, 60, 210
Second World War (*see* World War II)
self-efficacy/self-esteem, 22
self-identity (*see* identity, self)
Sellafield, 221
Seneca Falls, 47
sense of place, 6–7, 22, 112–32, 187
    see also identity, place; interpretation
        of place
Serbia/Serbs, 20, 159, 173–6, 179, 181,
    182
skills
    evaluation, 190, 195
    interpretive, 15, 92, 108, 109, 139,
        142, 143, 146–7, 250
    visitors', 65, 80, 81, 106, 107
smallest space analysis, 220
social construction of knowledge, 18,
    19, 186
    see also knowledge organisation,
        meaning construction, social
        mediation

social context, 57–9, 61, 62, 64, 67, 68, 84

social engineering, 206

social experience, 18, 56–76, 247

social identity (*see* identity, social)

social interaction, 18, 56–76, 84, 105, 247

social justice, 2, 11

social mediation, 38, 58–65, 70

social psychology (*see* psychology, social)

South Africa, 21, 165–7
    see also Africa

statistical procedures, 194, 195, 210, 225–6

statues/statuary, 41–6, 52, 136, 149

stewardship, 26, 29–34

Stone of Scone, 27, 30

stories, 84–5, 89, 91, 134, 140, 159–60, 168–9, 190, 235, 237–8, 242–3
    see also themes

summative evaluation (*see* evaluation, summative)

surveys, 190, 200, 210, 235
    see also focus groups, interviews, observation studies, questionnaires)

target audience (*see* audience)

technology in interpretation, 2, 148, 150, 232, 250

themes, 84, 85, 124, 125, 134, 135, 140, 191–2, 208, 210, 213, 226, 228, 235–40, 242, 243, 245, 246, 249
    see also stories

themes–markets–resources model, 235–40, 243

theory, 3–4, 11–25, 56, 62–70, 83–6, 98–101, 106, 153, 172, 186–7, 214
    see also Tilden

third world, 31, 32, 107

Tilden, 11, 12, 91, 106, 107, 153, 170, 232, 233, 235, 241, 245, 247, 248, 250, 251

tourism/tourist, 11, 14, 27, 98–111, 118, 120, 121, 124, 126, 127, 155, 178, 201, 249–50
    see also ecotourism

training manuals, 233

Tutankhamen, 32–4

Uluru/Ayers Rock, 31, 233
    see also Ayers Rock Resort Visitor Centre

urban design, 119, 148, 150

urban interpretation (*see* interpretation of urban environment)

Urban Studies Centres, 141

UK, 149, 162–3, 203, 221, 241
    see also Britain, England, Ireland, Scotland

USA/America, 27, 28, 30, 33, 34, 37, 41, 44–6, 51, 52, 69, 71, 101, 119, 134, 176, 232

vagueness, 195–6

validity, 195, 203, 226, 228

values, 11, 19, 20, 38, 39, 63, 68, 70, 78–90, 100, 106, 152, 154, 170, 172, 203
    see also attitudes, beliefs

viewing times, 206, 208

virtual reality, 139, 233

visitor behaviour, 58, 61, 66–70, 81, 199, 225, 227
    see also behaviour, behaviour change, behavioural mapping

visitor control, 206

visitor profile, 210, 211, 241

visitor-centred approach, 56, 57, 68

Vygotsky, 63–5, 72

war (*see* interpretation of war)

World War I, 45, 156, 179

World War II, 14, 45, 46, 158, 176, 180, 205

Yugoslavia, 20, 172–84